DARK HORSE

DARK HORSE

The Private Life of George Harrison

GEOFFREY GIULIANO

DUTTON   NEW YORK

DUTTON
Published by the Penguin Group
Penguin Books USA Inc.,
375 Hudson Street, New York, New York, U.S.A. 10014
Penguin Books Ltd,
27 Wrights Lane, London W8 5TZ, England
Penguin Books Australia Ltd,
Ringwood, Victoria, Australia
Penguin Books Canada,
2801 John Street, Markham, Ontario, Canada L3R 1B4
Penguin Books (N.Z.) Ltd.,
182–190 Wairau Road, Auckland 10, New Zealand

Penguin Books Ltd, Registered Offices:
Harmondsworth, Middlesex, England

First published in the United States in 1990 by Dutton,
an imprint of Penguin Books USA Inc.
Originally published in Canada by
Stoddart Publishing Company, Limited.

First printing, April, 1990

10   9   8   7   6   5   4   3   2   1

Library of Congress Catalog Card Number: 89-82521

ISBN: 0-525-24854-4

Printed in the United States of America

Illustrations used at the head of each chapter, in order, beginning with Chapter One:
"Rain," Stefano Castino, pen and ink, 1988; title unknown, medieval woodcut;
title unknown, detail of thirteenth-century woodcut; "Boar Incarnation,"
Bhaktivedanta Book Trust, pen and ink; peace sign, pen and ink; "Lord Ramachandra
Embraces Hanuman," nineteenth century, pen and ink; title unknown,
illustration from Sir Frank Crisp's Friar Park Guide; title unknown, Victorian poster
illustration; "Prince Siddhartha as Gautama the Buddha," Stefano Castino, pen and
ink, 1989; "Deus Non Fortuna," insignia of the Harrison family, rendered by Stefano
Castino, pen and ink, 1989.

SRI SRI GURU GAURANGA JAYATAH

*Dedicated to the memory of my
mother, Myrna Oneita Juliana.
To my father. To His Divine Grace
B.H. Mangalniloy Goswami Maharaj.
And to Michael Powers.*

*Leaves on a tree
Green to brown
Bud to ground
A life fulfilled*

ROBERT NOEL GIULIANO

OM TAT SAT

Contents

The man who hath no music in himself,
Nor is moved with the concord of sweet sounds . . .
Let no such man be trusted.

WILLIAM SHAKESPEARE

PREFACE
Down the Rabbit Hole

It's what you think you know about George Harrison that can fool you. Dedicated students of Beatle lore might well be able to rattle off chapter and verse of the enigmatic guitar player's most obscure recording work. Or the more philosophically inclined, details of his famous flirtation with Indian mysticism. Ex-lovers' caterwaulings, family squabbles, Beatle battles and stories of his druggie days piled up end to end might well stretch around something or other, but the real man always seems to elude us. Slipping away quicksilver-fast, afloat on a sea of eternal publicity, Harrison has thus far always had the last laugh. A quarter of a century later, all the many media pundits and pop soothsayers intent on bringing him in alive are still no closer to the mark. Old George, I'm happy to report, is just too clever for them. Twenty-five years on a treadmill like the Beatles' everwhirling helter-skelter will do that to you.

Harrison's Trojan horse approach to public adulation is not only extremely effective, but for the tight-lipped superstar, undeniably essential. "Look what happened to Lennon," one might be tempted to argue in defense of George's well-known lust for privacy. John was all over the streets of Manhattan almost daily for years. An easy target for the Beatle-obsessed. One look at the barbed-wire-and-brick fortress George calls home, however, should tell anyone he plans to live a very, very long time. A wilting Prince Prospero on the run from Poe's ever-advancing red death.

As for me, my initiation into the Beatles' magic circle way back in the burly winter of 1964 was to herald the beginning of my own inner voyage. It's not that the Beatles presented any great answers, but over the course of the last twenty-five years they have at least helped to solidify a number of very important questions. George Harrison, particularly, through his rather astounding body of work has contributed a great deal of insight into the amazing journey that is life. It is wrong, however, to think of Harrison as any sort of leader. Rather he is more a fellow traveler. He would be the first to admit that as a spiritual seeker he is a rank amateur. A mystical punk with his head and heart in the heavens but his feet still firmly fixed to the ground. Pete Townshend wrote me a letter years ago in which he said that to his mind punks were "especially close to God." If that's so, then perhaps George Harrison is closer to his ultimate goal than he thinks. Maybe we all are.

"I don't mind people telling my story," Harrison explained to me a few years back. "It's just that they never seem to get it right. To be honest, I've rather given up hope that anyone ever will." Seeing him sitting there in his old pal "Legs" Larry Smith's tiny bedsit in rural Oxfordshire, I remember thinking that I would never, ever want to trade places with this man. It was clear to me that his much-heralded, jet-set lifestyle no longer held any attraction for him. And that despite all the untold wealth and privilege, his soul was now almost completely barren. Long ago picked clean by the unrelenting backlash of diehard Beatlemania and a world that the cynical Harrison continually refers to as simply "loony."

Picking up the gauntlet of George's left-handed challenge to write a "really good book" about his topsy-turvy days as the Beatles' amazing rhythm ace was no small task, believe me. And it was only after much soul-searching of my own that I ever even dared to consider taking up the cause. I am, after all, mostly just a dedicated observer, one of the many from my generation who looked upon the Beatles as the psychedelic Pied Pipers of a new order; an order I hope based on more meaningful values than those of our parents. The reality, of course, turned out to be something quite different. From where I sit now, it looks to me like one generation is basically just as good or bad as another. It's apparently only the ad hoc circumstances of one's own karma that tend to tilt the scales, and so it is with our Mr. Harrison. As George's long-dead, invisible mentor and founder of Friar Park, Sir Frank Crisp, inscribed over the stone portals of the great manor, "Scan not a friend with a microscopic glass. You know his faults, but let his foibles pass. Life is one long enigma, true, my friend. So read on. Read on. The answer's at the end!"

GEOFFREY GIULIANO
Skyfield Manor
Western New York
September 1989

I

BLUE MOON OVER WAVERTREE

Childhood

George himself is no mystery. But the mystery inside of George is immense. It's watching him uncover it all little by little that's so damn interesting.

JOHN LENNON, 1968

"EVERY ONCE IN A WHILE I USED TO SEE GEORGE IN TOWN FOR A DRINK,"
drawled Nigel, the lanky ex-roadie for the seventies super group, Uriah
Heep, during a chance encounter late in 1983:

> Of course he's always so low-key that even many of the regulars never
> really caught on to who he was. I remember this one old jit rabbiting
> on and on about how the famous George Harrison of the Beatles
> lived in Henley and was even known to come into that very pub for
> a lager from time to time! *"No!"* said George, full of mock surprise
> and more than a little thick Newcastle Brown. *"Not him!"*

On Harrison's home turf of the pastoral Oxfordshire river town,
Henley-on-Thames, one is tempted to believe just about anything one
hears concerning the lauded guitar player, if only by virtue of the fact that
even those with an ear for such Beatle-related gossip hear so very, very
little at all. Even Henley's few crusty cabbies will tell you that although
they're often summoned to pick up a fare at Friar Park (or "the Park," as
the locals call Harrison's palatial Victorian manor), they're never sure
which of the several soiled groundskeepers marauding around the garden
is actually who he seems.

"More than once I've seen him digging around out there up to the
tops of his Wellies in shit," cooed one chain-smoking driver while taking
me on the ten-pence tour of Henley. "He's an odd one, is George. But
then they all were, weren't they?"

So very discreet are the many Harrison insiders in Henley about the
goings-on at George's that even *The Standard*, the tiny township's daily
paper, has managed only a few quick snaps of the reclusive Beatle in all
the twenty-odd years he's been in residence.

Even those rare birds who somehow summon up the courage to
amble cautiously up to the Park's massive wrought-iron gates and take a
poke at the estate's brass intercom button are almost always made to feel
most unwelcome. "Fuck off," ordered a voice from inside to one such ballsy
reporter from nearby Radio Reading following John Lennon's tragic
assassination in December 1980. And as if that isn't enough to discourage
intruders intent on an afternoon of up-close Beatle watching, then the
elegant green-and-gold sign posted just inside the main gate advising all
uninvited guests to "get you ass outta here" in ten major languages just
might. Despite the bravado, however, and although he has recently
installed an elaborate security system, Harrison steadfastly refuses to allow

any guard dogs on his property. As Ian Paice of Deep Purple has said, "To George, D-O-G is G-O-D spelled backwards," negative symbolism bound to be offensive to the religiously conservative Harrison.

In fact there seems to be at least two discernible George Harrisons. George One, the mild-mannered bus driver's son turned gardener, wouldn't be capable of attracting any more attention in a crowd than, say, your average upper-crust garden-club patron. Whereas George Two, the internationally adored rock-star philanthropist and philosopher turned movie mogul, most definitely would. Forever the odd man out as a member of the celebrated "Fab Four," George has often referred to himself and Ringo as "economy class Beatles." And on a purely financial level (John and Paul having both received a larger share of royalties from the sale of their albums) that may indeed be true. However, both as an artist and a sincere, time-tested truth seeker, Harrison is running way ahead of the game. About the name of his fledgling record label, Dark Horse, he once said, "That's the one who suddenly pulls out from behind the rest and barrels ahead to actually win the race. The one that nobody's bothered to put any money on. That's me, I guess. The very last one anyone would have ever expected to come out a winner."

George Harrison's father, Harold Hargreaves Harrison, first met his mother, Louise French, on a Liverpool street corner in 1929. On shore leave from his job as a steward with the famous White Star Line, he and several of his shipmates were larking about one afternoon when they happened upon Louise and a couple of her friends out for a stroll. "I'm going off to Africa in the morning," one of the boys shouted out to the giggly young girls. "Give us your addresses and I'll send you each a bottle of scent!" Louise, a shop girl at a suburban greengrocers, dutifully scrawled her house number on the back of a cigaret packet. Harry, never one to shy away from a potential conquest, immediately grabbed it out of her hand. "Thanks very much, ducky!" he said. "I'll write you as soon as we're out to sea."

A few weeks later the postman rang the bell of the Frenchs' neat little rowhouse and handed Louise's mother a crisp white envelope bearing the striking insignia of the posh commercial shipping line. Mrs. French had just allowed an old man who'd been struggling down the road into the kitchen to fetch himself a drink of water. Curious about the smart, official-looking letter lying there on the table, he casually peeled back the flaps and read aloud Harry's long soppy love note to the thoroughly embarrassed teenager. The letters continued to come, all from increasingly exotic ports of call, as the adventurous Master Harrison catered and waited his way around the world.

Born in Liverpool on May 28, 1909, Harry, the son of journeyman bricklayer Henry Harrison and Jane Thomson, left school at fourteen to work as a delivery boy, earning just seven shillings a week. Skimpy as it was, the money helped out, as his father had been killed at Mons during World War I and his mother was left alone with several children to care for. By the age of seventeen, Harry, like so many other young men from the rough-and-ready Liverpool port, was already at sea. Even after he and Louise were married on May 20, 1930, he remained a sailor, coming ashore some six years later only to wind up on the dole for the next fifteen months.

During a quick backstage interview in 1974, the elder Harry spoke of these years:

> Life at sea was rough all right. Every week without fail I always sent home my pay to Louise. As a first-class steward I used to take in some pretty good tips as well, so I would try and live off that. I was saving up to try and come ashore. The problem was, by the time I finally got round to making it in, there was a terrible depression going on, so I ended up collecting just over twenty-five bob a week . . . . We got by well enough. But life was never easy.

Despite the hard times, the Harrisons were a warm and loving family. Still working at the grocers right up until a few weeks before their first child, Louise, was born in 1931, Mrs. Harrison always tried to remain optimistic. "Lord willing, we'll be all right," George remembers her saying when he was a child. "It could always be worse."

By 1934 the Harrisons' second child, Harry, was born. Years later, as Friar Park's devoted estate manager, he would remember those early years as "wonderful." "Our little house was just two rooms up and two down, but, except for a short period when our father was away at sea, we always knew the comfort and security of a very close-knit home life."

Intent on finding an occupation that might afford his growing family the things they needed, Harry eventually found work as a bus conductor and after just a year was promoted to driver. In an interview conducted in late 1987, Paul McCartney remembered George's parents this way:

Harry was our local bus driver who was always great fun, but forthright and very straightforward. He would run over a dog in his bus rather than try and swerve a little to avoid it. Quite rightly, too, I suppose, as he was responsible for a lot of people's lives. But I remember always being a little disturbed about the hardness in his character.

Now Louise was lovely, though quite a hard lady too, in some ways, but soft as toffee on the inside, really. I remember her pouring a pan of water on some fellow she didn't want to open the door to. She'd always tell you how she felt, Louise.

Peter, the sibling George was closest to as a youngster, was born on July 20, 1940, the same year as John Lennon. All in all, it was a terribly tense time in Liverpool as World War II was now in full swing and Hitler's *Luftwaffe* was making nightly bombing raids over the city.

"In those days everything was in short supply," recalled George's father. "Sugar, butter, tea, meat, even clothes were all strictly rationed. As far as fresh fruits and vegetables were concerned, you could forget it. Every once in a while, though, one of my passengers would tip me with an apple or even an unheard-of banana."

With the coming of the summer of 1942, Louise discovered she was once again pregnant, a prospect that put an even greater strain on the family's limited resources. That is not to say that the baby was unwanted or unloved, but simply unexpected. It would be the couple's last child.

George Harold Harrison was born at 12:10 a.m., February 25, 1943. In George's autobiography, *I Me Mine*, the philosophically minded Beatle endeavored to put a finger on the metaphysics involved in this, his latest incarnation:

> To try and imagine the soul entering the womb of a woman living in 12 Arnold Grove, Wavertree, Liverpool 15. There were all the barrage balloons, and the Germans bombing Liverpool. All that was going on. I sat outside the house . . . a couple of years ago, imagining 1943, nipping through the spiritual world, the astral level, getting back into a body in that house. That really is strange when you consider the whole planet, and all the planets there may be on the physical level . . . How do I come into that family, in that house at that time, and who am I anyway?

Mr. Harrison's first impression of his little son wasn't quite so lofty. "I vaguely remember tiptoeing up the stairs to see him after he was born," he said. "All I could think of was that he looked so remarkably like me! A tiny, squalling, miniature replica of myself."

At his mother's insistence, baby George was baptized a Catholic like the other children, although the Harrisons were admittedly not overtly religious.

George's mother recalls him as a toddler:

George was good as a child. He was no trouble at all and seldom misbehaved. Lots of people think maybe I say this because he's famous now, but he *was* good, so it would be unfair to say he was a naughty boy!

George was very eager to start school. He was bright, intelligent and extremely independent. He was also very fair haired. He and his brother Pete were always together, and as a tot George would often look at photographs of his brother and think it was him. He never played about the streets as a child. He used to like swimming and always found something constructive to do in his spare time.

George's first school was Dovedale Primary, just a short hop from his home, across Penny Lane and down the street. John Lennon was there already, three years ahead of young George and just beginning to dabble on the guitar. The two never met at school. In Hunter Davies's definitive *The Beatles: The Authorized Biography*, Louise Harrison remembers her son's early days at Dovedale:

I took him to school that first day. He wanted to stay dinners right from the beginning. The next day, as I was getting my coat off the hanger, he said, "Oh, no, I don't want you to take me."

I said, "Why not?"

"I don't want you to be one of those nosey mothers, standing round the gate talking!" He's always been against that sort of thing. He used to hate all the neighbours who stood about gossiping.

One of George's earliest memories is of going to an outdoor market with his brothers, Harry and Peter, to buy live chickens. Each of the boys brought home his own hen but only Peter's survived. It was kept in a pen in the Harrisons' tiny back garden, but occasionally got free and scrambled

Peter and George in the back garden of their home at 12 Arnold Grove, Wavertree, Liverpool.

The modest "two rooms up and two rooms down" boyhood home of young George on Arnold Grove. Skyboot Productions Ltd.: G. Giuliano

around out front to terrorize unsuspecting visitors making their way to the door. George recalls that as the months passed the hen grew to a monstrous size, a fellow was hired to wring its neck and the bird was then dressed and roasted for the Harrisons' Christmas dinner. The image of the hen hanging on the clothesline to bleed dry was never to leave the impressionable little boy. Years later as a Beatle, George eagerly embraced vegetarianism. "Nowadays our Christmas dinner doesn't depend on the death of one of the millions of poor, innocent birds," George said late in 1988. "And it tastes all the better knowing that no blood was spilt."

The Harrisons' home on Arnold Grove was a cramped, rundown terrace house in Wavertree, a working-class section of Liverpool. George remembers some of the inadequacies of life there:

> The rooms downstairs were always extremely cold during the winter. We had only one fire in the entire house and other than that there was no heating at all. I remember . . . my brothers and I absolutely dreaded getting up [in the morning] as it was bloody freezing. On top of that, the toilet was outside next to my dad's little homemade hen house.

In 1949, the Harrisons moved from Wavertree to a brand-new, roomy council house in nearby Speke, which Harry had applied for some eighteen years earlier. The property, at 25 Upton Green, was lovely in comparison with Arnold Grove, but Louise didn't take to the sort of rough and tumble people who lived in the area and longed for the cozy familiarity of their old neighborhood.

Harry Harrison remembers his wife taking eight-year-old George to the cinema and the boy insisting that she give an old tramp half a crown. "Money didn't mean anything to him even then," says Harry. "If George had his way, every old boy we saw should be entitled to at least a few pence. He was always very compassionate like that." Even today, Harrison hates to see street people hanging about in doorways or sleeping on the pavement. Once in the early eighties, as he was leaving a trendy London restaurant with friends "Legs" Larry Smith and Rolling Stone Bill Wyman, he offhandedly presented a destitute old man with a crisp fifty-pound note. According to Larry, it wasn't the first time he had seen the guitarist give so freely.

Although money in those days was usually quite tight, the Harrisons still tried to take a little family trip together at least once a year. Usually they went to nearby towns on the northwest coast — Bidston Hill, Southport, New Brighton and that standard British holiday resort, Blackpool. In *I Me Mine*, George recalls several childhood visits to Wales, where he marveled at the country's natural beauty: "We went all over Wales, staying in little places, nice old stone cottages with slate roofs. Probably cost next to nothing to rent. You could actually live a whole happy life in a place like that."

On one holiday in Scotland, George was suddenly taken ill while swimming with his brothers at Inverness. A doctor was called and George was ordered into hospital. An ambulance arrived with two stretcher bearers, but George was adamant. "I'm not going on that," he said bluntly and walked out of the hotel, with the stretcher men in procession behind. In the hospital, George was far from a model patient. He hated the salt-free diet they put him on so much that he wrapped one meal in a brown paper bag and threw it out a window when no one was looking. Unfortunately for him, the matron happened to be passing underneath at precisely that moment and caught the parcel right on her head. She strode purposefully up the stairs and into George's ward, only to find him apparently fast asleep. "He was the first person I have ever seen smiling that broadly in his sleep," she said dryly to his parents afterward.

Although George was certainly very intelligent and capable, he was never really fond of school. Bearing in mind George's outstanding creative achievements of later years, one might well assume that, in the eyes of his masters, anyway, the seemingly disinterested Harrison was a bit of an anomaly. "Little polite rows of toffee headed robots," John Lennon once said. "That's all any of [the teachers] were after."

Despite George's natural reservations about school, he was at first a good student. In an interview with Hunter Davies in 1967, he aired some of his views on the subject:

> After we sat [for the entrance exam for grammar school] the teacher asked who thought they had passed. Only one boy put his hand up. He was a little fat lad who smelled. It was very sad, really. He turned out to be about the only one who didn't pass. Smelly kids like that were the sort teachers made you sit next to as a punishment. So the poor smelly kids really get screwed up. All teachers are like that. And the more screwed up they are the more they pass it on to the kids. They're all ignorant. I always thought that. Yet because they

were old and withered you were somehow supposed to believe they weren't.

To George, seeing through the illusion of so-called adult authority seemed to be all the justification he needed to forever reject its dictates even at such an early age. Like so many others in the creative sphere, it was George himself who ultimately found the courage to reject the mores and values he saw around him. From "those nosey mothers" standing at the school gate to the unenlightened, interfering masters he met at school, George Harrison has never borne fools gladly.

After leaving Quarry Bank High School for Boys in 1953, George was enrolled at the Liverpool Institute. On his first day there, he was jumped from behind by a local roughneck, which did little to bolster his enthusiasm for his new school. At first, Harrison did try to make the best of things by attending classes and keeping up with his homework. But soon, as George put it, "the old rot set in," and he once again declared a war of in-attention on all things relating to his life at school. As he told Davies in *The Beatles:*

> I hated being dictated to. Some schizophrenic jerk, just out of
> training college, would read out notes to you which you were
> expected to take down. I couldn't read them afterwards anyway.
> They never fooled me. Useless, the lot of them . . . . I had this mutual
> thing with a few masters. They'd let me sleep at the back of the class
> if I wouldn't cause any trouble. If it was nice and sunny, it was hard
> to keep awake anyway, with some old fellow chundering away on. I
> often used to wake up at quarter to five and find they'd all gone home
> long ago.

Hand in hand with the young teenager's rebellious attitude toward school went a sudden change in his appearance. Gone was the black blazer, gray flannel trousers and matching school tie. From now on his big brother Harry's wild canary-yellow waistcoat, secretly altered skin-tight pants and blue suede winkle-pickers, with their long pointed toes, were the order of the day — George's sassy new individualized school uniform. Another distressing addition to Harrison's look (or so his teachers thought) was his slicked-back hairstyle. Walking to the bus stop every morning with his school cap perched high atop his head, he looked every bit the gawky neighborhood hipster he fancied himself.

Mr. Harrison was definitely not amused. To him, career success, and ultimate financial stability, hinged on a solid education, which in turn depended on the impression one made. Harry, after all, had come up the hard way, and he wanted better for his children. Of his three sons, only young George had made it into grammar school, so naturally his father had high hopes for the boy. To most people of Harry's generation, conformity was the only acceptable way for a young man just starting out. "Don't rock the boat, sonny," he used to tell the rebellious and determined teen. "If you're not careful you just might drown!"

His mother, Louise, on the other hand, found George's mildly outrageous behavior both exhilarating and harmless. She was proud to see her son growing up to be an individual, with his own vision of the world. "There's more than enough sheep in this life, Dad," she would argue with her equally stubborn husband. "Just let the boy be." Speaking to Hunter Davies once again, George said of those early years:

> My mum did encourage me. Perhaps most of all by never discouraging me from anything I wanted to do. That was the really good thing about her and my dad. If you tell kids not to, they're going to do it in the end anyway, so they might as well hurry and get it over with. They let me stay out all night and have a drink when I wanted to. So I'd finished with all that bit by the time everybody else was just coming into it. That's probably why I don't really like alcohol much today. I had it all by the age of ten.

A true rebel, by his sixteenth birthday George was at the very bottom of his class at the Liverpool Institute, and often in deep water at home. Although he made no bones about his feelings for school, he was secretly nervous about leaving without benefit of even the most basic qualifications. To be able to sit for the General Certificate of Education, a student had to first pass a preliminary exam given by his teachers. The minimum requirement was successful completion of at least three subjects relevant to one's choice of career. George, however, failed dismally in all his classes, except art. "While most of the other students spent their Wednesday afternoons panting around the school track," says George, "I was content to take a notebook and dream up some sketches. They were mostly from my head, not from anything around me. I was fond of sports, too, especially swimming, but I guess I was fonder of art."

The institute's answer was to suggest that he be held back to try again next year. Afraid of what sort of unpleasantness this unhappy news might cause at home, George took the coward's way out and burned his report. During the last few months of the school year he seldom even bothered turning up for classes. Instead, he often spent the lunch money his mother gave him on week-day matinees at the local cinema, sitting for hours slumped down in the tattered theater seats hoping none of the grownups around would question his presence there. Other times, he would cycle over to the home of his big brother Harry's girlfriend, Irene (later Harry's wife), where they would happily chat away the afternoon. Promptly at 3:45 he would cycle back to the Speke estate, no one any the wiser.

Finally, however, the inevitable happened, and George was forced to own up to his parents about his failure at school. After the dust had settled, the Harrisons tried their best to understand. The only thing left now was for their youngest son to find himself a good steady job somewhere, qualifications or not, and make the best of it. George, though, couldn't think of any line of work he wanted to pursue. Harrison, increasingly cynical beyond his years, was not about to accept a position as a lowly bus conductor or a milkman. He was definitely meant for something better. Something with a real future.

Ultimately, however, George saw the wisdom of compromise and grudgingly accepted a one-pound-fifty-a-week position as an apprentice electrician at Blackler's, a Liverpool department store. His father was delighted and proudly presented his son with a first-class set of electrical screwdrivers that Christmas. Several of George's relatives have since said they felt Harry had it in his head that with all three of his sons busy working at vaguely related trades (young Harry was a mechanic and Peter an auto body worker), they might consider going into business together. A family-owned garage, Mr. Harrison figured, would be just the ticket. He, of course, would be the manager, his wife Louise the bookkeeper, and his sons would do most of the labor. A happy dream, to be sure.

After only a brief time on the job, though, George had had enough. He soon recognized that mindlessly cleaning endless strings of Christmas tree lights with a paintbrush or scrubbing out the gents' was certainly not appropriate work for a young man of his great potential — whatever that was. Although George's parents weren't pleased with this latest development, once again they were supportive. Of course, if George had stuck it out at school, received his certificate and then gone on to a steady job in Liverpool, the world might never have had the Beatles — a fact George has always been very much aware of.

Today, it is the funny little things George remembers about life in Liverpool, quirky, seemingly unrelated images strung together on a chain of golden memories. Pictures of pushy, tobacco-stained vicars chatting up housewives for donations. Little red-faced insurance salesmen toting their tatty imitation-leather briefcases around the noisy streets. Pot-bellied masters from the institute marching up and down the cricket fields followed by a scruffy band of schoolboy soldiers singing out their off-key cadence into Liverpool's late afternoon hustle-bustle. The rowdy merchant sailors, street vendors, pitiful alleyway drunkards, tight-lipped bobbies and, of course, the North's famous bounty of pretty girls. All characters right out of the Beatles' "Penny Lane." All striking by their own peculiar sense of normalcy and all still very, very real to George Harrison.

There are magical places, too, that still simmer fondly in George's consciousness. A highly polished giant meteorite set into cement outside the Wavertree Baths that, after careering around the Milky Way for a million years or so finished up its journey in a farmer's muddy field in suburban Liverpool. Young George used to scramble up on top and then gaily slide back down. It is still there today. Then there were Calderstone Park, the library and the mysterious tunnels leading the way to Childwall Five Ways. None of these places is on the tourist maps handed to out-of-town Beatle fans by the Merseyside Tourist Board. These are secret places reserved only for the people of Liverpool. The *real* Liverpool. The Liverpool Carl Jung called "the pool of life." The heady stuff that dreams are made of. And about which songs are composed and sung.

II

HIGHWAY OF DIAMONDS

Early Musical Discovery

We were made John, Paul, George and Ringo, because of what we did last time; it was all there for us, on a plate. We're reaping what we sowed in our last life, whatever it was. That's really all there is to it, Squire.

GEORGE HARRISON

BEHIND THE WHEEL OF HIS BIG GREEN BUS, HARRY HARRISON WAS A stern and cautious professional, methodically making sure every fare was paid, all elderly patrons safely seated and troublemakers quickly subdued or unceremoniously ejected. This motorized juggernaut of the roadway neatly knocked off its stops with a cool precision that passersby could set their watches to. "I was the best driver I could be," he said back in 1974. "It always meant a lot to me to do any job as well as I could. My dad was the same. We Harrisons have always taken a lot of pride in our work."

Off duty, though, Harry was just one of the lads. Gregarious and sociable, he spent a lot of time at the Liverpool Corporation Centre for Conductors and Drivers, at Finch Lane, drinking and carousing with his mates. His easy congeniality and genuine concern for workers' rights quickly led him to be elected a top union official. Once again, Harry's dedication to duty had paid off. By the mid-1950s the ambitious Harrison was the regular Saturday night master of ceremonies at the union's weekly social. Once on stage, the normally reserved driver suddenly came to life, all smiles and corny jokes. He later said:

> We always had a lot of fun back then. No one took any of it very seriously, though. Of course, it wasn't really show business at all, was it? Still, it was as close as I personally ever care to get! One thing I think we can take a little credit for, however, was helping to launch [comedian] Ken Dodd. He used to come in every once in a while for a drink, so of course, after a bit we all realized how marvelously funny he was.
>
> "Why don't you get up and do your act on stage, Ken?" I asked him one evening.
>
> "Not me, mate." Too nervous he was. Eventually, though, we wore him down and of course he ended up a big star.

In addition to Harry's duties as emcee, he and Louise conducted ballroom dancing lessons at the conductors' club for more than ten years. Louise, especially, was exceedingly fond of music, and their tidy home often swung to the Big Band sounds of Ted Heath or her personal favorite, Victor Sylvester. George remembers hearing Hoagy Carmichael's "Hong Kong Blues" as well as the old novelty tune "One Meatball." He even recalls standing on a little leather chair at about age four and singing his very own version of these songs at a friend of his parents' — the baby Beatle's very first public performance. George was also known to duck behind the sitting-room sofa from time to time for an impromptu puppet show, much to his parents' delight.

Louise's first indication that George was seriously interested in music came when he was thirteen; she happened to notice that his school exercise books were virtually covered with crude little sketches of guitars. Soon afterward, she bought her son a cheap three-pound acoustic from the father of one of George's schoolmates. Surprisingly, George didn't seem interested and relegated the gift to an upstairs cupboard for the next three months. When he eventually picked it up he found it frustratingly difficult to learn and almost packed it in several times before finally making a little progress. Sitting up some nights till nearly dawn, with his mum to encourage him, he practiced until his fingers bled.

With practice and determination — often listening to pop records and then trying to mimic what he'd just heard — George began to play quite well and outgrew the battered old acoustic that had served him so faithfully. His mum once again came to the rescue by saving up her extra household money to buy him another guitar. This one, a good, solid, wide-body acoustic with white inlaid trim, cost thirty pounds and featured a handy cutaway neck for easier maneuverability on the lower frets of the fingerboard. Proud and independent, young George was determined to reimburse his mother as soon as he could. It just wasn't in the lad's makeup to accept from anyone what he considered charity. As a result, he soon signed on as a Saturday-afternoon delivery boy for a local butcher. George's natural aversion to flesh as food slowly gained momentum as he cycled through the narrow back streets of Speke with a full load of raw meat packed into his dusty saddle bags. It is tempting to speculate whether these early memories later inspired his militant anti-meat eating song "Piggies" on the Beatles' "white" album.

It was during one of his deliveries that Harrison met Tony Bramwell who, like George, was an enthusiastic rock and skiffle fan. Tony happened to mention that he had been lucky enough to meet Buddy Holly during the singer's last whirlwind tour of Great Britain. George was greatly impressed, although he, too, had a similar tale to tell. His brother Harry explains: "In 1958 Lonnie Donegan was appearing at the Empire [Theatre] and of course George just had to go. In fact, he borrowed the money from our parents so that he could see every single show! Anyway, he found out where Lonnie was staying, which happened to be a house in Speke, so George went round and hammered on the door until he came out and gave George his autograph. Of course, he immediately raced home to show everyone. I bet you dollars to doughnuts he still has it safely tucked away somewhere."

With so much in common the two boys soon became chums, and their talk inevitably turned to music. "I used to lend George all my Buddy Holly records so he could try to learn the various chords and riffs," remembers Tony. "We played them all so much that by the time we'd finished they were just about ready for the bin."

Sometime later George set his sights on getting his first electric guitar. Candy-apple red, he thought, would be perfect. Just like the one his hero, skiffle king Lonnie Donegan, played. His brother Harry remembers that George's first guitar came to "a very sad end."

He had rested it up against a wall and was talking to a mate when someone suddenly pushed back a chair right into it! Although George had it repaired, it was never the same again. What he really wanted, though, was an electric guitar, but Dad wasn't keen on him having it on hire purchase. He always said you shouldn't buy anything unless you had the money to pay for it.

Anyhow, one night George, who was then working for Blackler's, came round to my flat. He went into a long speech about how much better an electric model would be. I realized he was working up to something, but said nothing. Then he finally came out with it. He knew Dad wouldn't let him have anything on hire purchase, so he wanted me to sign the guarantee forms. I wasn't very keen, but he persuaded me to go to Hessy's, the Liverpool shop where all the groups bought their instruments. There he showed me the guitar he wanted. It was priced at £120. George fiddled with it, trying to look like an expert, but no sound came out. So the salesman pushed a button on the amplifier, and suddenly there was a tremendous blast and all the instruments on the opposite wall crashed to the floor. After that, I just had to let poor George have his guitar!

Still marking time at the Liverpool Institute, George shuttled back and forth to school on his father's bus from Speke to Liverpool in a dreamy haze of guitars and pop stars. The long, rambling ride took up to an hour each way, which also allowed him the boyhood luxury of mucking about with the other lads. One of the boys, the son of a cotton salesman and the estate midwife from Allerton, was especially good fun. His name was Paul McCartney, and although he was a year ahead of George at school, the

George and John participate in a humorous skit included in the 1964 film, *Around the Beatles*.
DELIBERATE ALCHEMY ARCHIVES

Stone-faced, George stares down the media, 1964. DELIBERATE ALCHEMY ARCHIVES

two quickly became firm friends by early 1955. Like George, McCartney was also intensely interested in music and not only played the guitar but also held the proud distinction of owning his very own trumpet, which greatly impressed young master Harrison.

At home, George used to perch himself on a stool in the middle of the sitting room and strum along to his favorite skiffle tunes with his brother Pete, a fair musician himself. The two brothers even played a gig together at the British Legion Club in Speke in 1956 with Pete's school chum Arthur Kelly, and one or two others calling themselves the Rebels. This first engagement was memorable in that none of the other groups scheduled to play turned up, so the rocking Rebels were forced to entertain for the entire evening. Louise remembers the boys all ducking down behind the hedges on their way to the show that night, as George insisted that none of their nosey neighbors be clued in to what was up. "I remember the Rebels had a tea chest with a lot of gnomes around it," says George. "One of my brothers had a five-shilling guitar, which had the back off it. Apart from that it was all fine. Just my brother, some mates and me. I tried to lay down the law a bit, but they weren't having any of that. We thought we made a pretty good sound. But so did about four million other groups."

In those days playing such a prestigious gig was big news, so the next morning George excitedly scrambled to the bus stop to tell his mate, Paul, every detail. Not long afterward, Paul, too, was joining George in the Harrisons' cozy front room to struggle through the well-worn chord books the boys carried around in their school bags. George remembers:

> Paul was very good with the harder chords, I must admit. After a time, though, we actually began playing real songs together, like "Don't You Rock Me Daddy-O" and "Besamé Mucho." Paul knocked me out with his singing especially, although I remember him being a little embarrassed to really sing out, seeing we were stuck right in the middle of my parents' place with the whole family walking about. He said he felt funny singing about love and such around my dad. We must have both really been a sight. I bet the others were just about pissing themselves trying not to laugh.

Whether chatting up young ladies at the local chippy or spending school holidays together, the two boys became virtually inseparable. George recalls one such eventful outing from those early years:

When I was fourteen, Paul and I went to Paignton in Devon on a hitchhiking holiday. It was a bit of a laugh, too, because we ran out of money and had nowhere to sleep. So Paul suggested we sleep on the beach. Sand, however, is actually as hard as concrete when you lie on it all night.

Another year, when we were hitchhiking in south Wales, we did actually sleep on concrete. We ran out of cash again, and Paul, once again, had the idea that we could sleep at the police station in one of the cells.

Unfortunately the police refused but did suggest we could kip in the grandstand of the local football club.

With great difficulty we climbed the wall surrounding the football ground, and with even greater difficulty got to sleep on the concrete steps of the grandstand. Just as day was breaking I woke to see the caretaker standing over us.

"What are you doing in my grandstand?" he demanded.

"S-sleeping," Paul croaked.

"Well, you're not anymore!"

We didn't need telling twice.

With two pieces of the jigsaw puzzle the world would later come to know as the Beatles now firmly in place, it was John Lennon's appearance on the scene that broadened and solidified this magical partnership. Paul remembers:

As it turned out, John and I were both mates with a fellow from Woolton called Ivan Vaughan. One summer day [July 6, 1957], Ivan invited me to come along with him to a fete at the parish church in Woolton. I remember coming up from across the field and hearing all this great music, which turned out to be coming from [John's band] the Quarrymen's little Tannoy system. I just thought, Oh great, I'll go listen to the band, because I was very much into the music.

I remember John singing a lovely tune by the Del Vikings he'd heard on the radio called "Come Go With Me." Anyway, he didn't really know the words so he just made up his own. Good bluesy stuff like, "Come go with me down to the penitentiary." As I recall, he was playing banjo chords on his guitar, which only had about four strings at the time. Actually, he looked very good. He had his glasses off, so he was really quite suave.

As for me, that particular day I just happened to pick up an old guitar that was lying around and started to play "Twenty Flight Rock." I knew a lot of the words, which was really very unusual back in those days! Later, we all went down to the pub, and of course, I had to try and kid the barman I was really eighteen. A couple of weeks later, [John's friend] Pete Shotton cycled up to Allerton and invited me to join the group.

Paul McCartney first laid eyes on John Lennon at, of all places, the neighborhood chip shop. Beyond that he thinks he may have seen him once or twice as a young teddy boy climbing aboard a Liverpool bus bound for Woolton village. McCartney was invited to join the Quarrymen on the merit of his mastery of "Twenty Flight Rock," as well as his justly famous Little Richard imitation. His obvious talents were a welcome addition to the rag-tag group of schoolboy musicians. "John was really the only outstanding member," says Paul. "All the rest sort of slipped away, you know? I suppose the drummer was pretty good actually, for what we knew then. Frankly, one of the reasons they all liked Colin [Hanton] was because he happened to have the [Coasters'] record 'Searchin', and that was pretty impressive currency back then. I mean, sometimes you made a whole career with someone solely on the basis of them owning a particular record!"

Paul's tour of duty as one of John's Quarrymen continued almost a full year before George was introduced to Woolton's bad-boy bandleader. George recalls their meeting in late 1957:

I'd been invited to see them play several times by Paul but for some reason never got round to it before. I remember being very impressed with John's big thick sideboards and trendy teddy boy clothes. He was a terribly sarcastic bugger right from day one, but I never dared back down from him. In a way, all that emotional rough stuff was simply a way for him to help separate the men from the boys, I think. I was never intimidated by him. Whenever he had a go at me I just gave him a little bit of his own right back.

Deeply drawn in by the charismatic spell cast by the masterful Lennon, young Paul McCartney reveled in his role as John's onstage foil and steady street-corner accomplice. But though their musical efforts within the admittedly shaky structure of the Quarrymen were both admirable and ambitious, what they really needed was a good, solid lead guitar upon which to hang their funky back-street skiffle sound. Paul remembers the events leading up to their settling on George: "Well, he was always my little mate. Nonetheless, he could really play guitar, particularly this piece called "Raunchy," which we all used to love. You see, if anyone could do something like that it was generally enough to get them in the group. Of course, I knew George long before any of the others, as they were all from Woolton and we hung out with the Allerton set. I can tell you we both learned guitar from the same book, and that despite his tender years, we were chums."

John Lennon, however, was apparently quite skeptical about admitting such a veritable "baby" into the group. How would it look for someone as talented and popular as John to be caught consorting with someone so young and obviously undistinguished as George? What would his mates think, let alone the ladies? After all, the whole point of being in a band in the first place was to look like a big man, and that was admittedly a little tough to do playing with a teenybopper guitarist like George. In the end, however, Harrison's exceptional musical skill coupled with McCartney's insistence that George be brought on board overruled John's initial reservations.

George played "Raunchy" for them in a cellar club called the Morgue, then hung around the band until he was invited to play with them. He was formally accepted as a member on February 6, 1958.

McCartney, however, tells a slightly different tale. He says George's audition took place atop a Liverpool-bound bus: "George slipped quietly into one of the seats aboard this largely deserted bus we were riding, took out his guitar and went right into 'Raunchy.' A few days later I said to John, 'Well, what do you think?' And he finally says, 'Yeah, man, he'd be great!' And that was simply that. George was in."

Becoming a Quarryman though didn't mean George wasn't interested in playing with other people. Former bandmate Ken Brown recalls some of the particulars of George's musical curiosity:

It was summer 1958, and Harrison and I were playing in the Les Stewart Quartet with a chap called Skinner. We spent hours practising in the Lowlands Club, Heyman's Green. We would probably have gone on playing at clubs but for George's girlfriend, Ruth Morrison. George had never been really keen on girls. He was still only fifteen, and at school with Paul. Later, he suddenly seemed to go head-over-heels for Ruth, who later moved to Birmingham to become a nurse.

Anyway, one evening the three of us were sitting in the Lowlands drinking coffee, moaning about the fact that we had nowhere regular to play, when Ruth suggested we see Mrs. Best at the Casbah. Mrs. Best promised that the Les Stewart Quartet would play at the club when it opened. On the Saturday we were due to open, however, I went round to Les's house. George was sitting in the lounge with his Hofner guitar across his lap, idly plucking at the strings. The atmosphere seemed a bit tense.

"What's up?" I asked, but George just looked down at his guitar and said nothing. So I turned to Les. He looked daggers.

"You've been missing practice, Ken," he said.

"I know," I replied, "but only so's we can have somewhere to play. I've spent hours working at the club."

"You've been getting paid for it, too," challenged Les.

"No, I haven't."

"Well, I'm not going to play there," said Les, as our argument got steadily more heated.

"Look," I said, "the club opens tonight. We've spent months waiting for this, you're not backing out, too?"

George thought for a moment, then said he would walk home with me, so we left Les at his house. As we were walking down the road, I turned to George and said, "We can't let Mrs. Best down now. Let's try and get a group together ourselves. Do you know anyone?"

"Well, there's two mates I sometimes play with out in Woolton," ventured George.

"Okay, let's ask them," I said, and off George went on the bus, joining me two hours later at the Casbah with his two mates, who turned out to be John and Paul. This was the first time I had met them.

Paul was still at school, and had a schoolboyish haircut. But John was a bit of a beatnik, with his hair hanging well over his collar, dressed in a checkered suitcoat and old jeans. I told them we would each be paid fifteen bob a night. They seemed glad about that, as most groups played just for the experience . . . . We went down great, particularly when Paul sang "Long Tall Sally." Our most popular numbers were with Lennon and McCartney on vocals. I was the rhythm guitarist. John's pet solo was "Three Cool Cats," which he used to growl into the mike.

Now that the Quarrymen had finally found a steady place to play in Mona Best's accommodating black basement, all that was needed was somewhere reasonable to rehearse. For a while, Paul and John frequented the ceramic-tiled front entranceway to John's Aunt Mimi's house but sometimes got rather cold busking in such close proximity to Mother Nature. "As far as our music went," remembers Paul, "I recall playing our guitars out in front, inside the porch. I think we might have even learned the chords to 'Blue Moon' in there as well. From what John has told me, Mimi banished him out there from about the first day he brought home his guitar on account of all the noise. But it ultimately worked out okay, I guess, as we used to kind of like the echo in there with the guitars bouncing off the tiles."

Soon, however, this idea was abandoned in favor of full Quarrymen practice sessions in Springwood at the home of John's wonderfully free-spirited mother, Julia. Lennon's half-sister Julia Baird remembers the delightful ruckus: "Our toilet was probably one of the tiniest in all of Great Britain, and to see John, Paul, George, Pete Shotton, Ivan Vaughan and Mummy all scrambling around inside trying to find a place to sit was truly a wondrous sight indeed! Perched precariously atop the commode, tucked like sardines into the bathtub, or tentatively saddling up to the sink, they somehow managed not only to fit, but to actually play!" And as Paul remembers: "It was the best room in the house, hands down! Quite crowded, too, as I recall. Don't forget, it wasn't only us in there but also our instruments. Many a fine tune has been written in that little room, let me tell you." The lineup for these unusual sessions was generally John, Paul and George on acoustic guitars, Pete Shotton on string bass, and John's uninhibited mother on either washboard or playing percussion with the aid of her favorite kitchen utensils.

Another place the budding Beatles found sanctuary was with George's mum. Louise was more than willing to open up her drawing room to the boys for practice while she scrambled about serving bacon butties and, of course, endless cups of hot, milky tea. "I remember the very first time John came round," says Harry.

George had been going on about him for weeks. Telling us all how wonderfully clever he was and all about the various goings-on within the group. As far as young Lennon was concerned, he was the kingpin all right. That first evening he was at the house, George had apparently just got round to introducing him to Louise when he somehow tripped and landed right smack on top of her on the settee. At that exact moment I happened to come in from work and was frankly a little dismayed to see my wife and this scruffy-looking teen face to face in such a compromising position. George, however, immediately cried out, "Don't worry, Dad, it's only John!" Well, it was one hell of an introduction anyway, I can tell you!

Unfortunately, for all the support and goodwill showered on the boys by Julia Lennon and the Harrisons, John's Aunt Mimi (whom he lived with) still cast a decidedly dim view on this scruffy band of back-street Beethovens. To her, John's ever-increasing musical involvement was simply a boyhood hobby gone out of hand. "The guitar's all right, John," she used to chide her nephew in her now famous line, "but you'll never earn your living by it!"

Menlove Avenue and Mimi's comfortable middle-class lifestyle at home with John was a very long way from the tatty reaches of the Speke estate where George and his family lived, a distinction the ever class-conscious Mimi was keenly aware of. "He's not coming in!" she used to bark at John after an avalanche of begging to allow George entrance into her well-ordered, tastefully decorated home. "And why not, Mimi?" John would boldly reply, "Too common for the likes of such a grand lady as you?"

At length, however, Mimi relented and allowed the scruffy teenager to come in for one quick cup of tea and a piece of her famous apple pie. She says:

> He ambled cautiously in, wearing a crewcut and a shocking-pink shirt over a horrendous striped blazer. He said, "Hello, Mrs. Smith, how are you? You've got a beautiful home here."
>
> "You've been practicing, I see," I cut him off. "John, you did a lovely job at tutoring. Come along in then, if you must."
>
> "Go ahead, John," I used to say. "You won't be happy until you haven't a decent friend left. You really seem to attract the common types, don't you?"

By this time, John was a student at the Liverpool College of Art, and as such had outgrown the boyish name of Quarrymen for his group. "They went through a quick succession of names," remembers Julia Baird. "First it was the Rainbows. Then Johnny and the Rainbows. Then the Moon-dogs. Then Johnny and the Moondogs. And later the Silver Beatles. Finally, of course, they eventually settled on the Beatles. Sometimes they would even change it two or three times within the course of a single evening. As a result, one had to be very careful how you addressed them to friends. You never knew for sure what it would be this week! After a time, I remember Mimi giving up and simply calling them 'John's group.'"

The fledgling Beatles were well on their way to becoming one of Liverpool's top teenage groups, but the competition was ferocious and any financial rewards nonexistent. "We were usually skint most of the time," says George.

> That was one of the things that finally led me to taking the job at Blackler's. It was getting awfully embarrassing asking my dad for pocket money every time I went out. More and more we began entering these ridiculous talent competitions purely on the hope that we might win the two or three pounds offered in prize money. I remember we kept getting beaten out by a singing group with a midget fronting them called the Sunny Siders. I suppose if we weren't having such a good laugh at it all we could have easily become thoroughly depressed.

One of the boys' first big breaks came when Britain's "Mr. Star Maker," Caroll Levis, announced to the papers in November 1959 that he would soon be holding auditions at the Empire Theatre in Liverpool for his Caroll Levis "Discoveries" television program, which was to be filmed at a Manchester studio some weeks later. As expected, virtually every guitar-toting teenager in town turned out for the big event including, of course, John, Paul and George, this time billing themselves as the Moondogs. Louise Harrison remembers George being absolutely "over the moon" when he received word of their selection:

> They let us know by post. At first I couldn't make out why anyone would send us a letter addressed to the "Moondogs," but then I twigged. "You must have won, son!" I shouted to George, who happened to be just at the top of the stairs getting ready to go out.
> "I can't believe it!" he cried, almost flying down the stairs to read the letter. "We're really on the way now!"

The evening of the big show, the boys boarded the train from Liverpool's Lime Street Station to Manchester, struggling down the platform with their guitars and primitive amplifiers tottering precariously atop a luggage cart. "Where are we going, fellas?" Lennon sang out as they made their way into the already rolling train. "To the top, Johnny!" they yelled. "Where's that, lads?" "Why, to the toppermost of the poppermost!"

Although the Moondogs gave a rousing performance that night, they were in jeopardy of missing the last train back to Liverpool and couldn't, therefore, stay for the final judging. It was a crushing disappointment to the starry-eyed young musicians, being so close to what they considered "the big time," only to have it elude them through something so simple as the lack of reliable transportation. For this night, anyway, "the toppermost of the poppermost" would remain just a distant dream.

III

SECURELY IN THE J.F.K. POSITION

Worldwide Beatlemania

We were just a bunch of loonies, taking drugs and trying to be honest.

GEORGE HARRISON

"THERE WAS A TIME WHEN GEORGE REALLY HAD NO FAITH AT ALL THAT the Beatles would ever click," Harry Harrison senior has said. "I remember him going on about the lot of us packing up and emigrating to Australia. Then it was Canada, and even Malta for a time. 'Just stick with the music, boy,' I told him. 'If you really want it bad enough you'll catch your star.'" Of all the Beatles, George Harrison was perhaps the least likely to have stayed in show business if the Beatles hadn't finally caught on. Adventure was what he was after, and money. In their early days with manager Brian Epstein, it was Harrison who was most concerned with the business of contracts and record royalties. In the early days of rock and roll, playing music had not so much to do with artistry as with setting one's self above the crowd. Says Harrison wryly: "We looked at fellas like Buddy Holly and Elvis and thought, 'That looks like a good job.' Money, travel, chicks, nice threads — there's a great deal to be said for playing rock and roll."

The boys' first notable tour was in May 1960, when they backed pop singer Johnny Gentle in Scotland on what Harrison's buddy "Legs" Larry Smith has called "the cellotape and chewing gum circuit." The two-week tour took the band — now called the Silver Beatles — to the northernmost tip of Scotland, where they played dingy working-men's clubs and tatty teenage ballrooms all along the eastern coast. John's art-school chum, bass player Stuart Sutcliffe, by now had joined the band, as had drummer Tommy Moore. To affect a more "professional" air, the young men adopted stage names. George became Carl Harrison, after his rock idol, Carl Perkins; John was renamed Johnny Silver; Paul was now Paul Raymon; Stu became Stu de Stael. Tommy Moore did not change his name.

As undistinguished as that first tour may have been, it did give the band a little taste of fame, and they were hooked. "Someone asked me for my autograph," Paul proudly wrote home to his dad. George, too, had particular reason to brag. He and Gentle had become quite chummy, and when they returned from Scotland the singer presented George with one of Eddie Cochran's old stage shirts as a memento. "That tour was our first faint hope of actually making it one day," Harrison has said.

> But unfortunately it didn't really do much for us back home in Liverpool. After hanging out for weeks the only gig that came along was backing up a stripper named Janice in a club on Upper Parliament Street. It was work, I suppose, but definitely not what any of us had in mind when we got together. As for me, I was just about convinced it was never going to happen, which gave me great reason

for concern. After all, the only other reasonable alternative was to just go out and find a real job. Frankly, that was something all of us dreaded.

By the early summer of 1960, the prospects for the band were dwindling. By all accounts Tommy Moore had been quite good on the skins, but, being significantly older than the others, wasn't about to make a career of bashing about with a local two-bit beat group. A month after the tour (during which Tommy had the misfortune of losing his two front teeth when the group's van collided with a car full of senior citizens), Moore unceremoniously bailed out.

The effect on the band was devastating, for no one would ever hire them without a drummer. Fortunately, the answer to the Beatles' prayers soon came in the person of Randolph Peter Best, a strikingly handsome though sometimes uncomfortably quiet young man. Not only did he have a gear new kit but his mum, Mona, also had her own teen club, an irresistible combination.

A few months later, Allan Williams, the diabolical Welshman who had arranged some earlier bookings for the boys, was in a trendy London coffee bar called the Two I's, when he ran into German nightclub owner Bruno Koschmider. "Do you think you could fix me up with a Liverpool group to take back home?" Koschmider inquired. "Sure thing," Williams shot back. "One of the city's best."

The band he had in mind was Derry and the Seniors, a well-organized beat group much loved in Merseyside. Their gig went well, and soon Williams was again called upon to help import more of Liverpool's raucous brand of rock and roll to Hamburg's music-loving teens. This time, though, the boys were not passed over. Despite strong objections from their families, in August 1960 the Beatles piled into Williams's battered van and barreled off to the Channel ferry and on to Germany. Pete Best recalls their arrival in Hamburg:

> We immediately made our way down to the Kaiserkeller, the club we were supposed to be playing. The place was really jumping, had terrific atmosphere and was otherwise most impressive. Unfortunately, Koschmider was soon to burst our bubble.
> "Oh, no, lads, you're playing the Indra at the bottom of the street," he told us, which certainly took us down a peg or two.

Our next question, of course, was "Where are we all staying?" We were dead on our feet from the journey. We expected a hotel or maybe even rooms in the club, but instead, Bruno led us out onto the street and down a long narrow alleyway into what appeared to be the rear entrance of a noisy cinema house called the Bambi Kino. Down a black, smelly corridor, we were ushered into what had to be the dirtiest, most unappealing digs in all of Hamburg. We used to call it the Black Hole of Calcutta.

If the living was rough, the work was rougher still as the boys were expected to perform for eight hours every night, a far cry from the tidy forty-five-minute sets they played back home. In his biting memoir, *The Man Who Gave the Beatles Away*, Allan Williams recalls the Beatles' first days in Germany: "At the Indra, the clients had, of course, come to see a girlie show. Word hadn't yet got round that there were no girls anymore and that a beat group called the Beatles from Liverpool was the star attraction . . . . They did their best, but the clients just weren't interested. 'Bring on the girls,' they shouted. They felt cheated. That scene did the boys no good at all."

Within a week, Bruno had canceled the gig, and the Indra once again reverted to the fine art of the tease. The boys couldn't have been happier, as Koschmider now let them share the bill with Derry and the Seniors back at the Kaiserkeller. In a 1969 interview with rock journalist Ritchie Yorke, George said:

In my opinion, our peak for playing live was in Hamburg. You see, at that time we weren't so famous, so the people who came to see us were drawn in simply by our music and whatever atmosphere we managed to create. We got very tight as a band there, as most nights we played until the wee hours. We developed quite a big repertoire of our own songs, but still played mainly old rock 'n' roll tunes. Back in England all the bands were getting into wearing matching ties and handkerchiefs and were doing little dance routines like the Shadows. We weren't into that bit, so we just kept on doing whatever we felt like.

If the Beatles' music was transformed by their Hamburg period, so too were the boys themselves. To ease the pain of the torturous sessions they soon learned that an over-the-counter amphetamine nicknamed Prellies would not only keep them awake but also deliver a delicious wiry rush when washed down with the strong dark German beer. "Fuckin' Nazi bastards!" Lennon would howl at the drugged-up jiving audience as they crashed their way through their set. "Sieg Heil, you mothers!" Surprisingly, the Germans found this kind of verbal abuse exhilarating and cheered more wildly with each and every venomous obscenity hurled their way. According to Pete, it was John who was most often the instigator of this kind of spirited naughtiness, with Paul and George ever ready to egg him on:

> I always had a lot of respect for John because he simply didn't give a damn. Seeing as it was always so cold in our hovel, Lennon bought himself a pair of great wooly long johns. So anyway, George makes him a bet that he won't put them on and stand in the middle of the Herberstrasse. I remember he was getting ready for bed when he suddenly kicked the doors open, and strutted out into the street. It was the middle of the morning, so of course people were everywhere. Seeing John, naturally they were astounded, but Lennon was totally nonchalant. He just stood there in his long johns and sunglasses reading an English newspaper he brought back from the Seaman's Mission. I remember the five of us playing leap frog once outside the Kaiserkeller. These were the kinds of things we got up to just to help take the pressure off. Remember, we were basically just five naive young guys thrown together a very long, long way from home.

Hamburg was not all teenage fun and games, however. Without warning, the carefree atmosphere could suddenly turn ugly, revealing the seamy underbelly of Hamburg's nightlife. Like a gritty circus midway, the brightly lit streets of the Reeperbahn were a sideshow of excess and degradation. Everywhere there were small-time gangsters, pimps, hustlers, drug dealers, as well as an exotic range of prostitutes of both sexes. A peek into any one of the dozens of seedy, ill-kept nightclubs revealed the full spectrum of uninhibited, often perverted sexual pleasure available to anyone possessing the meager price of admission.

George Harrison once listed his tour of duty in Hamburg as his only "higher education," and he wasn't far wrong. To the Beatles, Hamburg's raw, uncensored lifestyle gave them a kind of carte blanche to act out their most violent and aggressive fantasies. For years, sources close to the group have told lurid tales of drunken barroom brawls, street fights with jealous boyfriends and all manner of explicit sexual escapades, both hetero- and homosexual. Undeniably, they were heavy drinkers. But there has never been even a single shred of evidence to suggest that the boys' bedroom habits were anything but one hundred percent heterosexual. They soon graduated from Prellies to more serious drugs such as Purple Hearts and Black Beauties and also experimented with barbiturates. There was a definite dark side to their life in Hamburg, as John Lennon confided to author Hunter Davies in *The Beatles*: "Once we chose a British sailor to roll, as I thought I could chat him up in English and kid him on [that] we could get some birds. We all got drinking and drinking and he kept asking where's the girls. We kept chatting him up, trying to find out where he kept his money. We just hit him twice in the end, then gave up. We didn't really want to hurt him."

George remembers how the smell of Senior Service cigarets wafting onto the stage from the audience, a tell-tale sign that lots of British seamen were on shore leave, often meant trouble:

> After a while, we strictly avoided any and all contact with our fellow countrymen, as we knew that by the end of the evening most of them would probably be lying there half dead. If the waiters or patrons didn't gang up on them then the street toughs roaming around outside definitely would. Realizing we were English, they would often try and pal around with us a bit. But we knew better. Most of the time they weren't just knocked about either, but bludgeoned or even knifed.

As time went by the Beatles began to attract a more interested and discerning following, winning over scores of adventurous students and would-be artists who had come to frequent the Kaiserkeller. Of these, three had grown particularly close to the Beatles by virtue of their artistic interest in the group: Klaus Voormann, Astrid Kirchherr and Jurgen Vollmer. Voormann, the son of a prominent Berlin physician, happened to be walking around St. Paulie one night when he heard what sounded like a pretty wild rock band coming from a smoky basement club, so he decided to duck in for a moment and check it out. Ironically, it was not the Beatles he heard but rather their arch competitors, Rory Storm and the Hurricanes — with drummer Ringo Starr.

Voormann was mesmerized by the raw excitement generated by the group and sat near the stage for the rest of the night right next to the Beatles, who regarded this unlikely patron in his artsy, expensive-looking clothes with mild amusement. Later that evening, Voormann saw the boys perform and even managed a few awkward, halting words with John and Paul. From the first moment the Beatles took the stage, Voormann was solidly hooked. He returned the next night, and the next, this time bringing along his girlfriend, photographer Astrid Kirchherr. Before long, the Kaiserkeller was all but taken over by Klaus and his friends. Astrid, in a rare interview conducted shortly after the Beatles' meteoric rise to the top, remembered her initial impression of young Harrison:

> George was lovely. Wide-eyed, innocent, open and very loving and warm. He was always extremely popular with the fans and even in Hamburg had a dedicated, affectionate following. He used to tell me that he'd never met a girl like me before, and he meant it. Here I was, a photographer, with my own little car, living that sort of carefree artist's life with my friends.
>
> I felt protective of George. He was a long way from home and seemed to miss the attention of his family. The other boys were more grown up and so were a little less concerned with all that.
>
> I know, for example, that he always looked up to John, and probably even Stu, as big-brother figures. And conversely, it was sometimes difficult for them not to see George as something of a pain for being so young. Still, in their own way, they loved him. We all did. Even when things were pretty rough they all stuck together. They often argued amongst themselves, but just let an outsider have a go at one of them and the sparks would fly. At first they were close out of necessity; later it was out of love.

Altogether, the Beatles' first trek to Hamburg lasted just over four months. Although they found playing the Kaiserkeller infinitely prefera-ble to the cramped and seedy Indra, they weren't entirely happy with Bruno Koschmider's bullying tactics, nor with the deplorable living con-ditions they were forced to endure. As a result, they approached local club manager Peter Eckhorn and requested an audition with an eye toward transferring their talents to his Top Ten Club, an even grander version of the somewhat scruffy Kaiserkeller. The Beatles weren't the first from Koschmider's camp to consider defecting, either. A few weeks earlier, the group's personal bodyguard and club bouncer, Horst Fascher, had left to work for Eckhorn, as had Rosa, the washroom attendant, along with several other key employees.

The Top Ten was anxious to have the Beatles as their star attraction, but Bruno Koschmider was very distressed at the thought of losing his biggest draw to the competition. Unfortunately for Koschmider, the Beatles' contract with him was about to expire, leaving the group free to perform wherever they chose. And they wasted no time. One evening, without any notice, the boys were gone, off to play the Top Ten for their new boss, Peter Eckhorn. As far as the Beatles were concerned, after having lived rough for so long, their only loyalty now was to themselves.

They were quite pleased with their new position. Their accommodations, supplied courtesy of Eckhorn, were far more comfortable than the smelly lodgings they had shared at the Bambi Kino, and the pay was top-notch. With a new extended contract in hand, it looked as though things were finally beginning to go their way.

Precisely twenty-four hours after the boys had moved into their new rooms, they were awakened by a loud knock at the door. "Police! You must open up!" The boys scrambled out of bed and hurried to get dressed. Lennon stumbled into the hallway and cracked open the door just enough to make sure their visitors weren't a team of Koschmider's musclebound enforcers sent round to make the lads an offer they couldn't refuse. That was the only invitation the police required, though, and suddenly the room was wall to wall uniforms. "We are looking for the one called Harrison," one of the cops barked. Everyone froze. "What the fuck do you want him for?" said Lennon, surprisingly belligerent in the face of such authority. "He hasn't done anything."

Apparently the police had received an anonymous tip that George was only seventeen and was therefore too young to be playing in an adult club past curfew. On top of that, the Beatles had not bothered to secure either visas or work permits before the band came to perform in Germany. George was to be deported immediately. There was no way out of this one; the boys had been had, by someone with a grudge. Someone very like Bruno Koschmider. Astrid remembers:

Stu and I drove George to the train station [on November 21]. He looked so lost and pathetic standing there on the platform holding his battered guitar case and his little duffle bag of laundry. Tears were welling up in his eyes, and just at the last moment he threw his arms

34

around me and gave me a big hug . . . .

Of course, this was the worst possible way for someone as proud as George to have to go home. As a failure. With nothing to show for all those months of hard work. I'm sure he dreaded seeing his father especially. After all, he had a lot of "I told you so's" to look forward to.

The loss of their guitar player left the Beatles in an awkward position. They couldn't very well perform without him, and there was little hope that the German authorities would relent and allow them to stay. They had no choice but to make their way home as best they could. Before leaving Hamburg, however, they attended to a little last-minute unfinished business.

Paul and Pete returned to the Bambi on the pretense of picking up a few things they had left behind. On their way out, they contrived to set fire to their old digs. Legend has it that Paul set alight a rotting tapestry hanging on the wall, and the fire spread from there. The police subsequently tracked down the arsonists and detained them until they could be booked on the first available flight home to England. That left only John and Stu. Though Lennon, as penniless as ever, was forced to sell off most of his belongings and almost all his extra clothing, he didn't even earn enough for the train fare back to Liverpool. His only avenue of escape was Astrid, who graciously made up the difference and even threw in some extra money to allow the beleaguered Beatle to eat as well.

By this time, Stu and Astrid had become romantically involved, so he was naturally more reluctant to leave than the others. When he did, however, it was first class by air as he was suffering from tonsillitis, and Astrid wanted to make sure that the strain of the journey didn't further deplete his strength. John was the last to go home, returning to Liverpool in early December 1960.

The boys were quite demoralized and didn't even bother getting in touch with each other for almost a week. Paul, meanwhile, had accepted a job on a delivery truck, hauling parcels around the city for a scant seven pounds a week. The lads eventually got back together to play a gig on December 17. But it was their December 27 show at the Litherland Town Hall that marked the beginning of the Beatles' rise to the top in Liverpool. Playing in Hamburg had had a profound effect on their music. Compared with the other groups knocking around town, they were brilliant. Their repertoire was extensive, their playing clean and succinct, and their vocalizing energetic and compelling as never before. "We just couldn't believe how much better we sounded than the rest of the lads," Harrison has rather immodestly recalled. "After a couple of gigs together, what happened to me in Hamburg became basically one bad memory in an otherwise very groovy scene."

Paddy Delaney, the former bouncer at Liverpool's famous Cavern Club on Matthew Street, still vividly recalls the Beatles' first appearance there on March 21, 1961. Like so many others once close to the phenomenon, he seems to be frozen in time. If you meet him for a drink at the nearby Grapes (a legendary Beatle watering hole), he will take out his wallet and show you his faded snapshots of the boys and bend your ear with stories of the good old days for as long as you let him:

> The first one I ever saw was George Harrison. In those days hairstyles were very strict and tidy, but George's hair was down to his collar. He was very scruffy and hungry-looking. I remember him ambling down the middle of the street, and for a minute I didn't think he was coming in. I stopped him at the door and asked him if he was a member. Of course I knew he wasn't and he said no, he was with the Beatles. Now we'd heard a lot about the Beatles over the previous weeks, and I knew they were on that particular night, so I let him in even though he was wearing blue jeans, which were strictly banned from the club. About fifteen minutes later, Paul McCartney tumbled down the street with John Lennon in close pursuit. Paul was carrying his bass guitar, and John had his hands dug deep into his pockets. I had an idea they were with George because they all had the same sort of hairstyle. It wasn't quite a Beatle haircut then, but it was still well past their collars. A little while after they strolled in, a taxi pulled up in front of the club and out came Pete Best. He was carrying the Beatles' first sound system, which consisted of two cheap chipboard speakers and a beat-up-looking amplifier. He also had a set of old drums, which he unloaded and took down the stairs. This is how the Beatles first arrived at the Cavern.

Even being asked to play the dank basement club was a triumph of sorts. The problem was that the owner, ex-accountant Ray McFall, was a traditional jazz buff in the extreme and looked down his nose on rock and roll. Prior to being invaded by the Beatles and company, the Cavern swung to the deep cool sounds of such artists as Acker Bilk, Johnny Dankworth and Chris Barber.

Ultimately, however, McFall had to give in to the expanding tastes of his audience and reluctantly opened the Cavern to what was then simply called Beat music. Former club deejay Bob Wooler remembers the Beatles' first appearance there:

> Originally I joined the Cavern for their lunchtime sessions only. I'd been onto Ray McFall about this group, the Beatles, for some time. I was really rooting for them. I said to him, "Furthermore, they are able to play lunchtimes because they don't work during the day." But unfortunately, he wasn't a very easy person to get through to. Now if you think I am sort of prim and proper, you should meet Ray! He's really the typical English gentleman. You wouldn't expect to find a person like him getting involved in the pop scene. Eventually, though, he agreed, and they played their first lunchtime session for the bargain basement price of just six pounds!

Tony Mansfield, original drummer and founder of the Dakotas, played on the same bill as the Beatles during those early days at the Cavern. He remembers the Beatles were very entertaining, "especially on the lunchtime sessions because it was so much more laid back. Many people were out of work, and I'll always remember John walking up on stage with a bacon butty in one hand and a cup of tea in the other, coming out with comments like, 'I've got to finish me butty first before we play, luv.' They used to perform television commercials, too. 'Omo washes not only white not only bright but clean.' They were just farting around, but it was a good laugh."

The Cavern soon became such a popular nightspot for live music in Liverpool that virtually every able-bodied teenager within a twenty-five-mile radius of Matthew Street had, at one time or another, jived at Ray McFall's most trendy of cellars.

To George Harrison, the Beatles' great success at the Cavern prophesied even better things to come. Gone were the nagging doubts that had plagued the young man, and also those of his father, who wasn't really keen on his son pursuing a career in music. Perhaps he could make a decent living playing guitar after all. The way Paddy Delaney remembers it, Harrison's newfound stature as the lead guitarist for Liverpool's top group didn't really seem to change the good-natured lad much at all.

George was always a big-hearted kid. I can just see him coming down
Matthew Street, driving his spanking new second-hand car, which
he had just bought with the first little bit of money that he'd made
from the Beatles. As he stepped out of his car and locked it up, I
happened to be arguing with two girls who didn't have quite enough
money to get in. Now this was a big night at the Cavern Club. The
place was packed, and these poor girls were just standing outside in
the street in tears. Well, George pushed past the two, into the club,
but paused at the top of the stairs and motioned for me to come over.
"What's the matter with those two, Pat?"

"Look, George, I'm sorry, but they haven't got enough money
to get in."

Chuckling, he pulled a pound out of his pocket and told me to
give it to them but to make sure they didn't find out who it was from.

By early spring of 1961, the Beatles were one of Merseyside's top
bands but were still virtually unknown outside their hometown. By now
George had turned eighteen, so the group returned to Hamburg to play
the Top Ten, from April through July 1961. While there, they had been
invited to sit in on a recording session with transplanted English pop
singer Tony Sheridan, who was perhaps Hamburg's most popular enter-
tainer. Although the Beatles had recorded a few times previously, once as
the Quarrymen in a friend's basement studio in Liverpool and then in the
fall of 1960 at Akustik Studios in Hamburg, these were their first truly
professional sessions. Produced by the well-known orchestra leader Bert
Kaempfert, the boys recorded eight tunes: six backing Sheridan, and two
others, a rocked-up version of "My Bonnie" and a Harrison-Lennon
original, "Cry for a Shadow." Released as a single in Germany in August
1961, a few imported copies of "My Bonnie" made their way back to
England and before long the obscure 45 was occasionally being spun in a
few Liverpool-area discos. All of which prompted eighteen-year-old Raymond Jones to wander into local businessman Brian Epstein's NEMS
(North East Music Stores) shop in the Whitechapel section of Liverpool
on October 28, 1961, and request a copy of the hard-to-find single.

Epstein had always prided himself on his ability to rustle up even the
most obscure records for his customers, but this particular order had him
stumped. What's more, none of Brian's many contacts in the music
business had even heard of the band, much less their fly-by-night single.
Coincidentally, a couple of weeks later, while chatting with one of his

At a Beatles recording session, 1965.
DELIBERATE ALCHEMY ARCHIVES

The Beatles pose in smog masks on a
particularly foggy night.
DELIBERATE ALCHEMY ARCHIVES

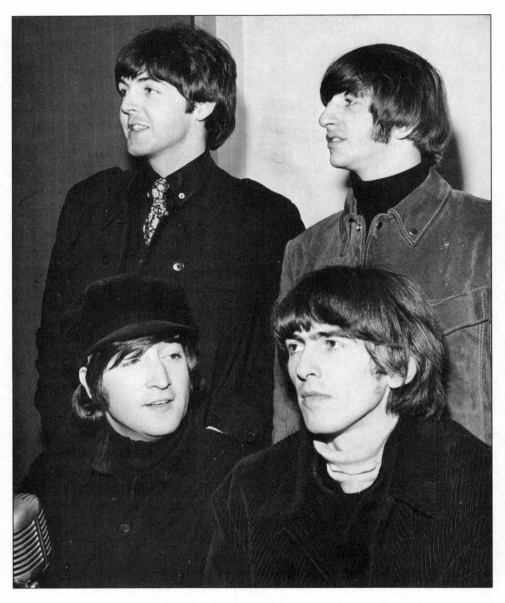

Meeting the press at yet another fab Beatle press conference somewhere on the road, 1965.

salesclerks, he learned that the mystery group was playing only a few hundred feet away at the tiny basement club on Matthew Street. He was intrigued.

A little after noon on November 9, 1961, Brian and his personal assistant, Alistair Taylor, visited the Cavern to hear for themselves this swinging ensemble known as the Beatles. Thirty-four days later, during a meeting at Pete Best's house, a formal management agreement was negotiated between the Beatles and Epstein's NEMS Enterprises. Brian didn't actually sign the document but simply shook hands as a show of faith. After all, unlike these four young scruffs, Epstein was a gentleman and his word was therefore his bond. At any rate, the deal was done. The Beatles finally had themselves an official manager and Epstein yet another pet project to occupy his otherwise tediously lonely life. Little did either party suspect what was to happen to them all in just a few short months.

In the April 1962 edition of Bill Harry's popular Liverpool music publication, *Mersey Beat*, Bob Wooler hinted at the profound impact he believed Brian Epstein's fastidious management was about to have on the group:

> They have gained immeasurably in prestige as a result of the inquiries of their manager. That they will secure a recording contract with a major British label in the near future is certain. Their outlook is now mature and professional. They are no longer only a local attraction . . . . If it is possible for a rock 'n' roll group to become a status symbol, then the Beatles have made it so. They are still a phenomenon, but now their appeal is legend!

That same month, the new, improved Beatles were to be flown to Germany under Epstein's auspices to begin their third stint on the Reeperbahn. This time they were booked into what was perhaps Hamburg's most upmarket venue, the Star Club.

On April 10, just as the boys were about to leave for Speke Airport, an urgent telegram was received from Astrid. Suddenly taken ill at her mother's house in Altona, a Hamburg suburb, Stu had collapsed and was rushed by ambulance to the hospital. He never made it, dying en route, cradled in Astrid's arms.

The ultimate cause of Stuart's death remains largely a mystery, although it was probably a brain hemmorhage. Paul, Pete and John immediately flew to Germany to be with Astrid. When they met Brian,

George and Stu's mother, Millie Sutcliffe at the airport the next day, "there wasn't a dry eye to be found anywhere," remembered Epstein years later. "That is, all except for John, who, I'm afraid, had drawn all his hurt deep inside in an effort to mask his true feelings."

"I always had lots of fights with Stuart, but I really liked him and we were very friendly before he died," George has said. This was the first time someone close to Harrison had passed away. "I know he felt just terrible for Astrid," George's mother commented. "I remember him writing home from Germany chock full of stories saying 'Stu and John did this,' 'Astrid and the lads went here.' In those days, anyway, they were all still very close." It was a measure of the Beatles' deep affection for the young artist that, five years later, his picture would be featured among the pantheon of famous faces appearing on the legendary *Sgt. Pepper* sleeve.

It was at this time that the first faint rumblings of the upheaval that lay ahead began to make an impression on Harrison. Hundreds flocked to see the boys perform nightly at the Star Club. Brian Epstein, meanwhile, in an all-or-nothing assault on London's jaded record executives, secured a recording contract with EMI through producer George Martin in July 1962. Upon their return to Liverpool, drummer Pete Best was soon sacked in favor of the charismatic Ringo Starr; Stu, however, did not need to be replaced, as Paul McCartney had taken over on bass. A Beatle fan club was formed, which took in dozens of new members monthly. Outside their homes, all the boys were besieged daily by swooning teenage girls and pushy autograph hunters. No longer could they even sit together with their girlfriends for a quiet night out at their favorite pubs. They were public property now — reasonably well paid for the privilege, but public property nonetheless. "Of course, at first we all thought we wanted the fame and that," George recalled at a launch party for his 1988 comeback album, *Cloud Nine*.

> But, very shortly thereafter, we began to think twice. Before we knew it we were parading about in those silly suits and ties, cranking out music that no one could hear anyway. After a bit we realized that fame wasn't really what we were after at all, just the fruits of it. After the initial excitement and thrill had worn off, I, for one, became depressed. Is this all we have to look forward to in life? Being chased around by a crowd of hooting lunatics from one crappy hotel room to the next?

One story from those days illustrates the unusual lengths the boys sometimes had to go to to avoid those "hooting lunatics." In July of 1963 the band played a gig at a local carnival in the Liverpool suburbs. Although the performance went smoothly enough, as usual the group had to rush offstage as soon as they'd played their last note, or else risk being torn apart by their fans. Tom McKenzie, one of the band's earliest emcees, wandered into the gents' toilet after the show only to find George locked in one of the stalls. "Oh, Tom," he moaned, "I'm sick as a bloody dog." "You're also stuck here," Tom replied. "The other boys have already left." There was another loud moan from inside. "Hold on a minute, mate," McKenzie said, "let me see what I can arrange." Tom scrambled out through the stage door and was met by a throng of young women all clamoring to meet the Beatles.

Making his way into the car park, he spotted a bus driver waiting to take a load of fans back to Liverpool. Suddenly Tom had an inspiration and invited the driver backstage, where, with the help of a crisp pound note he was persuaded to strip off to the waist. McKenzie then took the uniform into the bathroom and said to George, "Just put these on, son, and then we'll walk you out right through the crowd." Tom recalls:

> We walked quietly back outside to the bus and lo and behold, nobody noticed that it was him at all. Everyone thought it was just the driver coming back out again. About two hundred yards or so up the road the rest of the boys were waiting in the car for George, so we just kind of ambled out of sight of the crowd and ran up to the car. Now when the other Beatles saw George, they almost pissed themselves with laughter . . . . The driver was a rather stocky fellow, and of course George was mostly skin and bones anyway, so with the big coat on and the hat falling down over his ears, he looked absolutely ridiculous. So anyway, while the boys were hooting away at George, they all signed autographs for the driver, and off they went down the road in their beat-up old car.

By the fall of 1963, full-tilt, gut-wrenching, diehard Beatlemania had descended upon the British Isles. By Christmastime the band had played the prestigious Royal Variety Performance, toured Sweden, scored a number-one single with "I Want to Hold Your Hand" and consummated the deal for their first full-length motion picture, *A Hard Day's Night*.

Now that the Beatles were finally the household names they'd always imagined they wanted to be, all sorts of interesting offers regularly presented themselves through Epstein's NEMS office on Argyle Street, London. One of the most commercially viable to Brian was the *Daily Express*'s bid for George Harrison to front a weekly feature sensibly entitled "George's Column" and ghosted entirely by Beatle crony and crackerjack journalist Derek Taylor. Although the first installment wasn't even seen by Harrison until just before press time, thereafter the two co-conspirators met regularly on the pretext of discussing the particulars of each edition; more often than not they ended up whiling away the afternoons propping up the bar at some discreet back-street tavern. It was the beginning of a wonderful, lifelong friendship.

"George's Column" lasted only a little more than six months, yet it helped to set Harrison apart in the public eye from his three ever-present cohorts. In one of the first columns, George/Derek discussed the previously taboo subject of how much money a Beatle might expect to take home in a good year:

> This year I will probably earn, gross, upwards of £50,000 for appearances on stage and in other mediums. Big though it is, this figure is not final. Money comes in from our royalties on photographs, books, magazines, sweaters, badges, wigs, chewing gum, seasonal cards and discs . . . Our manager, "Eppy," Brian Epstein, takes his percentage, which is on a sliding scale up to 25% and I don't begrudge him a penny because he is the fifth Beatle and the best friend we have. We buy our own clothes and equipment out of the earnings and probably when the tax man finishes I'm left with about £9,000 a year for spends.

Epstein, needless to say, was not amused.

In those early days, the Beatles lived, in the words of John Lennon, "like kings of the jungle." Anything went so long as it could somehow be kept out of the papers. It was a super-sensual free-for-all set spinning by the seemingly impenetrable aura of power and success that enveloped these four very eager young men. "The Beatles' early tours were like the Fellini film *Satyricon*," Lennon revealed in *Rolling Stone* after the breakup of the group in 1970.

We had that image. Man, our tours were like something else. If you could get on one of our tours, you were in!

Wherever we went we always had a whole bedroom scene going, but we had our four separate bedrooms. We tried to keep them out of our room. Derek [Taylor]'s and [road manager] Neil [Aspinall]'s rooms were always full of junk and whores and who-the-fuck-knows-what, and policemen were with us! When we hit town, we hit it! There was no pissing about. There's photographs of me crawling about in Amsterdam on my knees coming out of whore houses and things like that. The police escorted us to the places because they never wanted a big scandal, you see.

Although the boys were doing their best to enjoy themselves despite the rigors of the road, nothing could subdue their almost obsessive desire to conquer America. George had already popped over to St. Louis, in September 1963, for a short holiday to visit his sister Louise, who had married an American in July 1954. He liked most of what he found, although he didn't really think much of the young ladies he met. "Very straight with braces on their teeth," he complained. George did enjoy walking around downtown, though, and taking in a drive-in movie in the family car. "We saw Cliff Richard in *Summer Holiday*," he has recalled. Louise was so staunch in her devotion to her baby brother's group that even though the band had yet to break in the States, she spent days ringing local radio stations requesting Beatle tunes. Epstein, too, made a short trip, to New York in 1963. Accompanied by Liverpool crooner and NEMS artist Billy J. Kramer, he met with television pioneer Ed Sullivan to discuss plans for the Beatles' appearance on his popular "really big shew." After a bit of respectable tussling over whether or not the Beatles would get top billing, a deal was finally struck for three appearances by the group on February 9, 16 and 23, 1964, for a total fee of $10,000. Later, New York promoter Sid Bernstein persuaded Brian Epstein to allow him to book the boys into Carnegie Hall for two big shows on February 12.

In January 1964 "I Want to Hold Your Hand" entered the American record charts at number 83. By the next week it had climbed steadily to 42 and showed no signs of leveling off. Days later, while the Beatles were holed up in their ritzy digs at the famous Hôtel Georges V near the Champs-Elysées in Paris, they received a call from New York informing them that their turbulent teenage love call had toppled Bobby Vinton's "There! I've Said It Again" and was now number one on the charts. Everyone was ecstatic. It was a dream come true. The boys had already experienced the thrill of topping the charts back home. Now they were taking America!

On board Pan Am flight 101 from London's Heathrow to New York's Kennedy Airport, on February 7, 1964, George Harrison and his three colleagues were very anxious. "America's got everything," thought Harrison out loud. "Why should they want us?" On top of feeling almost unbearable apprehension, George was also sick with the flu and concerned that his hair didn't look quite right following a last-minute shampoo back in London (no small worry to a group for whom hair was such an important part of the act). Brian Epstein, meanwhile, though trying to appear calm, was concerned that Harrison's ill health would prevent him from playing either "The Ed Sullivan Show" or Carnegie Hall.

From the moment they landed on American soil, everything went at breakneck speed. As the plane slowly made its way to the gate, the shrill screams of more than ten thousand hysterical teenagers penetrated the hull of the aircraft. Peering through the windows of the DC 10, the boys thought that perhaps the president was about to land on another runway. In her 1978 book, *A Twist of Lennon*, John's first wife, Cynthia, remembers the chaos. "We were all on cloud nine. When the door of the aircraft finally swung open the atmosphere and the reaction were indescribable. America truly belonged to us."

"Every kid from Broadway to the Bronx is here," observed one seasoned veteran of the New York press corps in an on-the-spot report. "They're wearing buttons that say 'I Like The Beatles,' and waving homemade banners. Teenaged girls are fainting by the dozens, and we've even seen a few of the older cops sticking bullets in their ears, for Pete's sake. As far as I can tell the four Beatles are standing at the door of the aircraft almost certainly completely and utterly in shock. No one, I mean *no one*, has ever seen or even remotely suspected anything like this before!"

Through an intense human crush, the bewildered Beatles were led into a specially laid-out lounge, where they went head to head with the American media in a wild, anything-goes press conference. Early on, John Lennon yelled at everyone to shut up and the entire room applauded.

"How do you like this welcome, boys?"

"So this is America," said Ringo. "They all seem to be out of their minds."

"Are you going to have a haircut while you're here?"

"I had one yesterday," replied George.

"Why don't you smile, George?"

"I'll hurt my lips."

"Will you sing something for us, boys?"

"We need money first," snorted John.

"What is your secret?"

"If we knew that we'd form a group and be their managers," Lennon growled into the mike.

"Do you hope to take anything home with you?"

"Yeah," said Paul. "Rockefeller Center."

"Ringo, what do you think of Beethoven?"

"I love him. Especially his poems."

"Some of your detractors allege that you are bald and those haircuts are wigs. Is that true, John?"

"Oh, we're all bald. Yeah. And I'm deaf and dumb, too."

"Where did the name 'Beatle' come from?"

"We were just racking our brains, and John came up with this name Beatle," replied George. "It was good because it was the insect and it was also a pun, you know, 'beat,' on the beat. We liked the name, so we kept it."

"John, is it all a fad?"

"Obviously. Anything in this business is a fad. We don't think we're going to last forever. We're just going to have a good time while it does."

"George, why do you wear your hair in such an unusual style?"

"Well, we've always liked it long, even when we were at school. I went to the swimming baths, and when I came out my hair dried, and it was just all forward like a mop so I left it like that. When Ringo joined the group we got him to get his hair like this because by then people were calling it the Beatle cut."

After a few minutes, press officer Brian Sommerville brusquely thanked the ladies and gentlemen of the press and the boys and their entourage were ceremoniously driven into the city in four plush Cadillac limousines. Outside the Plaza Hotel, thousands of screeching teenyboppers greeted their new idols.

As it turned out, Brian had good reason to worry about George's illness. Almost immediately after arriving at the Plaza, George took to his bed. A doctor was called and George's sister, Louise, moved into an adjacent room to nurse him. To further preserve the Beatle's strength, Neil Aspinall stood in for him at rehearsals for "The Ed Sullivan Show." In the end George rallied and, sustained by various medications, managed to get through the show. He even used his time in bed to do telephone interviews with deejays all across the country.

After their first appearance on "The Ed Sullivan Show," which was seen by a record 73 million viewers, the entourage boarded a train bound for Washington, D.C., on the morning of February 11. That night they played before twenty-thousand screaming fans at the Coliseum, another record audience and the first of many manic concerts the Fab Four were forced to endure. "It was bloody awful," says Harrison.

> Some journalist had apparently dug up an old quote of John's that I was fond of jelly babies and had written about it in his column. That night we were absolutely pelted by the fuckin' things. To make matters worse, we were on a . . . circular stage, so they hit us from all sides. Imagine waves of rock-hard little bullets raining down on you from the sky. Every now and then one would hit a string on my guitar and plonk off a bad note as I was trying to play. From then on everywhere we went it was exactly the same.

Despite their many triumphs, as the Beatles made their way from Washington, back to New York, and then down to Miami, the lunacy that surrounded them began to take its toll. John and George, in particular, soon grew cynical that the Beatles seemed to provide an excuse for kids to run wild in the streets, smashing phone boxes and climbing up elevator shafts in hopes of catching a glimpse of one of their idols.

On Friday, February 21, the Beatles ended their two-week mini-tour of North America, physically exhausted but basically relaxed, due in large part to a five-day holiday Epstein had allowed them in Miami. Now that America and England had clearly fallen under their spell, the remainder of the world was sure to follow. They were still in their early twenties, but already their vast experience had in many ways made them old men. Harrison, especially, who had only just turned twenty-one, was far more cynical and jaded than his years. "How fuckin' stupid it all is," he commented on the flight back. "All that big hassle to make it, only to end up as performing fleas." At the other end of the plane, Epstein was busily making plans for his next big coup, the filming of A Hard Day's Night.

Meanwhile, back in Liverpool, the Harrisons' tidy lives were being turned upside down by an avalanche of fans and fan mail that ended up daily at their door. Unlike the other Beatle parents, Harry and Louise were flattered by all the attention and genuinely seemed to enjoy kibbitzing with their famous son's many admirers. On George's twenty-first birthday, so many thousands of cards and presents were received that the post office had to dispatch several oversized mail vans to cope with the deluge. Outside the house, hundreds of screaming, swooning fans gathered to help celebrate the occasion, the teenage crowd eventually swelling to such proportions that the police had to be called in. "They put a bobby outside the front door," remembers Harry.

> Every few minutes Louise would make me run him out some tea, as it was very cold. "How do you live with all this?" he asked. What could I say? There were little girls queuing up to kiss our front door knob. "We love George!" they used to shout whenever one of us showed our faces.
>
> "Not half as much as we do," I'd reply. That would get them all right. Half of them would boo and hiss and the other half would applaud. Looking back, I suppose it was rather an odd way to live, but in the beginning it was just so damned exciting. The most exciting thing any of us had ever known.

Among the throngs of visitors who regularly flocked to bask in the hospitality offered by the Harrisons during the early years of Beatlemania was young Scott Wheeler and his family from New England. According to Scott, he and his parents were among the first American Beatle fans to travel to Liverpool and knock on Louise and Harry Harrison's door in August of 1964.

> We were completely unprepared for the astonishing reception that awaited us. They were busy making Sunday dinner, but they dropped everything and invited us in. Moments later, my parents and I were sitting in their parlor, gazing in stunned disbelief at the gold records proudly displayed on the wall and the stacks of fan mail piled on the tiny desk in the corner, while George's parents and his brother Peter cheerfully bustled about in the kitchen making us coffee and sandwiches. Later on, while I was sitting on George's bed, strumming one of his guitars, Lou gave me a typed Beatles set list she had found in one of George's coat pockets. It was the start of a wonderful friendship and a lively transatlantic correspondence that lasted until Lou and Harry passed away.
>
> My mother and I paid George's parents a second visit in June

1966. Once again we were overwhelmed by their hospitality and kindness. They met our train at Warrington Station and drove us out to the magnificent country bungalow that George had bought for them as a retirement present. Again they made us lunch, then played us a freshly arrived acetate of George's still unreleased sitar opus, "Love You Too" (originally entitled "Granny Smith"), on a deluxe stereo system George had personally selected. I will never forget watching Louise joyously dancing around the room to the thunderous strains of George's sitar music while Harry looked on admiringly. They both acted as happy as newlyweds in their honeymoon cottage.

So committed to the fans was Louise Harrison that she picked up her son's fan mail from the Beatles' Fan Club in Liverpool once a month and wrote one- or two-page replies to virtually every reasonable letter. Often she would work late into the night, even struggling through the foreign ones, picking up what she could of the content from the words she found that seemed similar to English. On average, she went through two-thousand letters a month from 1963 to 1966, slowing down only slightly during the final years of her life. In addition, both Harry and Louise enthusiastically participated in numerous charity events over the years, including judging local beauty contests, attending official openings, garden fetes and church socials all across England. "It was our way of saying thanks to all the people who helped make the Beatles the great success they were. Besides," said Harry, "we both thoroughly enjoyed ourselves."

Another young fan fortunate enough to make the acquaintance of Mr. and Mrs. Harrison during those first turbulent years of Beatlemania was Alanna Nash. Now a well known author and journalist, she remembered her first impressions of Louise following a 1966 encounter in a Cheshire restaurant.

She was a large woman with lovely white hair and a face that positively would not keep still; Mrs. Harrison constantly talked or laughed when she wasn't mugging for my super 8 camera. Clearly, she dominated the night's conversation, and in her stylish light blue dress, she didn't much resemble the fan-magazine pictures of the dutiful, loving mum who stayed in the background writing letters to fans around the world. She had fixed herself up a great deal with clothes and makeup — not to mention the fame, money and prestige

George provided — and I got the impression that she could be more than a little haughty if she chose to be.

Throughout the next six weeks the Beatles were hard at work portraying themselves in their film debut, *A Hard Day's Night*. At first, George was the odd man out, not really presenting a strong enough image for the writers to home in on while they were preparing the script. As a result, he was initially treated almost as a stand-in for himself, ambling his way through the scenes with a disinterested edginess. All that changed, however, when writer Alun Owen and director Richard Lester cleverly devised a scene in which Harrison wanders into the production offices of a trendy television casting director. After George is ejected for insulting the TV bigwig, the jaded director wonders out loud if perhaps the cheeky young man's attitude might not be a clue "to the new direction." Checking his calendar, he relaxes when he discovers that "*the change* isn't due for three weeks yet." It is a biting satire of the flipness of the emerging pop culture of the era, and clearly Harrison's most memorable scene.

A Hard Day's Night is still remembered as well for its original use of the new word *grotty*, pseudo-Liverpool slang for grotesque. Even John Lennon had to sit up and take notice: "I dug *A Hard Day's Night* although Alun Owen only came with us for two days before he wrote the script. He actually invented the word *grotty*. We all thought it was really weird, and George cringed with embarrassment every time he had to say it. But it's part of the language now, you hear society people using it. Amazing."

The film premiered on July 6, 1964, at the Pavilion Theatre in Piccadilly Circus, London. Apart from the Beatles and company, Princess Margaret and her husband, the Earl of Snowdon, were in attendance, and reportedly loved the fast-paced, off-beat comedy. Following the screening, there was a huge, elegant party planned to which the Royals had not been invited, on the simple pretext that they would never have agreed to come. But the film's producer, Walter Shenson, was loathe to offend such highly placed patrons and rushed over to invite them at the very last minute.

After the party got going, George leaned over to Shenson and whispered, "So when are we going to eat?"

"Listen, George, we can't possibly eat until Princess Margaret and Snowdon leave. Just be patient."

After another fifteen minutes or so, George got up from the table and casually walked over to the royal couple (who by this time were rather respectably tipsy) and said, "Your Highness, we really are hungry and Mr. Shenson says we can't eat until you two go . . ."

"I see," said the princess, nearly hysterical with laughter. "Well, in that case, we'd better run." With that, she and her entourage gracefully said their goodbyes and the hungry Harrison made a beeline to the dining room.

That June the Beatles toured the Netherlands, Denmark, Hong Kong, Australia and New Zealand. Just before leaving, Ringo developed a severe case of tonsillitis and subsequently missed most of the early dates. To replace him, Epstein recruited an obscure London session drummer, Jimmy Nicol, and the tour began. "I was dead set against carrying on without Ringo," says George. "Imagine, the Beatles without Ringo Starr! Anyway, I bowed to the pressure and off we went, but I was none too pleased, even though Jimmy was actually quite a lovely guy."

As expected, the tour was a whopping commercial success. In Adelaide, Australia, a quarter million of the faithful turned out to see the Fab Four glide triumphantly into the city center from the airport. Hospitals brought some of their patients outside to witness the great event and, in the sweltering heat, dozens fainted. George Harrison, sitting in what he called the "J.F.K. position" in the open limo, gaped in wonder at the long, winding ribbons of humanity so enraptured of these four long-haired musicians from Liverpool. Once again, the Beatles were greeted with unquestioning adulation. Once more they looked helplessly at each other and wondered, "Why?"

Harrison was fast becoming so fed up with it all that sometimes when the band was asked to greet the swelling crowds from their hotel balconies, he would silently motion Derek Taylor to step into his place at the last moment. "Who could tell anyway?" he muses.

That August, they returned to America to begin a month-long, twenty-three city tour that commenced in San Francisco. Although they had little new to say musically, there was still heaps of money to be made and lots of people ready to help them cash in. "We don't bother counting our money anymore," commented John Lennon sardonically. "We just weigh it." He wasn't far wrong.

This time around, the Beatles had the luxury of their own private jet, a Lockheed Electra, which gave them privacy — at least in the air. Back on the ground, however, it was the same old story. "Everybody wanted the image to carry on," said John later. "The press does too, because they want all the free drinks, the free whores and the fun; everybody wants to keep on the bandwagon. We were Caesars; who was going to knock us when there were so many millions of pounds to be made? All the handouts, the bribery, the police, all the fucking hype." Hype indeed. In Chicago, one firm was marketing "Canned Beatle's Breath." Following their Kansas City concert, an enterprising pair paid a thousand dollars for the bed linen on which the Beatles had reportedly slept. These were then cut into 150,000 one-inch squares and offered to the youth of the world for a mere ten dollars apiece. Over the next couple of years, a number of licensing deals were put together under the auspices of New York businessman Nicky Byrne, for Seltaeb Ltd. (*Beatles* spelled backward), which in turn had a deal with NEMS Enterprises in London. Altogether, 234 products were listed with Epstein's company at the time of his death in 1967, including Beatle egg cups, airbeds, cutlery, ladies' fancy garters with lockets, coat hangers, a Beatle bingo game, ladies' briefs, wallpaper, plastic disposable drinking cups and Beatle talcum powder. Among the bizarre proposals for which licenses were never granted was a Beatles sanitary napkin emblazoned with the likeness of each of the "Fabs."

In San Francisco, a tickertape parade through downtown was planned, but the boys adamantly refused to participate. After all, it had been only nine months since President Kennedy's assassination in Dallas. "Too many windows," said John at the time. "We would have been sitting ducks." While in Seattle, the lads only narrowly escaped when their limo was trashed by a mob of hysterical fans. Fortunately, they were pulled to safety, only seconds before the crunch.

"One had to completely humiliate oneself to be what the Beatles were," Lennon later stated. "It just happened bit by bit, gradually, until this complete craziness is surrounding you. Suddenly you're doing exactly what you don't want to do with people you can't stand. The people you hated when you were ten."

Bob Bonis, a burly, good-natured roadie, worked extensively for the Rolling Stones and the Beatles during those first turbulent years. He remembers going down to a hotel lobby for some towels while on this tour and overhearing a mother counseling her young daughter to try and sneak into Harrison's room and entice him into bed. "Then all you have to do is yell rape," she whispered. "We'll be rich!" Bonis could feel his stomach turning but all he could do was shake his head and try to forget it.

One of the most memorable highlights of this U.S. tour for George and the others was meeting Bob Dylan during their final American performance at the Paramount Theater in New York. Harrison and Lennon, especially, were self-confessed fanatics and listened to his albums almost with reverence. Although they had met briefly the previous February, this time they had a chance to get to know each other. It was during this meeting that Dylan first turned the Beatles on to marijuana. To George Harrison, Dylan was a revelation. Never in his short life had he met anyone so pervasively hip and untouched by the societal evils he so eloquently exposed in his songs. "Bob was always the gaffer as far as I was concerned," said George in 1988. "With all due respect to John, I don't think there's anyone in the business who's ever even come close."

For all things Beatles, 1965 was another banner year. Again there were the big shows, the frantic tours and the freaked-out fans. And by now the Beatles were quite bored. In February, Walter Shenson got together with Richard Lester and a couple of well-known screenwriters and concocted the film *Help!* The plot was a rather thinly contrived cartoon-like comedy pairing off our heroes against a crazy tribe of blood-thirsty Hindus intent on sacrificing a terrified Ringo Starr. Although it was filmed almost entirely on location in the Bahamas, Austria and England's Salisbury Plain, the company booked into Twickenham Film Studios on April 1 to shoot the movie's interiors.

It was there that George Harrison first attempted to play sitar. "I remember Lester hiring a small group of Indian musicians to try and perform some Beatle tunes in the background of one of the scenes," recalled the late Roy Kinnear, one of the film's co-stars. "George seemed very interested in it all, and before we knew it, he had someone run out and buy him a cheap sitar from one of those Indian shops near the British Museum. There they all were in a little clump, plucking away. None of it made much sense to me, of course, but it kept George happy, which was important as there was an awful lot of hanging about waiting to do your scenes. A testy Beatle could have meant big trouble for all of us."

In the end, the Beatles were less than pleased with *Help!* The filming had been long and arduous and not particularly rewarding for the boys, who complained that with all the exotic locations and involved scenarios, they felt like extras in their own movie. Lennon explained: "*Help!* was a drag because we didn't know what was happening. In fact, Lester was a bit ahead of his time with the Batman thing, but we were all on pot by then and all the best stuff ended up on the cutting room floor."

Perhaps the most dramatic happening of 1965 was George's and John's accidental initiation into the wonderfully wacky world of LSD, led by the group's London dentist. He and George had become friends and so was happy to accept an invitation for himself and the Lennons to dine at the doctor's fashionable Bayswater Road flat. Cynthia Lennon remembers thinking it strange that he had taken the trouble to line up four sugar cubes in a neat row atop his mantel, which he then carefully dropped into his guests' after-dinner coffee. For some reason, George's girlfriend, model Pattie Boyd, was reluctant to finish hers, but at the polite insistence of their host, graciously obliged. Retiring to the drawing room, they were casually informed that the cubes had each contained a rather respectable dose of LSD and were advised to settle back and enjoy the avalanche of distorted sights and sounds that would shortly follow. Cynthia and Pattie were immediately terrified. "What if this turns out to be some sort of aphrodisiac?" Pattie whispered to George. "Let's get the hell out of here," he said. "Perhaps he's trying for an orgy." Excusing themselves, the two couples piled into Harrison's car and were about to speed away when the dentist intercepted them at the curb.

"I would advise you not to leave," he said sternly. "You don't understand what's about to happen to you. If you stay here, I guarantee you'll be all right. If you go, anything could happen."

"We'll take our chances," yelled Harrison, and off they roared. Determined not to allow them to escape, the doctor and his girlfriend jumped into a taxi and took off in hot pursuit. Realizing that they were being tailed, George began careening through the rainswept side streets at breakneck speed. "It was like having the Devil following us in a cab," Cynthia recalled. "We were all panic-stricken." Not really knowing where to go, Harrison stopped off at the Pickwick Club to see their old friend, Klaus Voormann, perform with his group, Paddy Klaus and Gibson. Once they were inside, the large, dimly lit room suddenly began pulsing with the music, which had slowed itself down to an erratic, thumping soup. All eyes seemed to home in on the famous four. They felt as though they were being sucked into a great vacuum of disjointed sensory clutter. "Is everything going fast or slow?" wondered Lennon. Waves of euphoria rolled over them as they gasped in wonder at the swirling colors and patterns lighting up the darkened corners of the club. In the midst of it all, the dentist suddenly appeared and begged them to return to his flat. George looked upon what he considered the personification of evil itself and tore himself loose from his former friend's grasp. Once again they fled.

Their next stop, the famous Ad Lib Club, seemed to them to be lit up like a Hollywood premiere, complete with hundreds of screaming fans. As they drew closer, however, they realized it was just the usual one small light outside the club's entrance. John remembers:

> It was insane going around London. We were cackling in the streets, and Pattie was shouting "Let's break a window." It was insane. We were just out of our heads. When we finally got on the lift we all thought there was a fire, but it was just a little red light. We were all hot and hysterical, and when we arrived on the floor the lift stopped and the door opened, and we were all screaming. I had read some-body describing the effects of opium in the old days and I thought, "Fuck! It's happening." Then some singer came up to me and said, "Can I sit next to you?" And I said, "Only if you don't talk," because I just couldn't think. George somehow or other managed to drive us home in his Mini. We were going about ten miles an hour, but it seemed like a thousand, and Pattie was saying let's jump out and play football . . . . It was just terrifying, but it was fantastic. I did some drawings at the time of four faces saying "We all agree with you!" I did a lot of drawing that night.

George, too, was profoundly moved by his first psychedelic encounter and, like John, later became a dedicated advocate of the drug. "It was like I had never tasted, smelled or heard anything before. For me it was like a flash. It just opened up something inside of me, and I realized a lot of very heavy things. From that moment on, I wanted to have that depth and clarity of perception all the time."

Not surprisingly, their newly "enhanced" sensibilities only strength-ened their resolve to eventually leave behind the madness of touring once and for all. But for the moment, both George and John were unwilling prisoners of the Frankenstein monster that the group's incredible drive and talent had wrought. Still, Harrison realized that it was only a matter of time before the Beatles would call it a day — at least as far as live concerts were concerned.

The year 1965, for all its tension and insecurity, also brought with it a few surprises. First, there was the Beatles' investiture by Queen Elizabeth as Members of the Order of the British Empire, made public by Buckingham Palace on June 12. The announcement was soon followed by several protests, with MBEs sent back from all over the world by irate members. Among them, Hector Dupuis, a former Canadian member of Parliament, caused a furor with the fans when he called the boys "vulgar nincompoops." George responded, "If Dupuis doesn't want the medal, he had better give it to us. Then we can give it to our manager. MBE really stands for Mr. Brian Epstein." The boys' families, of course, were ecstatic, and everyone within the Beatles' sphere was exceptionally proud that they alone among rock's new gentry were chosen for the honor. That is, everyone *except* John Lennon. "Taking the MBE was a sellout for me," he later said, "and it was hypocritical of me to accept it." Harrison, on the other hand, was apparently ambivalent. "I didn't think you got this sort of thing for playing rock and roll," he told the media, unable to hide his amusement.

On October 26, 1965, the four Beatles were received by the Queen in Buckingham Palace's great gilded hall. After a brief ceremony, the lads reportedly retired to the sanctity of the men's room to smoke a joint. Rumor has it they also brought along an extra spliff just in case they happened to run into Prince Charles.

By the beginning of 1966, George Harrison's topsy-turvy life was beginning to show some signs of finally settling down. He and Pattie Boyd were engaged to be married; he owned his own home, Kinfauns in Esher, and Brian had agreed that that year's American tour would be considerably shorter than the last ones.

Still, there were problems. In an interview with journalist Maureen Cleave in the London *Evening Standard* that March, John commented that to his mind, the Beatles' influence over the young was greater than that of even Jesus Christ. By the time the news hit America that summer, there was a full-blown furor. All across the country there were record burnings, boycotts and big talk from dozens of Bible-thumping radio announcers and newspapermen. "Deport the Beatles!" cried the outraged publisher of one small-town Texas newspaper in a fiery editorial. "Parents in our country have no time for their lousy, low and lewd forms of so-called entertainment." Fearing that the boys might be injured if the tour proceeded as planned, Epstein contacted the various local promoters and offered to cancel their contracts and return their advances.

As it turned out, none of the promoters took him up on his offer, and the tour went ahead as scheduled. But not before Lennon and the rest of the group held an elaborate press conference in Chicago to try to explain his remark. "By the time I was nineteen, I was cynical about religion and never even considered the goings-on in Christianity," he said.

> It's only in the last two years that I — all the Beatles — have started looking for something else. We live in a moving hot house. We've been mushroom grown, forced to grow up a bit too quick, like having 30- to 40-year-old heads in 20-year-old bodies . . . The record burning was a real shock. I couldn't bear knowing I created another little place of hate in the world. Especially with something as uncomplicated as people listening to records and enjoying what the Beatles are . . . You can only hope that sometimes if you're truthful with people they'll stop all the plastic reaction and be truthful back. But it seems everybody is playing the game and sometimes I'm left naked and truthful with everybody biting me. It's disappointing.

Hard feelings smoothed over, the concerts commenced. Altogether, they performed in fourteen cities in just a little over two weeks. Ticket sales were brisk, and the Beatles made more money for their efforts than ever before. Still, to the boys, it was an ever-increasing drag.

From February 2, 1963, to August 29, 1966, the Beatles played more than 225 live shows in almost every country of the free world. They performed for millions of hysterical teenyboppers, were pelted with jelly beans and constantly harassed by fans looking for souvenirs — everything from autographs to bits of their hair, clothes and even fingernails. Crippled children were wheeled into the boys' dressing rooms in hopes that a dose of their mysterious power might restore or straighten lifeless limbs and twisted bodies. Airport terminals were continually dirtied by young women who became incontinent when at last they caught up with their favorite Beatle. It was, in all, quite a lot of madness for four provincial young men from the north of England to endure. And so, when the Beatles laid down their instruments after their last number at Candlestick Park in San Francisco on August 29, 1966, they said goodbye to public performing forever. From then on, John, Paul, George and Ringo would devote themselves exclusively to working their magic only in the privacy and sanctity of the recording studio. George Harrison, for one, couldn't have been more pleased.

IV

TWO HEARTS

George and Pattie

When George got together with Pattie, Mrs. Harrison and I were delighted. Of course, to the rest of the world it might have been "Beatle Marries Model," but to those that really knew them it was clear that this was a genuine modern-day love story.

HARRY HARRISON, SR.

IN 1964 PATTIE BOYD — BORN PATRICIA ANNE BOYD ON MARCH 17, 1945—was a pretty blonde print model enjoying great success in London, when Richard Lester, a transplanted American television director, saw her in a magazine and hired her to appear in commercials as the Smith's Crisps girl. In addition to her work on TV, she also did promotional appearances for the Smith firm all over England, appearing mostly at charity fetes and in department stores.

Following her great success as England's potato-chip princess, Pattie was cast by Lester in a tiny role in the Beatles' pseudo-documentary, *A Hard Day's Night*. George spotted her on the first day's filming and was overwhelmed by her big blue eyes, lovely long blonde hair and sexy, kittenish personality. Standing around behind the scenes in her scant Mary Quant micro-mini and pale dolly-bird makeup, she looked the epitome of Swinging London at its best. At the end of that first day, Pattie and a couple of her mates summoned up the courage to actually walk up to all the Beatles except John and ask for an autograph. To an innocent like Pattie, Lennon seemed entirely too caustic and cynical to run the risk of encountering in a bad mood.

"George signed one for my sisters and one for me," remembers Pattie. "Underneath Jenny and Paula's he drew a kiss for each, but under mine seven kisses. It was mildly embarrassing, but at the same time quite exciting."

During the next few days of filming, George's attention was definitely not on his work. Pattie often felt George's deep dark eyes staring at her as she waited to do her scenes. On the second day George invited her into the Beatles' private trailer for a cup of tea. She and her two younger sisters, Jenny and Paula, were from a steady middle-class home in the south of England, raised in a strict though affectionate environment where young ladies were taught to be both loving and loyal to their men. Pattie, therefore, politely declined the offer, telling the Beatle that she was already "semiengaged" to another boy. On the third day George tried again, this time asking her out for "a proper date." Once again she put him off, telling the thoroughly frustrated young man that she had an old-fashioned view of romance and couldn't see hurting her boyfriend over a casual night on the town. Later that afternoon George decided to approach her one last time. "She accepted," remembered George years later. "We went out to dinner together and then drove around London talking about everything we could think of. I don't know if you could actually call it love at first sight, but by the end of the first week I had already met her mum. Three weeks later we were looking at houses together, so I guess you could definitely call us a couple."

Pattie's initial exposure to the real-life world of Beatlemania came when Brian Epstein somewhat reluctantly engineered a whirlwind trip for George and Pattie to western Ireland during Easter 1964, along with John and Cynthia. In a bizarre cat-and-mouse game with the media, everyone flew under assumed names, the girls taking a separate flight from Manchester to Heathrow. From there the two couples boarded a private twin-engine plane for the bumpy flight to Dromoland Airport, safely tucked away in the outer reaches of the lovely Irish countryside.

They were looking forward to their stay at the exclusive Dromoland Castle Hotel but, despite all precautions, word soon leaked to the press that one half of the fabled Fab Four was in attendance. By the next morning the lobby was crawling with reporters and photographers, all intent on nailing down the identity of the beautiful blonde George had reportedly spent the night with.

Now that their secret romance was out, there was nothing left but to abandon their holiday and get back to London as quickly and discreetly as possible. The press, however, were posted at virtually all the hotel exits and stalked the corridors and stairwells in search of their prey. Meanwhile, the two couples were locked safely away in their rooms, planning their great escape.

George was furious that his privacy had been invaded on such a personally important outing. "Don't we give those bastards a big enough pound of flesh every goddamn day of our lives?" he exploded. "Why can't they just leave us alone sometimes?"

John could only agree. He and Cyn had been living this crazy life together for so many years that even this kind of callous intrusion seemed just a seamy, unavoidable fact of life.

A couple of hours later John and George fought their way through the media to the front desk and attempted to check out. The girls stayed upstairs, waiting for the right moment to make their getaway.

"Who's the blonde, George?" "What's her name?" "Do you love her?" "Will you marry?" "Come on John, where're the ladies?" The two young men were helplessly surrounded, flashbulbs going off all around them. "Just one picture with her. We've all come a helluva long way."

"Well so have we!" screamed Lennon, suddenly unable to contain himself. "Now leave off! You've had your fuckin' party, now we're gettin' the fuck out of here!" With that, John grabbed George by the arm and the two of them barreled head-on into the crowd.

The press knew they were licked, yet not only continued to hurl questions, but now added stinging insults. "You lot were finished anyway six months ago!" "Don't forget who made you yobbos in the first place!"

Upstairs Cynthia and Pattie had disguised themselves as chambermaids and were tiptoeing carefully through the halls, pushing an oversized laundry cart filled with dirty linen. They took the service elevator in the hotel's laundry room and then jumped into the hamper, concealing themselves among the used bedsheets. A primed bellboy then rolled the basket into the back of a laundry truck and sped madly through the rainswept streets on his way to the airport. So intent was he on pleasing his pop-star heroes with this good deed that it hadn't occurred to him that the two girls were still locked inside the hamper. Cynthia and Pattie all but gave up hope of ever making it out of the country alive.

John and George, meanwhile, had arrived by taxi at the airport some fifteen minutes earlier and were waiting rather impatiently for the girls to show up. "Good God, Cyn!" chuckled Lennon, when at last everyone was reunited. "You look like a couple of right scrubbers."

"Don't smell that great either," added George, just about falling down with laughter. "Let's get out of here once and for all."

Their little plane was met at London's Heathrow Airport by throngs of reporters and fans eager to pounce on George and his beautiful "mystery girl." Running the gauntlet between the press and the two Rolls-Royce limos Brian Epstein had hastily arranged, they scrambled inside, locked the doors and breathed a deep sigh of relief. "Well, Pattie," said George offhandedly, "I guess our secret's finally out. It's official now — Model Pattie and Beatle George have definitely become a very hot number!"

Hot enough that by early 1965 Pattie had already moved in with George to his extravagant Esher bungalow, outside of London, and was even writing a monthly column for 16 Magazine in America entitled "Pattie's Letter from London." All was not sweetness and light for the lucky couple, however, for as soon as word got around that the Harrison-Boyd liaison seemed to be serious, Pattie began receiving bags of hostile, even frightening, letters from George's loyal female fans. "It was terrifying," admits Pattie.

Hordes of wretched little girls used to lie in wait outside our gate waiting for me to go out to the shops. I was regularly kicked, bitten and even punched solely because I was George's girlfriend. "You'd better leave off our George or else!" they would shout as I drove away. George attempted to talk to them about it, but every time he came round they just fell about swooning and giggling. The next morning, however, once again they'd be out in full force, screaming insults and sometimes actually threatening to murder me!

Christmas 1965 was a whirlwind of activity for all those associated with the Beatles. Apart from their various recording dates and performances, there was the annual Beatle Christmas message to prepare for the fans as well as the general push and shove of the holiday season. The Beatles were seldom too busy to fit at least a little serious partying into their busy schedule and this yuletide was no exception. One of the highlights of this year's festivities was a big do at Brian Epstein's Chapel Street flat. "It was on the way that George proposed," remembers Pattie. "We were just motoring along listening to the radio when suddenly he very calmly told me he loved me and wanted us to get married. I think I just said yes or some such nonsense, but believe me, inside I was doing cartwheels. We really were very much in love."

George and Pattie were married on January 21, 1966, at the Epsom Registry Office in Surrey. Paul McCartney was the only Fab guest in attendance, but both John and Ringo sent along their best wishes in the form of flowers and several extravagant wedding presents. Mrs. Harrison once told Alanna Nash, "I felt as if I had lost everything. Quite silly, really, as we were in the car with them returning from the ceremony, George took my hand and said, 'It doesn't mean because I'm married I don't need you anymore, Mum. We need you more now.' He's such a lovable son, and cares about how people feel."

The couple honeymooned in Barbados just swimming, waterskiing and even doing a little deep-sea fishing. So happy and relaxed was the normally camera-shy George that he and Pattie graciously consented to pose for photographers on the beach. To all the world this was a match made in heaven: the sexy young guitar-playing millionaire and his vivacious super-model wife. As the British tabloids hit the streets of London, even some of George's most diehard fans began to soften. For George and Pattie, it was a deliriously happy time. Julia Baird remembers a Sunday outing to the Harrisons' home not long after the wedding:

Cynthia, fortunately, had volunteered to drive, so at least the ride over was not only very scenic but also much safer than if John was driving! It was John, [his son] Julian, [his other half-sister] Jacqui, myself and Cyn. Who, by the way was very good friends with Pattie in those days. I remember we sat on great huge pillows spread on the immaculate hardwood floor and enjoyed a lovely lunch of cold chicken, salad and spicy Indian rice accompanied by loads of fine red wine. It was a very cozy afternoon with lots of friendly conversation and good feelings all around.

George seemed really sweet, though maybe just a little quiet. (At least compared to our John with his mile-a-minute humor.) Pattie was certainly a very caring hostess as well, but Jacqui and I just couldn't get over seeing her at Woolworth's in Liverpool at what seemed only a few months before plugging away for the crisp company.

For George and Pattie, life in Esher was very happy. They had friends, the challenge of their exciting careers and of course each other. Often Pattie's sisters would come and stay for a few weeks at a time, keeping their big sister company evenings while George was in London recording with the Beatles. Later on the girls even operated a small boutique in Kensington Market, called Juniper in honor of Donovan's romantic ballad, "Jennifer Juniper." On those rare occasions when he was at home, George took an active interest in the garden and worked with his man, Maurice, to make sure everything was kept just so. Harrison and his old mate Klaus Voormann even painted a swirling psychedelic mural on the bungalow's stucco exterior. Some days when there were no other pressing engagements, George would reach into his antique ivory pillbox and pick out a small pastel-colored tab of LSD and trip out. Wandering through nearby Claremont Park, he would sink into a dreamy haze of good vibrations and warm sunshine. Other times he and Pattie would stay in and, after a hearty home-cooked meal, quietly pass the time with friends smoking bowls of Black Moroccan hash or nursing glasses of vintage wine.

The beginning of the end of the Harrisons' time at Esher came in the early evening of March 12, 1969, when Pattie answered a knock at the door and found a half-dozen policemen crowding the narrow archway.

"Drug squad, madam," announced Sergeant Norman Pilcher, the officer in charge. "We have a warrant." Immediately several constables and a couple of drug-sniffing dogs began their search of the house.

"I think perhaps I should ring my husband," said Pattie as calmly as

Celebrating George's twenty-fourth birthday, in Rishikesh, India. DELIBERATE ALCHEMY ARCHIVES

George and Pattie, still happy together in San Francisco, 1967. DELIBERATE ALCHEMY ARCHIVES

The Harrisons leave Esher Town Court following a brief trial that ultimately led to the couple's being convicted of possessing hashish. Although they only received a small fine, the drug conviction caused George, in particular, significant immigration hassles. DELIBERATE ALCHEMY ARCHIVES

possible. Darting into a small nook between the sitting room and the den, she quickly dialed the Beatles' special hotline number connected to Apple, the Beatles' corporate headquarters in London. After talking to his wife for a few minutes, George thoughtfully replaced the receiver and told Apple fixer Peter Brown what was happening. Not missing a beat, Brown immediately rang Martin Polden, one of London's top lawyers.

George, meanwhile, telephoned the Beatles' old crony Pete Shotton who lived nearby in Esher, and asked him to stay with Pattie until he could get there.

When George arrived with Derek Taylor awhile later, he found at least ten police cars and a paddy wagon crowded outside his house. "Everything was in an uproar," Shotton remembers. "The coppers had tipped over virtually all the furniture and were tearing through the closets when George suddenly burst in."

Everything came to an immediate halt as the bobbies jumped to their feet in rapt attention at the sight of Beatle George.

"Just what are all these men in silly felt hats doing in my home anyway, giving my friends bad vibes?" shouted George at the top of his lungs.

"Mr. and Mrs. Harrison," began the officer in charge, "I am charging you with the illegal possession of cannabis resin. I'm afraid I must ask you both down to the station for processing."

George sarcastically inquired if they had actually found any of *his* pot or were they instead featuring their own personal stash this evening. "And you needn't have turned the whole bloody place upside down either. All you had to do was ask me and I would have shown you where I keep everything."

Saying nothing, Pilcher just stuck out his hand as if to say "after you" and everyone filed out of the house and through George's garden en route to the Esher Jail. As they walked to the cars the coppers suddenly pulled in very close around George and Pattie, so much so that they could hardly walk.

"I'm not gonna run!" cried George. "Give us a little room will you?" Before anyone knew what was happening, a photographer jumped out of some nearby bushes and popped off a series of flashbulbs in George's face. Like Lee Harvey Oswald being blown away by Jack Ruby, George went down, but immediately bounced right back up and charged after the cameraman with the entire drug squad hot on his heels.

"I'm gonna fuckin' kill you, you bastard!" Harrison bellowed. The photographer was terrified, dropped his camera and never stopped running. Happily George managed to stomp on the camera once or twice before being forcibly restrained by the cops.

Once at the Esher Jail George and Pattie were quickly charged and subsequently released on bail. Not wishing such a fine spring evening to be a total waste, the couple were driven home and then quickly changed for a party given by London artist Rory McEwen at his studio in Chelsea. Arriving fashionably late, they were greeted by their host, who immediately steered them in the direction of his other two celebrated guests, Princess Margaret and her husband, Lord Snowdon. "Guess what?" said Harrison sheepishly. "We've been busted! Sergeant Pilcher and his goons planted a big block of hash in my bedroom closet."

"How terrible," said the princess sympathetically.

"Do you think you might possibly be able to get the charges dropped?" asked George.

"I don't really think so. It could become a little sticky. Sorry, George."

As if all this wasn't awkward enough for the princess, Pattie's youngest sister, Paula, casually strolled up and offered Her Royal Highness a toke on a joint that was being passed around the room. As one can imagine, this little gesture didn't go over all that well, and shortly thereafter the royals split the party.

Nineteen days later at Esher and Walton Magistrates' Court, the Harrisons pleaded guilty to unlawful possession of cannabis resin. Prosecutor Michael West said that the couple "had been of impeccable character hitherto." He also told the magistrates: "It is infrequent to find quite as much of the drug as one found in this case. There is something like 570 grains, which would result, when used, in a large number of cigarets. It would be wrong to draw the inference, however, that there was any intention to sell them. It is quite clear on the evidence that this was for personal consumption only and no more than a private supply."

The Harrisons' barrister, Martin Polden, pointed out that Pattie had allowed the police to go everywhere they wanted without obstruction and had made no attempt to hide the box on the living-room table found to contain nearly five hundred grains of hash. Polden also said the many powders, crystals and joss sticks the police had taken an interest in were all quite harmless and only emphasized the Harrisons' well-known interest in yoga.

Of the drugs subsequently found by the police in the Harrisons' wardrobe, he said: "The couple cannot explain this find. They know nothing about it to this day. The large amount of cannabis found, however, does not indicate that theirs is a household of corruption and debauchery. There is no question of addiction."

The magistrates fined Harrison and his wife each £250 and awarded ten guineas costs against each of them. The couple was allowed to keep an ornamental pipe confiscated in the raid.

As he left the court, George told the reporters outside, "We hope the police will now leave the Beatles alone."

It is interesting to note that in October of 1972 Sergeant Pilcher, the officer behind both the raid on Harrison and John Lennon earlier in 1968, was sentenced to several years in prison for planting drugs on an innocent suspect.

Shortly after the bust, the couple began the laborious task of house hunting, aided by a mountain of illustrated real-estate catalogs advertising some of Britain's finest properties.

Perhaps the most outlandish tale regarding the Harrisons' desire to find themselves a home comes via Alistair Taylor, who tells of the time Pattie appeared at Apple dressed as a dowdy upper-crust newlywed expecting him to play the part of her husband on an all-day country outing in search of a suitable property. Once inside the limousine, Pattie offhandedly introduced Alistair to "James," their uniformed chauffeur for the afternoon.

"Where to old boy?" the driver asked, turning to Alistair.

"Good Lord, George, it's you!" Alistair cried. "What's going on?"

"Well," Harrison jokingly explained, "you're the one who's always saying that everyone's out to screw the Beatles, so we decided to let *you* be the buyer this afternoon."

Motoring their way from one palatial country estate to the next, Pattie and Alistair played the part to a tee.

George and Pattie's attempt at anonymity, however, was short-lived. At one of the their last stops — an impressive Georgian estate just outside London — the agent casually inquired if "Mr. Harrison out in the car" might want to come in and look around as well. All George and Pattie could do was laugh. The Beatles' ever-expanding celebrity, it seemed, was bigger than the both of them.

V

EYE OF THE NEEDLE

Apple, Acid and
the End of the Beatles

Listen man, the Beatles were really breaking up from about day one. More than once in the early days I had to go out and find George. He'd just say, 'I'm not doing this anymore,' and he'd piss off, you know. I think the pressures got so bad towards the end I'm astonished they stayed together even as long as they did.

ALISTAIR TAYLOR, LONG-TIME APPLE AIDE

The split up of the Beatles satisfied me more than anything else in my career. Being a Beatle was a nightmare, a horror story. I don't even like to think about it.

GEORGE HARRISON

BACK IN THE LATE SIXTIES WHILE MANY OF THE WORLD'S YOUTH WERE busy getting loaded with their friends and living off student loans, George Harrison had already taken on a world of responsibility. He became one-fourth of the Beatles' international Apple Corps Limited, as well as being a fulltime professional musician, composer, record producer and husband. During this period, Harrison was now determined to forge a more meaningful role for himself within the group. Notwithstanding the Beatles' musical Midas touch, George became keen to launch his own solo career as well.

To a lot of people, the very idea of "corporate" Beatles was a contradiction in terms. After all, these four young men were the gurus of a generation, jubilant harbingers of a new age centered on music, love and a freer, less covetous lifestyle. What would be their next trend-setting fashion statement — bowler hats?

"I got back from [the Maharishi's retreat in] India a bit later than everybody else," George recalled in the mid-seventies. "They all split and started Apple. When I got back it was like a madhouse. In fact, to this day we're still trying to untangle it. At that time John and Yoko had just gotten together, and they had some guy throwing the I Ching every ten minutes. 'Oh, we're having a business meeting? Then let's play the I Ching!' The place was full of lunatics."

Apple Corps Limited was established late in 1967 chiefly as a device for lessening the Beatles' incredible tax burden. Paul McCartney came up with the name after apparently being inspired by an original Magritte painting he owned, which featured a giant Granny Smith apple locked inside a tiny room.

The genesis of the company was rather funky to say the least. Alistair Taylor remembers:

One Sunday we were sitting in Hille House, Brian's private office, having an Apple meeting. Just the boys, myself and Neil [Aspinall]. Suddenly they picked up the phone and said, "Hey, let's get hold of Derek!" They rang up Derek Taylor, who was then working with the Beach Boys in America, and they said, "Pack your bags and come on over, man."

I said, "What's he going to do?"

"Oh, well, we don't really know. I'm sure we'll find *something*."

Later, when Derek arrived, he said, "Okay, let's set some kind of business up." At one time there was even talk of doing one of those express delivery services. "Now," said the Beatles, "who are we going to get to run publishing?"

So Derek said, "There's this marvelous guy in the States."

"Well, get him on the phone and bring him here!" They were just pulling people in and saying, "Oh, shit, now what are we going to do with them? Oh, it doesn't matter. We'll think of *something*." So is it any wonder their money was flying out?

"Apple was never meant to try to save the world, despite popular myth!" roared Taylor in a 1984 interview.

Let's put Apple into perspective, right? A lot of nonsense has been spoken about Apple. Apple was set up purely and simply as a tax-saving project. Instead of paying nineteen and six on the pound, we only paid sixteen shillings. In the beginning there was an executive board, so the boys and Brian didn't want to know. It consisted of [Brian's brother] Clive Epstein, myself, Geoffrey Ellis, a solicitor and an accountant. The idea was that we would quietly announce to the tax authorities that we would soon be opening a string of shops. That was the original concept, but when the boys heard about it they decided that could become very boring — they didn't want their name above a string of ordinary shops. The original idea was greeting cards. Imagine Beatle greeting card shops! Gradually they started drifting in on the meetings, and Apple as we know it evolved from there. Later it all turned into this silly philosophy, admittedly, but even then it was not designed to save the world. All we wanted to do was to get rid of the hassle of big business. I mean, why couldn't business be fun and pleasurable?

Why not, indeed? Following the Beatles' retirement from live performance and their headlong foray into the exclusivity and isolation of the studio, the lads were more than game to try something different. When, in 1966, Harrison sang about the horrors of the English tax man, he wasn't kidding.

The Beatles, like most successful entertainers in Britain took a hiding when it came to taxes. Clearly, both personally and collectively, something had to be done. Apple, it now seems, was very much the inevitable outcome of an extremely difficult dilemma: where should the

Beatles put their ever-expanding millions? Despite Brian Epstein's well-known knack for packaging and promotion, his business sense was poor. He often worked with cash, lots of it, which of course made it extremely difficult to balance the books at the end of the day.

Paul McCartney remembers: "I think one of Brian's main faults, as I used to point out with a word he hated, was that he was a bit green. Some of the deals he struck, like the fact that Lennon and McCartney songs weren't our copyright, were *very* naive. The great thing about Brian, of course, was the flair."

"Maybe people think it's a drag that the Beatles are doing business," Harrison told Ritchie Yorke in 1969, "but we were always involved in it. We just didn't notice because Brian Epstein did it for us, and it was just becoming ridiculous. We had to try to solve these problems and sort it all out . . . . But the business side of it was always rather abstract to us because we'd always imagined, 'Well, Brian does all that, and everything is fine,' even when it wasn't fine. [After Brian died] it was directly up to us to work out what we had to do, and consequently we found out all these bizarre things going on, to our absolute horror."

"The aim of this company isn't really a stack of gold teeth in the bank," said John at a 1968 press conference in New York. "We've done that bit. It's more of a trick to see if we can actually get artistic freedom within a business structure, to see if we can create nice things and sell them without charging three times our cost."

The first Beatle-related venture to carry the Apple logo was the film *Magical Mystery Tour*, shown on English television on December 26, 1967. Artistically, it was years ahead of its time, employing many of the same surreal techniques so popular in today's rock videos. Commercially, however, it was a disaster.

From there Apple evolved into a trendy high-fashion head shop and boutique housed at 94 Baker Street, in Sherlock Holmes territory, with a small music publishing division housed above the store. In those days, Mike Berry, a middle-management music executive, and Beatle buddy Terry Doran were running the show, assisted by two attractive but largely ineffectual secretaries. A lot of dope was smoked and big ideas tossed back and forth, but precious little accomplished. And with the Beatles backing the venture to the hilt, expenses tended to run exceedingly high. Compared with what was happening downstairs, though, Apple Publishing was a veritable model of corporate efficiency.

The Apple Boutique opened its doors on December 7, 1967, with a gala celebration attended by John, George, their wives and about two hundred more trendy people than could comfortably fit inside the store. John nicknamed it the "psychedelic Woolworth's," and almost immediately it became the place to see and be seen in Swinging London. The shopfront featured a far-out, acid-inspired mural by a team of Dutch designers who called themselves The Fool. After endearing themselves to the Beatles, the flamboyant artists proceeded to put their creative touch to just about everything the boys owned. Suddenly, wild rainbow-colored designs showed up on George's living-room fireplace and on one or two of his favorite guitars. John even commissioned a fancy paint job for an antique upright piano. However impressed the Beatles may have been with The Fool's far-out creations, their Baker Street neighbors were less favorably disposed and promptly petitioned city officials to have the offending dreamscape removed from the building. About eight months later, the shop was closed down after a long history of petty pilfering and poor management, and the entire contents given away free to the public — that is, after the boys stopped by to do a little last-minute shopping themselves.

Paul McCartney, ever the freewheeling entrepreneur, was by all accounts the driving force behind Apple Corps. Working with Alistair Taylor, he devised a clever ad featuring an old-fashioned one-man band busking his heart out with several offbeat instruments. Above the photo was the obtuse legend, "This man has talent." And below it, "One day he sang his songs into a tape recorder (borrowed from the man next door). In his neatest handwriting, he wrote an explanatory note (giving his name and address) and, remembering to enclose a picture of himself, sent the tape, letter and photograph to Apple Music, 94 Baker Street, London, W.1. If you were thinking of doing the same thing yourself — do it now! This man now owns a Bentley!"

The poster was plastered all over London and the surrounding area. In addition, half-page ads were placed in all the English music magazines. To no one's surprise (except perhaps the Beatles'), within two weeks the Baker Street office had become little more than a post office, with hundreds of tapes, manuscripts and bits of film piling up everywhere. Alistair Taylor explained: "Everything collected dust in the corner. We just couldn't cope. Of course we tried. Eventually we got hold of a few good people — Billy Preston, Badfinger, James Taylor and Mary Hopkin. The kids were sending all sorts of tapes and sheet music in constantly. You'd come in in the morning, switch on the answering machine and get some guy auditioning on the message tape! We used to send a lot of them around to the [Lew] Grade organization."

By February of 1968, Apple Corps had outgrown its Baker Street digs and moved to an entire floor of a smart office building at 95 Wigmore Street. But within a few months, even these offices proved too small for the Beatles' ever-growing empire, and on June 22 the London papers reported that Apple had purchased Number 3 Savile Row for more than half a million pounds. Known the world over as London's preeminent tailoring strip, Savile Row didn't exactly embrace the Beatles and company when they heard the news. They knew that where the Beatles went their fans would follow — an unsettling thought for an industry to whom very proper "appearances" were so important.

Of course, the Beatles' move did see a sudden influx of fans into the area. Waiting at the curb for a precious fleeting glimpse of one of their idols, the "Apple Scruffs," as they were soon called, rapidly became fiercely territorial. They shunned "ordinary" tourists who hoped to sight a Beatle in between treks to Madame Tussaud's or lunch in Covent Garden. The level of devotion exhibited by the Scruffs, however, was indeed extraordinary. They printed their own magazine, the *Apple Scruff Monthly Magazine*, and even issued professional-looking membership cards to proven converts. Although the Scruffs were obviously taken with all four members of the group, the girls seemed to hold a special place in their hearts for George. *New York Post* columnist Al Aronowitz, who came to be about as close to the boys as was possible for an outsider, realized the intimate nature of this bond and wrote about it in his column:

I remember sitting through some of the overdub and mixing sessions [in 1970, for Harrison's triple album, *All Things Must Pass*] in London's Trident Studios . . . . Somehow George reminded me of a holy man going to his temple in the most sinful part of town. What did it matter that he went in a Mercedes?

Outside the studio door, whether it rained or not, there was always a handful of Apple Scruffs, one of them a girl all the way from Texas. Sometimes George would record from 7 p.m. to 7 a.m., and there they would be, waiting through the night, beggars for a sign or recognition on his way in and out. In the morning they'd go off to their jobs and in the evening they'd be back outside the studio door again. Their grapevine was infallible.

So taken was George with their devotion that he even immortalized them on *All Things Must Pass* with the aptly entitled tune, "Apple Scruffs."

According to one of the group's charter members, Carol Bedford, the one from Texas, the depths of George's emotional attachment to these young women was perhaps a bit deeper than even he would care to admit. In her 1984 autobiography, *Waiting for the Beatles*, she reveals yet another side to the intensely private Harrison: "Around 7:30 p.m., after I had eaten, the doorbell rang. I went to the front door. When I opened it, there he [George] was, grinning from ear to ear . . . . Before I could gather my wits, George stepped into the threshold and threw his arms around me! I was shocked. I hugged him back. We stood like this for several minutes. Then he stepped back to look at me. I was wearing jeans with a soft, fluffy pink sweater. I was embarrassed. Here was George alone with me. Now what?"

They walked slowly to Carol's tiny bedsit at the end of the hall, where George sat nervously on the end of her bed and seemed, in her words, "frightened." Following a few awkward moments of airy chitchat, the Beatle made his move. "He looked shy," Carol remembers. "He stepped towards me and placed his arms around me. I thought he just wanted to hug me, as he had when he arrived. But he kissed me. Needless to say, I happily responded."

Of course at that time, 1972, George was still married to Pattie Boyd. His only saving grace was that, physically, things went no farther with Carol. The two continued to see each other, as friends, off and on. Once, Carol writes, Harrison may have even dispatched the Beatles' roadie, Mal Evans, to her flat with what turned out to be a very unexpected offer. Her autobiography continues:

"George wants you to move to Los Angeles," he said without any warm-up conversation. "He has an apartment there you could have."

"Why?" I asked.

"He can't take you out places here. You know, he'd like to take you out to restaurants and places, but he's married. Reporters are everywhere . . . George can't get a divorce right now, so he doesn't want to be seen visiting some other girl."

"Why not 'right now'? What's he waiting for, the great flood?"

"He doesn't want to lose the house. If she petitions him, the house goes to her," Mal explained.

When Carol dismissed the offer as insulting, Evans allegedly made a pass at her himself, which she also rejected. Thereafter, she was never really sure if Mal was just playing her up by inventing the story, or if Harrison had really meant it.

At any rate, the idealistic young woman was so upset by the episode that she consciously put the two-timing Harrison out of her mind for good and her days as an Apple Scruff behind her, ultimately going on to a successful career as a record company executive.

Meanwhile, back on Savile Row, life with the Fab Four proved just as demanding as ever. Asked in a 1969 interview to explain the philosophy behind the development of Apple, Harrison offhandedly relegated the question to the seemingly ever-present Derek Taylor. Seasoned publicist that he was, Taylor came up with a suitably inscrutable answer: "It's an organization which has developed without anyone really planning it that way, as a service which exists to implement the whims of the Beatles, which fortunately often turn out to be very commercial. However, if they didn't, we'd still have to do it, and that's okay as well. That's the gig. The gig is *not* Apple, the gig is working for the Beatles. You come here and you work for the Beatles. Now the latest whim is to take the world's worst minority religionists' cult in England, the Hare Krishnas, and get them a Top Thirty record within ten days! It's nothing else, you know, and that's what it will ever be."

The Beatles' "whims" were often born of some very individualized thinking. Pete Bennett, a latter-day Apple promotion czar, remembers George and Pattie driving the out-of-town executives crazy with their constant proselytizing about the advantages of a strict vegetarian diet:

We had just arrived from New York and caught a cab right over to Apple, where George was doing some work in the studio. As we were sitting around listening, all of a sudden Pattie shows up with a tray of carrot sticks, celery, raw broccoli, all sorts of crap, and starts passing it around the room. Well, I had just endured an eight-hour flight and I was starved . . . . But of course I had to be polite. There we sat, three big, grown-up businessmen, holding these tiny little pieces of carrot in our hands not knowing what to do.

"How do you like the eats?" George calls out from the drum booth.

"Fine. Great, George. I can't tell you how long it's been since we ate like this."

After about an hour or so of this, I had had enough, so we told George and Pattie we had a very important Apple meeting to attend so we would have to catch up with them later. Of course, we raced back to our hotel and immediately ordered the biggest sirloins in the house. Then we caught another cab back to Apple.

"Everything okay lads?" Harrison shouted out again.

"Fine George," I said, and gave him a big thumbs up. He just laughed. I've often wondered if he somehow figured out what we were up to.

Artistically, Apple was always a very mixed bag. At one end of the spectrum, such artists as the Radha Krishna Temple, soul singer Doris Troy and Jackie Lomax may have been somewhat out of the mainstream, but nevertheless meant a lot to George. As a musician, Harrison was inventive and ever willing to experiment with new sounds. A self-confessed perfectionist, he would often lose himself in his work, going over and over the same riff until he got it just right. And as a producer, his job demanded that he oversee virtually every detail of the often laborious recording process.

Of all the acts he was involved with producing during those Apple years, it was in fellow Liverpool pop singer Jackie Lomax that he invested the most time and trouble. Harrison was so sure the lanky singer-song-writer would break out and become a big star that he threw the full force of his extensive web of show-business connections behind the project. Lomax's album, *Is This What You Want?*, tastefully draws on the performing talents of superstar sidemen Paul McCartney, Eric Clapton, Ringo Starr, Nicky Hopkins, Klaus Voormann and of course George, but unfortunately the overall effect is surprisingly rather abysmal. One astute critic noted, "Apparently, over at Apple all that glitters is *not* gold." Despite a massive, overblown publicity campaign, the Lomax album went nowhere. Insiders say that Harrison, while maintaining his usual public facade of detachment, was privately very disappointed.

Is This What You Want? was Lomax's one and only Apple LP. He later emigrated to America, recorded two more albums for Warner Brothers and a third for Capitol, and then drifted into obscurity. When last heard from, Apple's superstar-that-never-was was still playing nightclubs and living the good life in sunny California.

Mary Hopkin, an Apple recording artist whose monster hit "Those

Were the Days" took her to the top of the charts in 1968, describes George from this period:

> I remember one time going along to the sessions for "Happiness Is a Warm Gun" at Abbey Road and seeing John sitting there strumming away. I guess I'd been there just watching for about an hour before the session really started. George had this beautiful acoustic guitar inlaid with mother-of-pearl and I complimented him on it. After a while George suddenly got up and left the studio for about an hour and then came back without saying a word. Later, Mal [Evans] appeared and said, "Mary, come with me," and led me out of the studio. There, sitting on the reception desk, was this beautiful classical guitar, a Ramirez, which is an absolutely superb instrument and very expensive. It was from George. He'd just spent an hour hunting around town for a new guitar for me and didn't say a word. It was only later on, the day of the premiere of the film *Yellow Submarine*, that I had a chance to thank him. George is a good man.

Still cautiously optimistic about their future together, from 1966 to 1969 the Beatles racked up an incredible list of worldwide smash recordings, the titles of which read like a table of contents for the dope-filled dreams of an entire generation: *Rubber Soul, Revolver, Sgt. Pepper's Lonely Hearts Club Band, Magical Mystery Tour, The Beatles* (the "white" album), the *Yellow Submarine* soundtrack, *Abbey Road* and *Let It Be* — an astounding array of ground-breaking, intelligent and artfully conceived music. The problem was that the evolving talents of the four artists could no longer be so easily contained on one LP every twelve months or so. There is no doubt that George Harrison possessed the innate ability to perhaps even commercially surpass the Lennon-McCartney songwriting cartel, but the chance never came, and Harrison was relegated by fate to the back of the Beatles' bus to ride out the remainder of the Mystery Tour as a second-class citizen. "I believe that if I'm going to sing songs on record, they might as well be on my own," commented George in 1969.

> I also feel you can say more in two minutes of a song than in ten years. The first song I ever wrote was "Don't Bother Me." It wasn't

very good, but I was sick in bed and I thought I might as well write something, and it went on our second album [*With the Beatles*; released in America as *Meet the Beatles*]. The most difficult thing for me is following Paul's and John's songs. Their earlier songs weren't as good as they are now, though, and they obviously got better and better, and that's what I have to do. I've got about forty tunes that I haven't recorded, and some of them are quite good. I wrote one called "The Art of Dying" [later to appear on *All Things Must Pass*] three years ago, and at the time I thought it was too far out. But I'm still going to record it.

I used to have a hang-up about telling John, Paul and Ringo I had a song for the albums, because I felt mentally, at that time, as if I was trying to compete. And in a way, the standard of the songs had to be good, because theirs were very good. I don't want the Beatles to be recording rubbish for my sake . . . just because I wrote it. On the other hand, *I* don't want to record rubbish, just because *they* wrote it. The group comes first. It took time for me to get more confidence as a songwriter, and now I don't care if they don't like it. I can shrug it off. Sometimes it's a matter of whoever pushes hardest gets the most tunes on the album, then it's down to personalities. And more often, I just leave it until somebody would like to do one of my tunes.

If nothing else, George Harrison is an honest man, sometimes painfully so. Several years after Apple's demise he had this to say about the ill-fated company: "It wasn't *me* who wanted to do Apple. Paul decided to do Apple and was aided and abetted by John . . . . Of course, it *was* a good idea, but it wasn't subtle enough. Shouting to everybody about what you're going to do before you even know what you're doing yourself. I loved it because it was what we wanted to do, and what I'm still trying to do."

While Harrison might have been reserved when it came to pushing himself to the fore creatively, he had no such inhibitions when it came to climbing behind the wheel of a good, fast car. Ever since he was a little boy he had been consumed by the thrill of speed and the careful negotiation of a hairpin turn.

Like so many other kids of that time, he used to lie in bed at night and imagine racing around and around a dusty dirt track on a souped-up motorcycle, careering almost out of control, only to pull the monster back just in the nick of time. Unlike most youngsters, however, that fantasy only grew stronger as time went on. From the very moment he could afford it, George sought out only the very best cars available, eventually owning some of the finest machines on four wheels. At various times, he has tooled around London in Ferraris, Porsches, Lamborghinis, Rolls-Royces and BMWs as well as several extravagant, customized Mercedes. He might claim to be a simple gardener in his heart of hearts, but behind the wheel he was without question the undisputed king of the road — a distinction, he'd be the first to admit, that has caused him his share of troubles over the years.

One of the most dramatic was a spectacular one-car collision on February 28, 1972, when George was driving from his Henley home to a Rick Nelson concert in London. A strike by electrical workers had led to a blackout, so George couldn't see where he was going and slammed into a roundabout at ninety miles an hour. Neither he nor Pattie was wearing a seat belt. Thrown into the windscreen and crushed up against the steering wheel, George was momentarily dazed. Pattie, however, was out cold, slumped over in her seat. For a moment Harrison thought she was dead. Panic-stricken and feeling none too well himself, he knew he had to get help immediately. His own door was jammed shut, so he had to gingerly climb over Pattie to get out through the passenger door.

At that moment, a car pulled up and turned on its emergency blinkers. Staggering over to the horrified motorist, Harrison tapped on the man's window, but the driver wouldn't roll it down. "Look at you!" he cried from inside his car. Straining his neck to peer into the side mirror, George suddenly felt faint. Staring back at him in the foggy glass was a badly bruised face framed by bloodstained hair. "It took a moment to realize it was actually me," George has said. "By then I was pounding away on this poor chap's window begging him to get an ambulance."

Harrison sustained a cut on his scalp which required eight stitches, a minor concussion and a bruised shoulder. Pattie, though, was more seriously injured. She remained unconscious for some time following the accident and required several days in hospital as well as two additional weeks in a London nursing home. She not only suffered a concussion but also broke several ribs. Despite the trauma of this incident, however, George still has apparently never learned his lesson and continues driving very fast to this day.

Throughout the years 1966 to 1969, George Harrison struggled with an on-again, off-again drug problem that included an array of nonaddictive substances such as LSD, mescaline, peyote, psilocybin, marijuana and hashish. John Lennon has admitted he and George were "pretty heavy" on acid: "We are probably the most cracked, Paul being a bit more stable than George and I." To his credit, though, George never got involved in harder drugs like heroin or morphine. A deeply ingrained fear of needles helped, but beyond that, he had seen too many good friends become hopelessly addicted or end up dead to take that risk himself.

As with most things in George Harrison's life there was method behind his drug-taking. Unlike the youth of today, who seem intent on using drugs to numb themselves to the reality of life around them, the youth of the sixties considered dropping acid as a key to inner knowledge and heightened self-awareness. Their drug-taking, then, was not necessarily an escape from anything, but often an attempt to reach a subtler, more meaningful reality. "LSD was just like lots of doors in my mind were flying open," said George at the time, and he meant it. Aided and abetted by such vocal advocates as former Harvard professor Dr. Timothy Leary and long-time associate Dr. Richard Alpert (later to become Baba Ram Das), many of the Beatles' generation were convinced that pharmacological nirvana was not only the surest means to "tune in" to this elusive higher consciousness but without doubt the most vividly colorful. In his famous counterculture manifesto, *The Psychedelic Experience*, Leary wrote:

> The scope and content of the experience are limitless, but its characteristic features are the transcendence of verbal concepts, of space-time dimensions, and of the ego or identity. Such experiences of enlarged consciousness can occur in a variety of ways: sensory deprivation, yoga exercises, disciplined meditation, religious or aesthetic ecstasies, or spontaneously. Most recently they have become available to anyone through the ingestion of psychedelic drugs. Of course, the drug does not produce the transcendent experience. It merely acts as a chemical key — it opens the mind, frees the nervous system of its ordinary patterns and structures.

It was in pursuit of his new awareness offered by hallucinogens that George and his cohorts kept getting high. After a time, fighting for the legalization of many of these substances became a sort of cause célèbre for London's show-business elite, prompting several big names to sign a

Catching forty winks during the filming of *Magical Mystery Tour*.
DELIBERATE ALCHEMY ARCHIVES

Running a gauntlet of fans outside Apple.
DELIBERATE ALCHEMY ARCHIVES

John and Yoko pose with some of the performers participating in a charity gig at the London Lyceum Ballroom in 1969. George Harrison and "Legs" Larry Smith are on the extreme left.
DELIBERATE ALCHEMY ARCHIVES

The controversial dreamscape masterminded by the Dutch designing team: *The Fool* adorns the Apple boutique in London.
DELIBERATE ALCHEMY ARCHIVES

George, Pete Bennett and Ringo at a press reception heralding the release of the film version of the Concert for Bangla Desh.
PETE BENNETT INTERNATIONAL

petition that ran in the *Times* on July 24, 1967, stating that "the law against marijuana is immoral in principle and unworkable in practice." The document bore the names of all four Beatles as well as Brian Epstein. Not surprisingly, the advertisement caused a furor in the media, with the *Times* sharply criticized for agreeing to publish the piece in the first place.

That July, George and Pattie flew to Los Angeles and took up residence in a house on a pretty suburban street called Blue Jay Way (immortalized in song on *Magical Mystery Tour*). Teaming up with old friends Derek and Joan Taylor, "Magic" Alex Mardas and Neil Aspinall, the Harrisons enthusiastically took in the sights of Hollywood, kept smiling with the aid of a steady supply of heady California grass.

For much of his time in L.A., George kept company with a gregarious teenybopper fan named Rodney Bingenheimer. Together they cruised Hollywood in a little two-door Corvair, soaking up the good vibrations and the steaming California sun. "We literally drove all over town," Rodney recalled, "and of course went to Jerry [Hopkin]'s psychedelic store in Westwood, called Headquarters. George bought everything there: all kinds of beads, weird roach clips — that's where we got the heart-shaped sunglasses . . . . He bought some round ones, too, several pairs. Then we went up the street to a place called Sat Purush, which was the place the Strawberry Alarm Clock did their album cover. George bought a bunch of Nehru-type things and shirts with ribbons in them and stuff like that." *Tiger Beat* magazine, a syrupy teen rag, reported that while at the boutique, George was "running all around the store in his underwear and even went into the window display in his underwear to try on shoes." So much for his image of being shy and reserved!

From there, Rodney, George and Jerry took off for a nearby Orange Julius stand on Santa Monica Boulevard, where Harrison had trouble ordering from the menu, apparently unable to fathom how much anything cost. The Beatle was so used to having an aide around to take care of his everyday affairs that he also had difficulty figuring out how to work the juke box and even tried to pay the bill with pound notes.

The next day, August 7, 1967, the entire entourage boarded a private Lear jet bound for San Francisco to pay a visit to Pattie's sister Jenny, then married to drummer Mick Fleetwood, and have a look at Haight Ashbury, the city's famous hippie haven. In the rented limo after lunch, George carefully divided several bright orange tabs of LSD among his guests. He downed one himself and then leaned back in happy anticipation of both the impending acid trip and the overwhelming love vibes he expected to encounter in Haight Ashbury. "I'd thought it would be something like King's Road [London], only more," George has said. "Somehow I expected them to all own their own little shops. I expected them all to be nice and clean and friendly and happy." Instead, as the limousine glided to a stop, George and his pals stepped out onto the curb and into another world, a world Harrison has likened to New York's Bowery. He was confronted by a legion of "hideous, spotty little teenagers," as he called them, all deluded into thinking that he was one of them, and he was not impressed.

In fact, George soon found he had a problem with the entire hippie ethic. "I don't mind anybody dropping out of anything," he has said, "but it's the imposition on somebody else I don't like. The moment you start dropping out and then begging off somebody else to help you, then it's no good. It doesn't matter what you are as long as you work. It doesn't matter if you chop wood as long as you chop and keep chopping. Then you get what's coming to you. You don't have to drop out. In fact, if you drop out you put yourself further away from the goal of life than if you were to keep working."

Making their way through the throngs of stoned-out, panhandling youngsters, George and Pattie huddled close. At the entrance to Golden Gate Park, someone thrust a beat-up old guitar in George's hand and commanded him to play. Harrison tried his best to decline politely, but a wave of jittery hostility rolled through the crowd until he finally acquiesced. Strumming out the first few quirky chords to the Beatles' "Baby You're a Rich Man," George tried to sing but the words just would not come. The acid was coming on strong, and all he wanted was to get away. As he handed back the guitar, the crowd saw this as some kind of rejection and started to boo the freaked-out singer. George and company sprinted to the waiting limousine, the wild band of jeering hippies in hot pursuit. They escaped unhurt, though ironically, this was not to be the only close call of the day.

On the road to the airport, Harrison was still very high from the acid. He has since said that afternoon was like "living in a Hieronymus Bosch painting" complete with "fish with heads" and "human vacuum cleaner faces coming out of shop doorways." As the private jet took off, George was very nervous, never being at ease while flying at the best of times. He began chanting Hare Krishna quietly to himself as he often does when on a plane. Suddenly, the aircraft banked sharply and the engines stalled. The instrument board lit up and a red sign began blinking UNSAFE.

Screaming out the rather mixed-up mantra, "Om, Christ Om," Harrison was joined in this impromptu prayer meeting by "Magic" Alex, who began chanting Hare Krishna at the top of his lungs. The engines sputtered for a couple of seconds and then miraculously regained power. Exhausted by the ordeals of the day, George staggered to the back of the plane under the pretext of trying to get some sleep. The acid, however, would not let go. The unnerved guitarist could only stare blankly out the window at the passing clouds. It had easily been one of the worst acid trips of his life.

Upon returning home to London, George confided to John that he was giving up drugs for good and suggested that his friend should, too. "It's not fucking me up yet," said Lennon, "so I'll carry on."

"Just wait," warned Harrison, "it will. You'll see." Despite George's laudable intentions, he was to continue taking psychedelic drugs off and on for several more years. George has said of the mysterious drug, LSD:

[It] can help you go from A to B, but when you get to B, you see C. And you see that to get *really* high, you have to go it straight. So this was the disappointing thing about LSD. In the physical world we live in, there's always duality — good and bad, black and white, yes and no. There's always something equal and opposite to everything, and this is why you can't say LSD is good or it's bad, because its good *and* bad. It's both of them and it's neither of them altogether. People don't consider that. We've all got the same goal whether we realize it or not. We're all striving for something called God. Everyone is a potential Jesus Christ, really. We are all trying to get to where Christ got. And we're going to be in this world until we get there.

The hippies are a good idea — love, flowers, and that is great — but when you see the other half of it, it's like anything. I love all these people, too, those who are honest and trying to find a bit of truth and to straighten out the untruths. I'm with them one hundred percent, but when I see the bad side of it, I'm not so happy.

The late sixties seemed to be rather an era of disillusionment for George Harrison. First it was the broken promise of drug-induced enlightenment, followed closely by the inevitable wilting of flower power. The Beatles' trek to India in 1967 to sit at the feet of the Maharishi turned sour almost immediately, and even George's fairy-tale marriage to Pattie Boyd began to suffer under the strain of the constant demands made upon George's time and energy. When the Beatles finally began to collapse in

1969, Harrison's new declaration of independence was tempered, it was safe to say, with some very real doubts.

Perhaps one of the saddest changes during this time was George's eventual estrangement from his great friend John Lennon. When the inscrutable Yoko Ono entered John's life, many of the Beatles' former friendships were set aside to make room for her larger-than-life presence. To say John was bewitched by Yoko is perhaps too strong, but there is little doubt that he was heavily influenced by this bullish opportunist who almost from day one set about isolating him from his loved ones. Many disturbing stories about Ono have circulated over the years. Foremost among them was the tale told by Julia Baird concerning her younger sister, Jacqui Dykins. Following Lennon's tragic murder in 1980, Jacqui phoned Ono and asked for some help in keeping the utilities turned on in the flat she shared with her young son, John. Without so much as a thought for Lennon's family, Yoko reportedly slammed down the receiver in disgust.

Another equally pathetic postscript to the life of John Lennon concerns his elderly uncle, Norman Birch. Way back in 1964, John was good enough to purchase a lovely new home for his Aunt Harrie's family in the Gatachre section of Liverpool. The Birches lived there happily for years (along with Lennon's two half-sisters) but again, following John's death, Yoko, apparently a little short of funds, sought to legally remove the dottering, destitute old man from the property on the pretense of "settling the estate." Toward that end she had one of her high-powered New York attorneys, David Warmflash, send John's uncle a terse one-paragraph letter informing him of Mrs. Lennon's desire to dispose of the property. Birch then immediately wrote to Ono in an attempt to try to work out some sort of compromise. His letters, however, were subsequently returned unopened. The last time I spoke to him, Birch had no idea what he was going to do.

No, Yoko Ono is *not* a nice lady, a fact well known to just about everyone within the Beatles' magical inner circle. That is, of course, everyone but the gullible, lovesick John Lennon. He had fallen for the charismatic conceptual artist hook, line and sinker, and vehemently repelled virtually everybody who wasn't as enamored as he of his new wife. Harrison apparently disliked her from almost the moment they met, and so much as told Lennon so one afternoon outside Apple. "We've asked around about her to a few people in New York," said Harrison. "Dylan, for one, says she gives off very bad vibes. I happen to agree." Lennon's answer went unrecorded, but he later commented in an interview with *Rolling Stone's* Jann Wenner, that "I should have hit the bastard!"

For some time thereafter an icy chill set in between the two. But Harrison deeply valued his relationship with John and eventually swallowed his pride and was at least outwardly cordial to Ono. Privately, however, it remained a different matter. Ono's presence in the boys' lives certainly wasn't the only reason for the demise of the Beatles, but it was clearly a prominent influence. While it's unfair to say that Ono actually split the Beatles, she certainly helped to put a wedge between John and the others, a fact not lost to the sometimes coldly unforgiving George Harrison.

Another nail in the Beatles' coffin, George felt, was Lennon and McCartney's stranglehold over the material that made it on to their records. The "white" album, for example, featured thirteen songs by John, twelve by Paul, but only four from George and one by Ringo. When it was later decided that a number should be cut from the lineup, Harrison's snazzy, soul-filled "Not Guilty" was summarily chosen to go. In view of the number of Lennon-McCartney tunes slated to appear, this hardly seemed fair. Harrison's compositions were certainly up to par. To cut "Not Guilty" in favor of something as inconsequential as, say, "Why Don't We Do It in the Road" was unjustifiable. "We were so isolated together," said Harrison in 1974. "It became very difficult playing the same old tunes day in, day out. When I made *All Things Must Pass* it was so nice for me to just be able to work with other artists. I really don't think the Beatles were all that good, you know."

Like the sweet twirling smoke of an Indian joss stick, the swinging sixties faded into the uncertain seventies and scattered to ashes any hopes the world might have had that the Beatles would stay together. When at last it came, on December 31, 1970, with the suit McCartney brought against his three former partners, the end was long overdue. In even the most bitter of marriages, the mechanics of the final dissolution are always painful. Anger is the first emotion to be overcome, and in the case of John, Paul, George and Ringo, that alone took years.

People, of course, are desperate to try to pinpoint a specific cause of the split — something absolute to tidy up all the loose ends in their minds. The truth is it was many things, but mostly just the inevitable ebb and flow of time washing away what was and replacing it with what is.

One of the most profound reasons, however, seems to be the introduction of New York show business accountant Allen Klein into the picture back in 1969. Eventually, John, George and Ringo were convinced that Klein just might be the answer to the Beatles' problems with Apple and as a group. Paul McCartney, however, and apparently quite a few other Apple insiders definitely did *not* agree. "Allen Klein was a creep, a real creep," remembers Mary Hopkin. "I didn't like him at all. He was very smarmy. He never did anything to me but his personality was enough. I was never directly involved with him financially. I don't like people who patronize me. He was trying to manipulate me. He'd say do this and that. I remember walking away from him in the middle of a meal once. I like to think I'm a good judge of character. He was very transparent."

Being in the Beatles, in Harrison's words, was like "being in a box," and once the way was finally made clear, he ran like the blazes and never looked back. Although they are all genuinely loving, none of the Beatles is particulary sentimental or nostalgic. On the surface, at least, there is a hardness that probably owes much to being from the north of England, but even more to having lived through the lunacy of Beatlemania. When they went their separate ways, George was only too pleased to try to deflate the group's mighty myth at every turn.

"I realize that we did fill a big gap in the sixties," he has said, "but all the people who we really meant something to are all grown up. It's like anything people grow up with, they get attached to it. I can understand that the Beatles, in many ways, did some nice things, and it's very appreciated that people still like them. But the problem comes when they want to live in the past."

As a roving one-man anti-Beatles propaganda machine, George had a mighty tough row to hoe. Still, he makes a lot of sense. "Even if I were to be a Beatle for the rest of my life, it would still be only a temporary thing," he says, referring to the transitory nature of life itself.

As the years slipped away, however, Harrison's hard-line view on the Fab Four loosened up considerably: "Maybe one day we'll get the Beatles together and just put them in a room having tea, satellite it all over the world and charge twenty dollars each to watch it. We could make a fortune."

By the mid-seventies Harrison was able to see the whole amazing period with at least a measure of good humor.

VI

DEEP PEARL RISING

A Spiritual Journey

Of purifiers, I am wind; of wielders of weapons I am Rama; of fishes I am the shark; and of flowing rivers the Ganges; of letters I am the letter A, and among compounds the dual word. I am also inexhaustible time, and of creators Brahma, whose manifold faces turn everywhere. I am all-devouring death, and I am the generator of all things yet to be. Among women I am fame, fortune, speech, memory, intelligence, faithfulness and patience. I am also the gambling of cheats, and of the splendid I am the splendor. I am victory. I am adventure, and I am the strength of the strong.

SRI KRISHNA from *The Bhagavad Gita, As It Is*

EVER SINCE GEORGE HARRISON WAS A LITTLE BOY HE SUSPECTED THAT
there might be a God. Once, while deep in meditation at the Maharishi's
Rishikesh *ashram*, he experienced what he called "a slowing down of the
thought process followed by a blinding acceleration of consciousness." It
was frightening, says Harrison, but it was nothing new. As a child he had
often felt the same thing. Only then he was terrified, as he had absolutely
no idea what it meant. Years later, he could understand it as a lightning
flash of divine awareness. "It's something to do with feeling really tiny,"
says George:

> But at the same time I also felt I was a whole thing as well. It was
> like being two completely different things at the same time. Soon
> this feeling would begin to vibrate right through me and started
> getting bigger and bigger and faster and faster. Before I knew what
> was happening it was going so far and so fast it was mind-boggling
> and I'd come out of it really scared. I used to get that experience a
> lot when we were recording *Abbey Road*. I'd go into this big empty
> studio, get into a soundbox and do my meditation. It was here I had
> a couple of indications that this was the same thing I went through
> as a kid.

After the party was well and truly over, the brain drain of having
been a Beatle twenty-four hours a day was overwhelming. Shell-shocked
by a whirlwind celebrity that never subsided, the four were compelled to
find other outlets or fizzle away. John eventually collided head-on with
Yoko Ono, Paul with his solo career, Ringo with acting. And George with
himself. It is said in the *Vedas*, the sacred Hindu texts, that "whatever a
great man shall attempt, common men will follow." Harrison's well-pub-
licized spiritual trek to India became a catalyst for a lot of people's own
inward journey. Once again, the Beatles led the way.

"The first time I heard Indian music," George recalled in 1967, "I
felt as though I knew it. It was everything, everything I could think of. It
was like every music I had ever heard, but twenty times better than
everything all put together. It was just so strong, so overwhelmingly
positive, it buzzed me right out of my brain."

From the first eerie twang of the Indian sitar in the motion-picture
soundtrack of the Beatles' second feature film, *Help!*, George Harrison was
forever hooked. From that moment on, all things Hindu — philosophy,
diet, fashion, literature and art — held their transcendent sway over the

young man, who shuttled his revelations across the Indian subcontinent into the appreciative arms of a turned-on generation of seekers. Suddenly, in tiny bedrooms and cluttered crash pads around the world, young people were ripping down their tattered M.C. Escher posters in favor of brightly colored representations of an array of multiarmed benevolent gods from Buddha to Brahma. And at the very hub of this spiritual revolution was George's friend and mentor, sitar virtuoso Ravi Shankar.

"I met him at Peter Sellers's house in London for dinner," recalled George of their introduction in 1966, "and he offered to give me some instruction on the basics of sitar. It was the first time I'd ever actually approached music with a bit of discipline. Later, I started really listening to Indian music, and for the next two years I hardly even touched the guitar, except for recording. Having all these material things . . . I still wanted something more, and it suddenly all came to me in the form of Ravi Shankar."

In the early summer of 1966 George humbly requested that Shankar accept him as a student. It was a challenging undertaking, but he applied himself admirably and came away with a newfound knowledge and respect for Hindu culture.

I went over [to India] partly to try to learn the music, but also to absorb as much of the actual country as I could. I'd always heard stories about these old men in the Himalayas who were hundreds of years old, levitating yogis and saints who were able to be buried underground for weeks and live. Now I wanted to see it all for myself. I'll tell you one thing for sure — once you get to the point where you're actually doing things for truth's sake, then nobody can ever touch you again, because you're harmonizing with a greater power. The farther into spiritual life I go, the easier it is to see that the Beatles aren't really controlling any of it, but that something else has now taken us firmly in hand.

George's deep faith in an innate spirituality was only strengthened by his association with Shankar and marked the beginning step of a lifelong quest to understand the life he was living. "Ravi," he says, "is probably the person who has influenced my life the most. Maybe he's not that aware of it, but I really love Ravi and he's been like a father as well as a spiritual guide. I got involved with Hinduism because Ravi Shankar was a Hindu. And I came to understand what Christ *really* was through

Hinduism. Down through the ages there has always been a spiritual path, it's been passed on and it always will be. It just so happens that India was the place where the seed was planted."

Shankar, too, was most grateful to George for the great boost their friendship gave to Indian music throughout Europe and America. Soon music stores everywhere were scrambling to stock not only sitars but also *tablas*, *tambouras* and *sarods*. Suddenly, Shankar was playing to large, appreciative audiences everywhere from Carnegie Hall to the Fillmore. Perhaps his most celebrated performance was at the famed Monterey Pop Festival in 1967. He also played Woodstock. In his book, *My Music, My Life*, Shankar recalls George's early interest in Indian music and his initial trek to India in 1966 to study with the mystic maestro:

> Within twenty-four hours, almost all of Bombay came to know that George Harrison was there. In another day or so, huge crowds of teenagers gathered in front of the hotel, headlines appeared in the papers and my telephone started to ring non-stop. One caller even pretended to be "Mrs. Shankar" and demanded to talk to George. She changed her mind, however, when I took the phone myself. After a few days, I knew the situation was only going to get worse. I couldn't teach and George couldn't practice. Things reached such a state that we had to call a press conference to explain that George had not come as a Beatle but as my disciple, and he asked to be left in peace to work on his music with me.

Few realized that most of the day-to-day instruction George received from Shankar in the late sixties was overseen by Ravi's long-time right-hand man, Shambu Das. Practicing together for hours on end in luxury quarters in Kashmir and Rishikesh, the two men soon became fast friends. Shambu still gets a chuckle from remembering the first time George attempted to eat Indian-style — with one hand — during his initial stay with Shankar in Bombay. "I was teaching at Ravi Shankar's school," said Shambu in 1982, "and Ravi suggested that I personally look after George's progress. Once in a while, though, he would come in and see how the lessons were going. Sometimes all three of us would sit together and practice. We had a fantastic time. Pattie was often there, and she was always very friendly to everyone. We used to visit some ancient Hindu temples in the area and then head back home for yet more practice.

George was very intelligent. Sometimes he would play up to eight hours a day."

Even after George's marathon instruction was completed, he and Shambu remained close. Harrison invited Shambu to visit the Beatles' entourage while they were meditating at the Maharishi Mahesh Yogi's ashram, and inadvertently became a pawn in an apparent philosophical conflict of interest between Shankar and the giggly Hindu master. He explains:

> I was only there four days, but the Maharishi quickly became very close to me, because George wanted me around, I think. One day, as he was sitting there talking to the Beatles, he said to me, "We would like you to do some special work for us." The next day I wanted to leave, but the Maharishi insisted I stay a little longer. On the plane home I met this big industrialist from Bombay who showed me a headline that said one of Ravi Shankar's very close associates had bowed down to the Maharishi as if he had become his disciple.
>
> "Well," I said, "this is the Indian custom. When you meet a religious person you should always touch their feet, and that's what I did."
>
> Later that afternoon I was driving to the hotel with Ravi when I noticed he was acting a bit stiff. I didn't realize he had already seen something in the papers about me visiting the Maharishi. I asked him why he was so upset, and he said, "How was your ashram visit?" in a very funny way, so I said, "It was very good."
>
> "I saw the item in the newspaper, Shambu, so what is your plan now?"
>
> "There is no *plan*, Ravi," I replied, "I just visited the Beatles, that's all."

The Maharishi was the first real-life spiritual master most of us had ever seen, and he fit the bill as a Hollywood-style Indian guru to a tee. Long, stringy, shoulder-length hair, salt-and-pepper beard, flowing robes and that laugh! If nothing else, his cosmic cackle was worth the price of admission alone.

It is not that the Maharishi is a charlatan. Quite the opposite. He is unquestionably most sincere in his beliefs and in his Spiritual Regeneration Movement. Those who became enamored of the Maharishi's fifteen-minute-a-day meditation were adamant that whatever it was you wanted out of life, TM (Transcendental Meditation) could, and most definitely *would*, enhance your chances of getting it.

By the late summer of 1967, both George and Pattie Harrison had become absorbed in cultivating their spiritual lives. They had already endeavored to teach themselves meditation from books but weren't really making much headway. So when a girlfriend of Pattie's suggested that she attend a lecture on Transcendental Meditation at Caxton Hall, London, she readily accepted and afterward signed up to become a member.

George, meanwhile, had alerted the other Beatles that the Maharishi Mahesh Yogi was coming to London and they could hear him speak at the Hilton Hotel on August 24. They went, and were impressed by what they heard. Afterward, the Maharishi met the boys and invited them to a ten-day conference in Bangor, North Wales, the next day. Traveling with the guru by train (or "The Mystical Special" as the London *Daily Mirror* called it) were Mick Jagger, Marianne Faithfull, and Pattie's younger sister, Jenny Boyd, among others. George especially was genuinely excited about the prospect of finally hooking up with someone who, it seemed, might be able to provide some answers to the Beatles' nonstop, topsy-turvy existence. Naturally, the platform at Bangor was mobbed by hundreds of screaming fans. John Lennon later confided that the naive yogi actually thought the crowds had turned out to see *him*.

On August 27, 1967, the Beatles were formally initiated into his society but some distressing news suddenly came through from London — Brian Epstein was dead.

Although the Beatles were naturally concerned about how Epstein's untimely demise might affect their careers, and thus their staggering collective fortunes, for George Harrison the tragedy only encouraged his further retreat into the yogic philosophy that by now consumed him. To many close to the Beatle, his curry-flavored rhetoric could no longer even be considered preaching but, rather, out and out raving. "Everything's a cycle!" George told a reporter for *Look* magazine in 1967:

> It's up to us to get off that cycle, because it's going to be going around forever. You have to say, "I've had enough of this roundabout, and I'd like to get on now to something else." People are making it to the astral plane, but those who don't just keep dying and coming back and dying and coming back. It's all action and reaction.
>
> Finally you've got to get on the astral plane, go around there

for a bit, get rid of your astral karma, and then on to the causal plane, until you get rid of that one, then you're right in there!

Not to say there mightn't have been an element of truth in George's mystical meanderings, but with hindsight even Harrison agrees that his ability to "talk the talk" rather significantly exceeded his power to, as the born-again Christians say, "walk the walk."

Still, it was with great enthusiasm and optimism all around that George, John, their wives and a few close friends arrived at New Delhi Airport on the morning of February 16, 1968, to begin serious study with the Maharishi at his extravagant Rishikesh retreat. At the end of a rugged 150-mile drive in three cars from New Delhi to the ashram, the celebrated disciples were warmly welcomed by the diminutive guru with a shower of encouraging words and endless cups of steaming almond drupe tea on the veranda of his comfortable stone bungalow situated in the heart of the rambling camp. Mal Evans gives us a hint of the many amenities available to the meditators in an article first published in *The Beatles Monthly Book* in May of 1968: "I suppose a total of about forty people were employed at the academy — including joiners, a full-scale printing works, numerous cooks and cleaning staff. The room service was marvelous. On my first day there I unpacked dozens of the Beatles' shirts and other clothing and piled them up on shelves in my room. An hour later the lot had disappeared. The same evening they were back, all freshly washed and pressed. And I hadn't even asked!"

A couple of days later Ringo, Paul and their entourage of lovers and friends arrived along with a throng of representatives from the world's press to a tumultuous welcome from the entire camp. Although no provisions had been made for the newspapermen, the Maharishi happily slotted them in when and where he could. Not surprisingly, the attendant publicity didn't seem to upset him too much either.

As one day slipped casually into the next and the initial excitement of the trip subsided, the boys' pent-up tensions slowly began to unravel under the magic spell of the meditation. Most days it was the normally sluggish John who was the first up, and after about a half-hour of meditation he would go for a leisurely stroll around the compound with Mal or George. "The Maharishi really was a wonderful teacher," recalls Cynthia. "His lectures and talks were humorous, enlightening, and provided truly halcyon days. John and George, particularly, were in their element. They threw themselves totally into the Maharishi's teachings, were happy, relaxed and above all found a peace of mind that had been denied them so long." Paul, too became very much absorbed in the Maharishi's philosophy, but Ringo didn't particularly like the simple Indian food or the many insects, and complained that the stifling midday heat was keeping him from meditating properly.

Many of the Beatles' long-time friends also joined them on the pilgrimage: Donovan and his ever-present friend Gypsy, the eccentric Greek inventor "Magic" Alex Mardas, Beach Boy Mike Love, Neil Aspinall and Mia Farrow and her younger sister Prudence (Lennon's inspiration behind the song "Dear Prudence"). From all accounts, at that point anyway, it was as perfect and peaceful an interlude as anyone could ever hope for. Quite a curious contrast to the rather menacing Hindu guards who stood watch just outside the main gates under a huge cloth banner that said, simply, "Welcome."

The ashram itself, a half-mile south from the heart of the famous little mountain town of Rishikesh, sat on two levels amidst a grove of sheshum and teak trees, surrounded by yards of menacing barbed wire. The lower tier was highlighted by a random series of several long, low stone buildings, one of which was labeled Enquiry Office. It was here that potential aspirants were stopped to have their spiritual credentials checked by a soft-spoken young man called Suresh. Those lucky enough to pass the impromptu inquisition were given a warm blanket and directed to one of the many tiny cottages that ringed the grounds, there to await word on whether or not their "vibrations" were sufficiently pure to allow them entrance to the upper echelon of buildings, where the Maharishi and his superstar faithful held forth. Those who didn't pass Suresh's spiritual twenty questions were told abruptly to go away.

For those inside the Maharishi's select inner circle of meditators, the key word was endurance. Students were encouraged to meditate for longer and longer periods, only to gradually taper off near the end of the course in an effort to "reconnect" with the material plane. "To make sure we would meditate in peace," wrote Mal, "we had little printed cards saying MEDITATING, PLEASE DO NOT DISTURB, which we stuck outside the doors of our bedrooms." Within the Beatles' clique it was marathon meditators John and George who led the rest, clocking in respectively at seven and nine solid hours of tuned-in cosmic awareness.

Soon, however, the inevitable happened, and the Beatles' fascination with TM slowly began to subside. After all, sitting hour after hour silently muttering a Sanskrit syllable to oneself (no matter how exotic the

Hessy's Music Centre in the heart of Liverpool, where George and all the Beatles bought their first guitars.
SKYBOOT PRODUCTIONS LTD.: G. GIULIANO

Phoning home from New York during the Beatles' first American tour, 1964.
DELIBERATE ALCHEMY ARCHIVES

Shooting a promotional film to accompany the tune "Paperback Writer."
DELIBERATE ALCHEMY ARCHIVES

On the road again, 1965. DELIBERATE ALCHEMY ARCHIVES

With "My Guy" vocalist Mary Wells. DELIBERATE ALCHEMY ARCHIVES

George and Ravi Shankar backstage during Shankar's performance at the Royal Albert Hall, 1967.

On tour in the USA, 1966.
DELIBERATE ALCHEMY ARCHIVES

The Beatles in August 1967, upon receiving the devastating news that their longtime manager, Brian Epstein, had died of an apparent drug overdose in London. DELIBERATE ALCHEMY ARCHIVES

Discussing the intricacies of eastern philosophy and Transcendental Meditation with TV talk show host David Frost, 1967.
DELIBERATE ALCHEMY ARCHIVES

Knocking off for lunch during sessions for the "white" album, 1968.
DELIBERATE ALCHEMY ARCHIVES

"Thumbs up" at the historic first international satellite broadcast for the program "Our World," in 1967. As England's contribution to the show, the Beatles performed the classic "All You Need Is Love." DELIBERATE ALCHEMY ARCHIVES

A wistful George during a break in filming for the Beatles' critically disastrous 1967 TV Boxing Day special *Magical Mystery Tour*.
DELIBERATE ALCHEMY ARCHIVES

George Harrison, "when he was Fab," in the psychedelic sixties. DELIBERATE ALCHEMY ARCHIVES

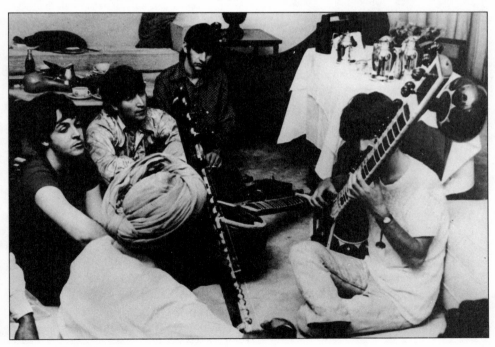

Entranced with the mysterious sitar, 1966.
DELIBERATE ALCHEMY ARCHIVES

In Bangor with His Holiness, the Maharishi Mahesh Yogi.
DELIBERATE ALCHEMY ARCHIVES

George on his return to London following an intensive two-week crash course on the sitar with Ravi Shankar.
DELIBERATE ALCHEMY ARCHIVES

Recording *Wonderwall* in India. Harrison's sitar tutor Shambu Das is seen holding the stopwatch.
DELIBERATE ALCHEMY ARCHIVES

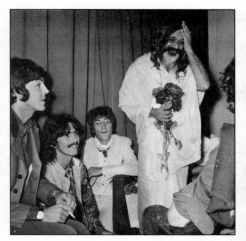

Three Beatles and "Sexy Sadie" at the Hilton Hotel in London.
DELIBERATE ALCHEMY ARCHIVES

The Harrisons arriving in L.A. with Ringo, Maureen and several members of the Byrds in tow, 1967. DELIBERATE ALCHEMY ARCHIVES

With the Maharishi, August 1967. DELIBERATE ALCHEMY ARCHIVES

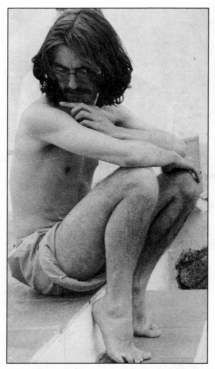

On the run at London's Heathrow Airport, to see off old friends Bob and Sara Dylan.
DELIBERATE ALCHEMY ARCHIVES

Relaxing on the front steps of Kinfauns.
DELIBERATE ALCHEMY ARCHIVES

Kinfauns, George and Pattie Harrison's psychedelic Esher bungalow.
DELIBERATE ALCHEMY ARCHIVES

locale) did tend to become a little boring. Ringo and his wife, Maureen, left after only ten days. Arriving at London's Heathrow Airport, Starr's only comment to the assembled media was that it had reminded him of Butlins, the famous working-class English holiday resort. And, yes, he was going right home to tuck into a generous plate of bangers and mash, thank you.

McCartney, meanwhile, was becoming increasingly anxious over the preliminary organization of Apple, a pet project of the singer's meant to bring at least a semblance of order to the Beatles' rapidly declining business empire. Despite the distractions, however, Paul and his girlfriend, actress Jane Asher, managed to stick it out for six weeks before jetting off home. Were they disillusioned with the teaching? they were asked upon their return. "No," said Paul, "just a little homesick."

That left John and George, the Maharishi's most ardent believers. So besotted were they with the bearded holy man that even when "Magic" Alex first introduced a rumor that the Maharishi had made a very definite bid for the earthly affections of Mia Farrow, they were loath to believe it. Within a week Farrow had gone on a tiger hunt in the south. It was suggested by the Maharishi's staff that she would be returning shortly thereafter. She never did.

John and George were extremely hurt and confused by the whole sordid affair, all the while enthusiastically counseled by their mate "Magic" Alex to drop the guru once and for all and go home. "It was obvious to me," recalls Cynthia Lennon, "that Alex wanted out and more than anything he wanted the Beatles out as well. An entire evening was spent trying desperately to sort everything out in their minds. That night of soul-searching by John and George produced a victory for Alex but great unhappiness as far as I was concerned. Out of confusion and accusation came anger and aggression. Doubt and subterfuge had replaced our joy and hard-won peace of mind."

Once the penny had dropped, the two remaining Beatles were convinced that there was nothing left but to confront the elderly master with the charges. The job fell to John Lennon. He explained in a 1970 issue of *Rolling Stone*:

> There was a big hullabaloo about him trying to rape Mia Farrow or somebody and attempting to get off with a few other women. Anyway, we went to see him after trying all night to figure out if it was possible. When George started thinking it might be true, I

thought, well, it *must* be true, because if George thinks it might be true then there's got to be something to it. So I said to him, "We're leaving."

"Why?" he asked, and all that shit, so I said, "Well, if you're so bloody cosmic, then you'll know, won't you?"

"But I don't know why. You must tell me," he replied.

I kept saying, "You ought to know" and he gave me a look like, "I'll kill you, you bastard." I knew then.

The Beatles stormed out of the bungalow and rang for a taxi from the ashram's dining hall before racing back to their quarters to pack. As they were filing out the main gate, a disciple was sent by the Maharishi to make one last pitiful plea for them to calm down and talk things over. But it was too late. The Beatles, like so many times in the past, had burned their bridges and were moving on. As Paul's brother, Mike McCartney, has said, "With that lot you only get one chance and then you're finished." Within thirty-six hours the Harrisons and the Lennons were safely back home on their estates in suburban London. The magical Maharishi Mahesh Yogi and company had become just another in a long series of bum trips.

Syamasundar Das, a broad-shouldered, strapping young American devotee of Krishna, sat patiently in Apple's crowded reception area quietly fingering his prayer beads, awaiting a precious moment or two with George Harrison. In any ordinary business, the sight of a saffron-robed, shaven-headed Hindu monk tapping out mantras in the lobby might have at least raised an eyebrow, but this was Apple circa 1969, the hip center of the hippie world, and nothing was too far out. Nor was this the Hare Krishnas' first overture to the ascetically inclined Harrison. Ever since the first feeble wave of devotees shuttled across the Atlantic from America the year before, they, like most of the world's youth, had Beatles on the brain. Still, this was no ordinary teenage hero-worship. The devotees shared a serious, single-minded devotion to the Lord Sri Krishna and, as such, felt it imperative to try to link up with a celebrity of global stature like George. Earlier attempts at attracting the attention of the Beatles had included sending them an apple pie with the words *Hare Krishna* scrolled across the top in green icing, as well as dropping off an inscribed wind-up walking apple and a homemade audition tape of their hypnotic Vedic chants (for which they received the standard Apple Records' rejection letter). Bounding down the stairs from a late-afternoon conference, George stopped dead in his tracks upon seeing the yogi. "Where have you lot been?" he called out excitedly, making his way through the crowded room. "I've been trying to connect up with you people for some time. It's great to finally see you."

For the next two hours George and Syamasundar sat talking, completely oblivious to the dozen or so hangers-on crowding around this transcendental odd couple. As he rose to leave, George invited all the devotees to his Esher bungalow the next afternoon for lunch with his mates, John, Paul and Ringo.

Racing back to the dilapidated headquarters of the London Radha Krishna Temple in an old warehouse near Covent Garden, Syamasundar was ecstatic, with the hope that the movement would now begin to take hold in Britain. After all, with the Beatles' good wishes and the blessings of Krishna, nothing was impossible.

The next day, the devotees, complete with flowing robes, cymbals, tambourines and Indian drums, boarded London's public transport bound for Waterloo Station and the wilds of Esher. After a hearty vegetarian smorgasbord and a brief chanting session, everyone settled down to a friendly chat.

"Why the robes and that?" wondered Lennon. "This is not that culture. Won't you tend to turn off more people than you attract?"

"Why compromise?" countered George. "There's no reason for them to try to fit in with everyone else. Besides, yogis have dressed this way for thousands of years."

Syamasundar remembers feeling warm toward not only his host but the other Beatles as well. "They were always very nice people," he commented years later, "but George was always the one who was really sincere about trying to know God. This wasn't just a casual sort of curious intellectual inquiry either, but rather, a deep, deep longing for the truth."

As the weeks passed, George and Syamasundar became increasingly close. George also formed friendly relationships with two other devotees, Mukunda and Guru Das. "I feel at home with Krishna," says George. "I think that's something that has been there from a previous birth. So it was like a door opening to me at the time, but it was also like a jigsaw puzzle and I needed all these little pieces to help make the complete picture. And these are some of the reasons why I responded to Syamasundar and Guru Das when they first came to London. Let's face it, if I'm going to have to stand up and be counted, then I'll be with the devotees rather than the straight people who are the so-called saints."

During the heady days of 1969, George's newfound belief in Krishna was absolute and he never hesitated to do whatever he could to help promote the temple or its erudite founder, His Divine Grace A.C. Bhaktivedanta Swami Prabhupada. In 1922, Prabhupada met his spiritual master, Srila Bhaktisiddhanta Saraswati Goswami Maharaj, who instructed him in the devotional science of Bhakti Yoga and fostered within him a sincere desire to dedicate his life to propagating the transcendental message of the Lord Sri Krishna. By 1933 he was formally initiated into the cult of the great Bengali *avatar* (incarnation of godhead), Sri Chaitanya Mahaprabhu, and in September 1965, at the age of seventy, traveled to America to try to fulfill his master's sacred mission. As part of his enduring legacy to his disciples, Srila Prabhupada established more than one hundred Krishna Consciousness centers around the world and also wrote more than eighty scholarly books on Vedic philosophy and culture.

Since the Krishna devotees were all foreigners who lacked the necessary connections or finances, George instructed Apple to back them by leasing a proper building in which to house their temple. After a lengthy search, they finally settled on a brownstone tucked away in Bury Place, a little side street near the British Museum. Of course, renting a house and turning it into an authentic Krishna temple were two entirely different matters, but once again Harrison was anxious to help. Hearing that Syamasundar was having difficulty raising the money to purchase enough marble to finish the temple's ornate altar, George generously donated £2,000 for a huge slab of golden sienna plus two smaller pieces for the terraced base.

When he learned of Harrison's generosity and goodwill toward the devotees, Srila Prabhupada immediately wrote Syamasundar a long letter outlining some of his thoughts on the potential benefits of the Beatle's involvement with the International Society for Krishna Consciousness (ISKCON):

It is understood from your letter that Mr. George Harrison has a little sympathy for our movement, and if Krishna is actually satisfied on him surely he will be able to join us in pushing on the Sankirtan [congregational chanting] movement throughout the world. Somehow or other the Beatles have become the cynosure of the neighboring European countries and America also. He is attracted to our philosophy and if Mr. Harrison takes the leading part in organizing a huge Sankirtan party consisting of the Beatles and our ISKCON boys, surely we shall change the face of the world so much politically harassed by the maneuvers of the politicians.

And in another letter some weeks later he wrote: "I am so glad that George Harrison is composing songs like, 'Lord whom we have so long ignored.' He is very thoughtful. When we actually meet I shall be able to give him thoughts about separation from Krishna, and they will be able to compose very attractive songs for public reception. The public is in need of such songs, and if they are administered through nice agents like the Beatles, it will surely be a big success."

As George's involvement with the temple grew, the idea that the devotees might eventually join George and the other Beatles for some recording work soon was in the air. "Still," said George, "I think it would be preferable if you guys got the money instead of us. It might actually be better if you made your own record for Apple. How about it?"

Mukunda Das Goswami, a long-time associate of Harrison's and today the head of ISKCON's public affairs office in San Diego, remembers those early sessions in 1969: "The first time we got together to record was at George's place on Claremont Drive in Esher. He had a very nice vegetarian meal prepared and afterward we all chanted with him and Billy Preston. Billy was playing an early type of Moog synthesizer, George was playing his guitar and we were on drums and *kartals* [hand cymbals]. I remember us doing a bit of cooking together that night, and I think he may have even played us a Lenny Bruce record."

Later that same week the devotees again joined Harrison and Preston for yet another preparatory session, this time at Trident Studios in St. Anne's Alley, a particularly seamy section of Soho's notorious red-light district. Once again, George and the devotees went through their repertoire of up-tempo Sanskrit chants, and when it was over, Harrison and Syamasundar both felt the time was right for what they called "a real session." In Srila Prabhupada's official biography, *Every Town and Village: Around the World 1968-1971*, His Holiness Satsvarupa Das Goswami recalls the big event:

On the day of the recording about a dozen devotees, including some newly recruited Britishers, assembled at EMI recording studios on

Abbey Road. When the first group of devotees arrived in George's white Mercedes, a crowd of teenagers began singing Hare Krishna to the tune popularized by the rock musical *Hair*. While Yamuna applied *Vaisnava tilaka* to the foreheads of the recording technicians, Malati began unpacking the picnic baskets of *prasadam* [vegetarian foodstuffs first offered to Krishna] she had brought, while some of the other devotees put up pictures of Krishna and lit incense. The studio was now Krishna-ized.

With Paul McCartney and his wife, Linda, operating the control console, the recording session began. Everyone worked quickly, making side one of the 45-rpm record in about an hour. George played organ and Mukunda played *mridangam* [an Indian drum]. Yamuna sang the lead with Syamasundar backing her, with the other voices blending together in a chorus.

On the fourth take everything went smoothly, with Malati spontaneously hitting a brass gong at the end. Then they recorded the flip side of the record. Afterwards, George dubbed in the bass guitar and other voices. The devotees, engineers, everyone felt good about it. "This is going to be *big*," George promised.

Now officially signed to Apple Records as a recording act promoted under the name of the Radha Krishna Temple, the devotees finally felt they were on their way. With a five-story townhouse in the heart of central London and the promise of an upcoming visit by their spiritual master, Srila Prabhupada, they were very optimistic. But they were soon to discover that not everybody in London was as enamored of Krishna consciousness as they. Just weeks before the renovations to Bury Place were to be completed, they received word from city officials that because of various complaints from local residents the Ministry of Housing was holding up their building and zoning permits pending a lengthy investigation.

Once again the Beatles came to the rescue. John Lennon suggested to Syamasundar that the devotees might consider coming out to stay at Tittenhurst Park, Lennon's seventy-six acre estate in Berkshire, next door to the famous Ascot raceway. Lennon had only recently purchased the eighteenth-century mansion and was anxious to begin renovating and redecorating to the tastes of his new bride, Yoko Ono. If the devotees were willing to help with the work, then they would be more than welcome to take over the estate's massive conservatory as a temporary home until all the formalities regarding Bury Place were sorted out.

"We were given the Park's guest houses, which had all been done up very nicely," remembers Mukunda. "We were far enough toward the other end of the property that we never seemed to bother John and Yoko. They pretty much kept to themselves in the main house. We actually had very little contact with them because Yoko had it organized that way."

About this time, Apple Records released the devotees' first single, "The Hare Krishna Mantra," with "Prayers to the Spiritual Master" on the B side.

The very first day it was out it sold seventy thousand copies and immediately started making its way up the charts. But that wasn't the important thing to the spiritually inclined Harrison. "When the record came out, a man who had stayed locked in his room for twenty years heard it on the radio, and now he has joined the movement," George has recalled. "It didn't matter to me whether the record was a commercial success or not. The fact is that it helped one person, and that was what counted for me."

Apple staged a launch party in the back garden of a large Georgian mansion in south London. An impressive blue-and-white-striped tent was erected, under which London's top media types enjoyed a gourmet vegetarian meal as well as a rousing chanting session with George and the devotees. In an interview conducted by Mukunda for his 1982 book, *Chant and be Happy: The Story of the Hare Krishna Mantra*, Harrison remembers the profound impact that chanting Hare Krishna was to have on his life:

> I once chanted the mantra all the way from France to Portugal nonstop. I drove for about twenty-three hours and chanted all the way. It gets you feeling a bit invincible. The funny thing was that I didn't even know where I was going. I had bought a map, and I knew basically which way I was aiming, but I couldn't speak French, Spanish or Portuguese. Strangely, none of that seemed to matter. Once you get chanting, things start to happen transcendentally.
>
> I remember once I was on an airplane that was in an electric storm. It was hit by lightning three times, and a Boeing 707 went right over the top of us, missing by inches. I thought the back end of the plane had blown off. . . . As soon as the plane began bouncing around I started chanting Hare Krishna. The whole thing went on for about two hours with the plane dropping hundreds of feet, all the

lights were out and there were all these explosions. Everybody was terrified. I ended up with my feet pressed against the seat in front yelling "Hare Krishna" at the top of my lungs.

I know for me the difference between making it and not making it was chanting the mantra. Peter Sellers also swore that chanting Hare Krishna had saved him from a plane crash once.

"I remember singing the mantra for days, John and I, with ukulele banjos sailing through the Greek Islands together," says Harrison in Mukunda's book. "Like six hours we sang, because we couldn't stop once we got going. As soon as we stopped it was like the lights went out. It went on to the point where our jaws were aching singing the mantra over and over. We both felt absolutely exalted. It was a very happy time for us."

On a rainy, windswept September 11, 1969, Lufthansa Flight 707 from Hamburg arrived at London's Heathrow Airport carrying a very special passenger. Srila Prabhupada had at last fulfilled his promise to visit his London followers as well as meet his newest and most celebrated disciple, George Harrison. Following a brief airport press conference sponsored by Apple Records and Lufthansa, the aging Indian guru was whisked away to Tittenhurst Park in John Lennon's immaculate white Rolls.

After a relaxed luncheon with several of his close disciples, Srila Prabhupada agreed to meet with George, John and Yoko in his private quarters on the second floor of the expansive outbuilding. Smiling broadly from behind a long, low desk, he greeted his hosts warmly with a throaty "Hare Krishna" and softly asked them to please enter and be seated. Prabhupada gently removed the beautiful red and white garland of carnations presented to him at the airport and indicated to Syamasundar that he should carefully place them over George's head.

"Thank you," said George, clearly a little overwhelmed at meeting his spiritual mentor face to face. "Hare Krishna."

"This is Krishna's blessing," Prabhupada replied.

George nodded in silent agreement. The touching moment had genuinely humbled the introspective superstar. Fortunately someone in the room had the foresight to record their conversation, an edited portion of which went as follows:

PRABHUPADA (*to Lennon*): You are anxious to bring about peace in the world. I've read some of your statements, and they show me that you're anxious to do something. Actually, every saintly person should try and bring peace, but we must know the process. What kind of philosophy are you following? May I ask?

YOKO: We don't follow anything. We are just living.

GEORGE: We've done meditation. Or I do my meditation — mantra meditation.

PRABHUPADA: Hare Krishna is also a mantra.

JOHN: Ours is not a song, though. We heard it from Maharishi. A mantra each.

PRABHUPADA: His mantras are not public?

JOHN: No, it's a secret.

YOKO: If Hare Krishna is such a strong, powerful mantra, is there any reason to chant anything else?

PRABHUPADA: There are other mantras, but Hare Krishna is especially recommended for this age.

JOHN: If all mantras are just the name of God, then whether it's a secret mantra or an open mantra, it doesn't really make much difference, does it, which one you sing?

PRABHUPADA: It does make a difference. For instance, in a drug shop they sell many types of medicines for curing different diseases. But still you have to get a doctor's prescription in order to get a particular type of medicine. Otherwise, the druggist won't supply you. You might go to the drug shop and say, "I'm diseased. Please give me any medicine you have." But the druggist will ask you, "Where is your prescription?" Similarly, in this age, the Hare Krishna mantra is prescribed in the scriptures. And the great teacher Sri Chaitanya Mahaprabhu, whom we consider to be an incarnation of God, also prescribed it. Therefore, our principle is that everyone should follow the prescription of the great authorities.

YOKO: If the mantra itself has such power, does it matter where you receive it?

PRABHUPADA: Yes, it does matter. For instance, milk is nutritious. That's a fact everyone knows. But if milk is touched by the lips of a serpent, it is no longer nutritious. It becomes poisonous. If you don't receive the mantra through the proper channel, it may not really be spiritual.

JOHN: But what if one of these masters who's not in the line says exactly the same thing as one who is? What if he says his mantra is coming from the Vedas and he seems to speak with as much authority as you?

PRABHUPADA: If the mantra is actually coming through a bona fide disciplic succession, then it will have the potency.

JOHN: But the Hare Krishna mantra is the best one?

PRABHUPADA: Yes. We say that the Hare Krishna mantra is sufficient for one's perfection, for liberation.

GEORGE: Isn't it like flowers? Somebody may prefer roses, and somebody may like carnations better. Isn't it really a matter for the individual devotee to decide? One person may find that Hare Krishna is more beneficial to his spiritual progress, and yet another person may find that some other mantra may be more beneficial for him.

PRABHUPADA: But still there is a distinction. A fragrant rose is considered better than a flower without any scent. You may be attracted by one flower, and I may be attracted by another flower. But among the flowers a distinction can be made. There are many flowers that have no fragrance and many that do. Therefore, your attraction for a particular flower is not the solution to the question of which is actually better. In the same way, personal attraction is not the solution to choosing the best spiritual process. You've been speaking of the Maharishi. Hasn't he written some book on *Bhagavad-gita* [a sacred Vedic text]?

JOHN: Yes, that's the one we've read.

PRABHUPADA: So, why is he using Krishna's book to put forward his own philosophy? *Bhagavad-gita* is Krishna's book. Why is he taking Krishna's book?

GEORGE: Well, he didn't. He just translated it.

PRABHUPADA: Why? Because Krishna's book is very well respected.

JOHN: I've also read part of another translation by Paramahansa Yogananda.

PRABHUPADA: Yes, all these men take advantage of Krishna's book to lend an air of authority to their own speculations. Vivekananda has done it, Sri Aurobindo has done it, Dr. Radhakrishan has done it, Mahatma Gandhi has done it. Thousands of them have done it. But why do they use *Bhagavad-gita* as the vehicle for their own ideas?

GEORGE: In the versions I've read, the authors all claim that theirs is the best. And sometimes I get something from one which I didn't get from another.

JOHN: I found that the best thing for myself is to take a little bit from here and a little bit from there.

YOKO: I mean, we're not just saying that. We want to ask your advice. In other words, what is your answer to this question of authority?

PRABHUPADA: If we don't take the *Gita* from the authorized disciplic succession, it won't help us. In our introduction to *Bhagavad-gita* we have carefully explained that aside from Krishna there is no authority. Krishna is the authority, because *Bhagavad-gita* was spoken by Krishna. Can you deny that?

JOHN: What about Yogananda, Maharishi and all these other people who have translated the *Gita*? How are we to tell that their version isn't also Krishna's word?

PRABHUPADA: If you seriously want to understand this, you should study the original Sanskrit text.

JOHN: Study Sanskrit. Oh, now you're talking. (*Laughter*)

GEORGE: But Vivekananda said that books, rituals, dogmas and temples are secondary details anyway. He said they're not the most important thing. You don't have to read the book in order to have the perception.

PRABHUPADA: Then why did Vivekananda write so many books? (*Laughter*)

JOHN: Who says who's actually in the line of descent? I mean, it's just like royalty — Yogananda also claims to be in a line, he talks about his guru's guru's guru's guru, like that. Maharishi claimed that all his gurus went way back. I mean, how are we to know?

PRABHUPADA: Whatever Maharishi may be, his knowledge does *not* extend up to Krishna, not up to His personal feature.

JOHN: That's what he used to say in exactly the same way about everybody else.

PRABHUPADA: But factually he cannot be an authority, because he does not speak anything about Krishna. If a postman comes and does not know anything about the post office, what kind of postman is he?

YOKO: But he does talk about *his* post office.

PRABHUPADA: No, you cannot create your own post office. There is only one post office, the government post office. If a postman comes and says "I belong to another post office," then at once you can know he is unauthorized.

JOHN: In the Bible or any other holy book, they talk about one God. So it's just the one Being everywhere, in all the books. So why isn't Hare Krishna or something similar in the Bible?

DISCIPLE: It is in the Bible. In Psalms it says, "Praise the Lord with every breath. Praise the Lord with drum and flute."

JOHN: But they haven't got very good tunes. They haven't been passing on any good chants, have they? (*Laughter*) I mean, would it be effective to chant, "Lord Jesus, Lord Jesus, Hail Lord Jesus?"

PRABHUPADA: Lord Jesus says that he is the Son of God. He's not God but the Son of God. In that sense, there is no difference between Krishna consciousness and Christianity. There is no quarrel between God and God's Son. Jesus says to love God, and Krishna, the Supreme Personality of Godhead, says, "Love me." It's the same thing. All right?

Despite the auspicious beginning, however, within about seven weeks Prabhupada began to feel the devotees had overstayed their welcome at Tittenhurst. Although John was always exceedingly kind and interested, Yoko, it was thought, felt somehow threatened by their presence. After a word one day from John concerning the Lennons' "great need for privacy," Prabhupada's men immediately began searching for an apartment for their leader. One can only assume that this latest wrinkle in the on-going personality clash between the new Mrs. Lennon and the rest of the world proved deeply embarrassing to George. Prabhupada soon relocated to a comfortable furnished apartment on Baker Street to await completion of the Bury Place temple.

In 1959 the scholarly spiritual master had begun the mammoth task of translating the tenth canto of the great scripture, the *Srimad Bhagavatam*, into English. The result, a lengthy, lavishly illustrated volume entitled *Krishna: The Supreme Personality of Godhead*, was now ready to publish after ten years of painstaking work. There was a problem, however. Srila Prabhupada was short of funds for the first printing. Although Syamasundar was extremely hesitant to ask George for the money, his guru insisted. Harrison only reluctantly agreed, and arrangements were made through Apple to pick up the swami's $19,000 printing tab. In addition, George was also asked if he would be kind enough to pen a brief introduction to the text. "I didn't really think I was qualified," says Harrison, "but because I am known the devotees thought it would help.

A rare smile from the normally somber George, 1969. DELIBERATE ALCHEMY ARCHIVES

His Divine Grace A.C. Bhaktivedanta Swami in 1975. Affectionately known as "Prabhupada," this gentle intellectual scholar was the founder of the much misunderstood Hare Krishna movement and one of George's closest friends. STEVEN ROSEN

Sri Krishna, Harrison's preferred image of God as the mystical cowherd boy, Govinda. JADURANI DEVI DASI

From another point of view, though, not everyone wants to listen to what I say. I mean, if I picked up a book on Krishna and the foreword was written by Frank Zappa or somebody like that, I would think, 'God, maybe I don't want to know about it.'"

With so much Krishna consciousness in the air, the devotees' records steadily rocketed up the international charts with an intensity that surprised even the most jaded critics. The "Hare Krishna Mantra" single reached number one in West Germany and Czechoslovakia while making the Top Ten in Japan and most of Europe. A great deal of the temple's success, of course, had to do with the passion with which George Harrison promoted his mantra-made protégés. "George plugged the record to virtually anyone who would listen," commented Mukunda in a 1983 interview. "He was always very well known for his savvy of media promotion tactics."

George's new love for Krishna was also having its effect at home. Unlike most transplanted Indian philosophies, the tenets of Krishna consciousness made no allowances for the flickering, undisciplined Western mind. The rules and regulations were the same for everyone. No meat, fish or eggs. No alcohol. No gambling. And no illicit sex. That is, no sex other than for reasons of procreation. In addition, aspirants were not allowed to take coffee, tea, chocolate, garlic or onions — all of which were thought to arouse unwanted sexual passion.

Most important, however, was the regulated chanting of Hare Krishna on wooden prayer beads, called *japa mala*, similar to the Catholic rosary. Devotees are required to repeat the holy name 1,728 times daily, a feat that generally takes about two solid hours. "In the beginning, when I was heavy into chanting and I had my hand in my bead bag all the time," George says, "I got so tired of people asking, 'Did you hurt your hand, break it or something?' In the end I just used to say, 'Yeah. I had an accident,' because it was easier than explaining everything. Using the beads also helps me to release a lot of nervous energy."

Initially, Pattie was favorably disposed toward Prabhupada and the devotees, though she soon found the day-to-day lifestyle incredibly restrictive. Mukunda, however, remembers her as always "very warm and gracious" whenever they met, though he also noted that she "didn't particulary exhibit any kind of overt spiritual characteristics."

Beatle confidante Peter Brown witnessed first-hand Harrison's conversion to Krishna consciousness, but is skeptical about its lasting influence on the singer:

> I think he was sincere all right, but I don't really feel they changed him in the least. When George got on any subject he was involved with, he became a little boring. He's one of those people who, when he's telling you about something, just doesn't know when to stop, he goes on and on. Whether he's talking about Transcendental Meditation, Hare Krishna or *whatever* it's the same — he just goes on. I'm sure he genuinely believes in the philosophy, but that doesn't mean he's going to always practice what he's preaching. I mean, you can talk to a good Catholic and they'll know what they want to do, but what they actually achieve is sometimes a slightly different matter.

There isn't much doubt that the Harrisons' admittedly jet-set life-style was both a blessing and a curse to their yoga practice. On the one hand, their social mobility gave them access to virtually anyone they wanted to meet; on the other, it threw a lot of fuel on the fire of passions they were both struggling to control. For George and Pattie Harrison, Krishna consciousness was a double-edged sword. The transcendental power of the mantra was both liberating and inspirational, but the rigid dictates of Srila Prabhupada's no-nonsense philosophy tended to expose faint cracks in their already shaky marriage.

By early 1973 George was more involved than ever with the temple. When Srila Prabhupada noted that because of growing attendance the Bury Place property was no longer suitable, Harrison readily agreed to finance the acquisition of yet another house. This time it should be something really grand, some place with prestige to help attract a more select following, and preferably in the country with large grounds to accommodate the many outdoor festivals held each year. In short, a real showplace for Krishna consciousness. A place where people could get a taste of the splendor of devotional service to the Supreme Lord. A tall order, to be sure, but after all, it wasn't every day a Beatle got to go house hunting for God!

Eventually they found the perfect site in what was to become Bhaktivedanta Manor, in Letchmoore Heath, just outside London. George negotiated down the exorbitant asking price, then bought the property. In early March 1973, the devotees moved in.

Harrison's journey into Krishna consciousness has taken him all over the world, but it is his various pilgrimages to holy sites in India that he sees as the highlight of his devotional life. In a 1974 questionnaire published in England's *Melody Maker*, he describes seeking Sri Krishna in His sacred homeland of Vrndavana as his all-time most thrilling experience. Retracing the footsteps of this entrancing, rain-cloud-colored cowherd was to George indescribably ecstatic. Mukunda recalls one such occasion: "He once met Guru Das and Prabhupada in Vrndavana. He came with Ravi Shankar by bullock cart and Guru Das took them around to see our new temple, which had only recently been built. George visited with the devotees and seemed very, very happy to be there. He loved the temple and spent hours talking with Srila Prabhupada."

Another time, George and Ravi were shown around by Sripad Maharaj, a local ascetic. Arriving just before dusk, the two men were led by a giggling little girl to the aging Goswami's one-room mud hut near where the sacred river Yamuna long ago flowed. Stopping only briefly for a cup of tea and a polite chat, Harrison and Shankar then accompanied the long-haired, barefoot yogi on an impromptu walking tour of the area just after dark. As they made their way through the village's ancient, twisting side streets and narrow alleyways, George was amazed at how almost everyone they passed bowed low with folded hands at the sight of the *dhoti*-clad, mud-caked mystic. After a lengthy tour of many of Vrndavana's most sacred temples, the pious ascetic directed his two guests to a simple stone bungalow immediately adjacent to one of the best-known temples, where they could sleep for a few hours. At about four the next morning the man silently reappeared and beckoned to the pair to get dressed and follow him into the temple room to join the morning service or *puja*. "I was a stiff Westerner when we started off," said Harrison in his *I Me Mine*, "but there was a moment when the atmosphere of the place got to me, melting all the bullshit away . . . . It was the deepest sleep I had ever had in my life and all through it I could hear choirs singing . . . . I don't think it was the temples I could hear — I think it was something else. It was a fantastic experience."

By the early fall of 1977, the eighty-one-year-old Srila Prabhupada's health was beginning to deteriorate. George was informed of his guru's condition by his old friend Syamasundar during one of Harrison's semi-regular visits to Bhaktivedanta Manor.

"Will he live?" George asked.

"He's in no immediate danger, but it doesn't really look too promising," replied the devotee sadly.

That afternoon, George revved up the engine of his jet-black Ferrari and took a long, fast drive through Oxfordshire's winding back roads — something he often did when he needed to get away from the unrelenting swoosh of his lifestyle. Meanwhile, a world away in India, a small band of Prabhupada's key men were silently chanting to themselves outside their guru's private quarters in ISKCON's Krishna-Balaram Temple in Vrndavana.

In his bed, surrounded by several solemn devotees, Prabhupada very slowly inched a simple gold ring from his finger and pressed it into the hand of one of them. "Please, give this to George Harrison. He was a good friend to us all. He loves Krishna sincerely and I love him. He was my archangel!"

Srila Prabhupada passed away on the evening of November 14, 1977. As his final instruction to his disciples, he left this mortal world serenely, situated in perfect Krishna consciousness. For more than a decade, this kindly Indian gentleman had personally undergone great hardship so that the world's troubled youth might have at least a chance of coming to know God. He taught by example that man was not only a body and mind but an eternal spirit as well. George Harrison heard this simple teaching and took it to heart.

Months later, he had this to say about his relationship with the great master:

He was a friend. He is my master, who I have great respect for . . . . The thing that always impressed me most about Prabhupada was his saying "I am the servant of the servant of the servant." I like that. A lot of people say "I'm it. I'm the divine incarnation. I'm here, and let me hip you." But Prabhupada was never like that. I liked Prabhupada's humbleness. None of us is God — just His servant.

I was always very relaxed with him, and I felt more like a friend. Even though he was at the time seventy-nine years old, working practically all through the night, day after day, with very little sleep, he still didn't come through to me as though he was a very highly educated intellectual being, because he had a sort of childlike simplicity. Even though he was the greatest Sanskrit scholar and a saint, I appreciated the fact that he never made me uncomfortable . . . I always thought of him as sort of a lovely friend, and even now, he's still a lovely friend.

It is to George Harrison's great credit that he has shown himself to be liberal and generous enough to have embraced the teachings of so many seasoned and enlightened masters over the years. Of them, three present perhaps the greatest challenge to our understanding.

Paramahansa Yogananda, long recognized as a sincere and highly evolved advocate of the science of Kriya Yoga, is to many the quintessential spiritual guide. Throughout his brief lifetime he traveled the world extensively, teaching its precepts and, along the way, establishing the Self Realization Fellowship (SRF). Perhaps his most significant achievement, however, was authoring the widely read *Autobiography of a Yogi*, an introspective look at the incredible life of one who has traveled far along the often perilous spiritual path. Ever since George first received a copy from a friend in 1966, it has seldom left his side. When his mother was dying of cancer in a Liverpool hospital, George used to sit by her bedside reading the insightful book out loud. He has often described it by saying it has "a miracle on every page." Even today Harrison routinely presents lavish leather-bound inscribed copies to all his associates, carefully drawing his signature Sanskrit Om sign just below his name.

Strangely, Harrison rarely discusses his great affection for the guru. It is perhaps a measure of his genuine regard for the master that though in his music he regularly comes out with passing references to Yogananda's teachings, he has never really publicized his association with the SRF. He did, however, have this to say in the late seventies:

> Yogananda . . . in 1952, as opposed to dying . . . left his body. And he's been probably the greatest inspiration to me . . . . Yogananda I never met personally in this body, but he had such a terrific influence on me for some very subtle reason, I can't quite put my finger on it . . . . A lot of my feelings are the result of what he taught and is teaching *still* in his subtle state.

Perhaps in light of the media circus created around the Beatles' flirtation with the Maharishi or his tenure with the Krishna consciousness movement, Harrison has thought better of going too much out on a limb with his precious inner life. As he said in Toronto in 1988, "You don't actually do it in the road. [Spiritual life] is a way of just trying to get in touch with yourself."

Many people first came in contact with Yogananda after spotting his picture tucked away in the montage of famous faces on the *Sgt. Pepper* cover. His spiritual forebears Sri Yukteswar, Lahiri Mahasaya and the ledgendary invisible Himalayan *premavatar* (incarnation of love), Mahamuni Babaji Maharaj, are also depicted. Harrison has recorded several musical tributes to Yogananda, including the songs "Dear One" (on *Thirty-Three & 1/3*), "Life Itself" (*Somewhere in England*) and the upbeat "Fish on the Sand" (*Cloud Nine*).

Such was the great power of the guru that upon his death in 1952, his mortal remains were reportedly spared the decay normally witnessed by undertakers. The mortuary director of Forest Lawn Memorial Park in Los Angeles was so astounded that he immediately dispatched a notarized letter to the SRF headquarters in San Rafael, California, outlining his remarkable findings:

> The absence of any visual signs of decay in the dead body of Paramahansa Yogananda offers the most extraordinary case in our experience. No physical disintegration was visible in his body even twenty days after death . . . . This state of perfect preservation of a body is, so far as we know from mortuary annals, an unparalleled one. At the time of receiving Yogananda's body, the mortuary personnel expected to observe, through the glass lid of the casket, the usual progressive signs of bodily decay. Our astonishment increased as day followed day without bringing any visible change in the body under observation. Yogananda's body was apparently in a phenomenal state of immutability.

This incredible tale has always fascinated George, who has been known to relate the bizarre particulars to even casual acquaintances, using the story to convince the listener of the validity of yogic mysticism. If nothing else, it says something about Harrison's long-held hope of the possibility of life after death and a great deal about the unique spiritual status of Paramahansa Yogananda.

The second of the masters, Sathya Sai Baba, the alleged reincarnation of the well-known Hindu saint Sai Baba, is a different matter altogether. Highly controversial, but still immensely popular with Indians around the globe, he claims to have attained the same level of consciousness as Christ. That is, he says he is an avatar, or the divine prophet of God for our time. As in the case of Jesus, there is also a body of rather convincing evidence that over the years he has performed numerous miracles, from producing jewelry and sacred ash out of thin air, to healing the sick, reading minds and allegedly even raising the dead.

Very little is known about George Harrison's connection to Sai Baba. Most Harrison observers first became aware of the former Beatle's interest after seeing George wearing a Sai Baba button on the inside cover of his *Thirty-Three & 1/3* LP. It is believed that the guru once granted Harrison a rare personal audience at his Anantapur ashram in India sometime in the mid-seventies. John and Yoko also met with Sai Baba around that time. It was from this experience that Lennon later made the quizzical comment, "Guru is the pop star of India. Pop stars are the gurus of the West."

Finally, young Guru Maharaji may also claim some allegiance from Harrison. George's second wife, Olivia, reportedly introduced him to the corpulent teenage guru sometime in the mid-seventies, and Harrison rapidly became intrigued with the philosophy and meditational techniques of his Divine Light Mission. Although never a serious disciple, Harrison was sufficiently impressed with the master that he signed several of his followers to his Dark Horse label under the name of Jiva. They recorded just one album, *Jiva*, and then dropped from sight. "Sri Maharaji," says his press biography, "is empowered to impart practical knowledge of Divine Light and the Imperishable Word of God to all sincere aspirants who seek for perfect tranquillity of mind through spiritual insight. He says, 'Give me your love, I will give you peace. Come to me, I will relieve you of your suffering. I am the source of peace in this world.'"

Despite such grand claims, the guru's movement ran into a great deal of difficulty in the late seventies following a tiff between the master and his mother over the leadership of the organization. Coupled with mounting legal entanglements there was also trouble with scores of disgruntled parents who were reclaiming and then "deprogramming" their devotee children with alarming regularity. Very shortly thereafter, Maharaji's "Divine Light" suddenly went out.

George, however, was quick to come to his defense: "When people are presented with ideas they don't understand, fear takes over," he told *Rollling Stone* in April 1979. "They want to destroy it, chop it down. Just like that guy in America [Ted Patrick] who claims to go around deprogramming people from Krishna and the Divine Light Mission. That's *his* fear coming out, because if you understand something, you don't have to fear it."

Still, Guru Maharaji wasn't really able to overcome the death blow dealt his movement and by the early eighties was forced underground with his new wife, a former mission secretary. Apparently, the couple has frequently visited George, meeting, and allegedly even converting for a time, several of the Harrisons' closest friends, including long-time aide Terry Doran and former Apple roadie Robbie Cain. To this day a photo of the guru sits prominently atop George's prized grand piano.

During my own encounter with George in 1983, Harrison commented that although he still certainly believes quite strongly in all these philosophies, his approach these days is far different:

> I was at the airport in Honolulu and I met a guy dressed in these old saffron corduroys who approached me with a book and said, "My guru wants you to have this." I couldn't make out if he recognized me or not. I said, "What do you mean, your guru wants me to have this book? Does he know I'm here?" The book said, "(*Something Something*) *Guru, The World's Spiritual Leader.*" Now I read it, and this guy doesn't like *anybody*. He ran down Sai Baba, Yogananda, Guru Maharaji and everybody. Although he did quote Prabhupada's books — and everyone else's for that matter. It seemed very dogmatic. I'm just not into that. It's the organization of religion that turns me off a bit. I just try to go into myself. Like Donovan said, "You've got to go into your own temple once a day." It's a very personal thing, spiritual life.

The road to hell, they say, is straight and broad. The road to heaven, however, is narrow, rough and treacherous. One is easy; the other difficult. George Harrison's arduous spiritual trek was fraught with disappointment and pain almost from the beginning. In 1967, after finally coming to grips with the tug of his inner voice, he began a frantic search for someone or something that could help him on his way. "I used to laugh when I read about Cliff Richard being a Christian," Harrison said in *The Beatles: The Authorized Biography*. "I still cringe when I hear about it, but I know now that religion and God are the *only* things that exist. I know some people think I'm a nut case. I find it hard not to myself, sometimes, because I still see so many things in an ordinary way. But I know that when you believe, it's real and nice. Not believing, it's all confusion and emptiness."

George's search has led him at times in some very strange directions. In 1966, after reading a book on cosmic communication, he set off on a solo pilgrimage to scale a rugged mountain peak in a remote corner of Cornwall. He had hoped that, being in such close physical proximity to

God, he might be given some sort of sign. He was not. It was the first of many disappointing episodes in the Beatle's spiritual life. "When the student is ready," Harrison often found himself silently repeating, "the master will appear." Ready or not, the Maharishi burst into the Beatles' lives, offering salvation with a price tag of only fifteen minutes of devotion a day. "It seemed too good to be true," Paul McCartney later quipped. "I guess it was."

It was in Krishna consciousness, though, that George invested the most faith, so it was particularly troublesome when several of Srila Prabhupada's disciples approached him over the years with so many apparently trivial requests. Saffron-robed Krishnas began turning up at his front gates at all hours of the day and night, demanding over the intercom to see the singer. One young devotee needed the money to buy false teeth for her husband. Another asked for backing to convert an old truck into a traveling Krishna temple. Of course, there were also the usual schemes to get George to do this and that musically. "How about an album of children's songs to Krishna?" "Do you think you and John might get together next month at *Rathayatra* to lead our chanting party?" All such suggestions, however, fell on deaf ears. George Harrison is not a man to be trifled with. Push him too far and sooner or later he will cease being polite. It was at this time that ISKCON, recognizing the problem, asked George's old ally Mukunda henceforth to deal exclusively with the intensely private Harrison. Movement officials were intent on ensuring that George would no longer be harassed by devotees saddling up to their precious superstar convert.

When George visited the temple, things were evidently no better. Once, while worshiping before the deities of Radha and Krishna, his shoes were stolen by a fan. It was raining, and despite offers from the devotees to lend him their own footwear, he hobbled off down Bloomsbury Way in a huff, much to the amazement of passersby. Thereafter, whenever Harrison came around, the temple president made sure all extraneous personnel, as well as any guests, were tactfully asked to leave.

Mukunda, though, relates the most ridiculous tale of all. The Beatles were rehearsing at Abbey Road once in 1969 when suddenly the lounge's suspended ceiling caved in and a young man with a shaved head, dressed in flowing robes, landed right in the middle of the astounded musicians. After he brushed himself off, he very respectfully began offering formal Hindu obeisance to Harrison, who was struck dumb with wonder. Looking slowly first from one to another, it was Lennon who finally broke the silence. "He must be with George," he said sardonically. But Harrison was not amused and gruffly offered the wacked out would-be devotee a stern ultimatum. "Either you get up and leave now or Mal calls for security." The man then bowed low and began slowly walking out backward, all the while muttering to himself in Sanskrit. George looked helplessly at the others, who were by then all laughing hysterically.

Eventually, all this madness almost caused ISKCON to lose Bhaktivedanta Manor to Yogananda's SRF. "George came by the manor a few times without ringing and was none too pleased with the state of the place," remembers one senior devotee. "Our original agreement with him called for us to make sure that not only the house be kept up but also the extensive grounds as well. The tennis courts were overgrown, the greenhouse about to fall down, and the flower beds had all been trampled by the kids. George was furious and told the president that if things didn't very quickly shape up he might consider turning the property over to Yogananda's people." Happily, the movement took George's mandate to heart and today the manor is the very model of a gracious, well-run estate.

Perhaps most exasperating to Harrison, however, was ISKCON's penchant for using George's name to market projects he had little or nothing to do with. For a time in the early seventies, some devotees even went so far as to collect money by posing as agents for George in an effort to "feed hungry children." Not surprisingly, when Harrison caught wind of this tactic, he was none too pleased.

For all its shortcomings, however, ISKCON and the teachings of Srila Prabhupada remain close to George's heart. "Create and preserve the image of your choice" goes one of his favorite quotations. To Harrison, that ideal image is one in which he is free to be what *he* wants, which is definitely not an ex-Beatle, a rock superstar or even a wealthy film executive.

Late in 1985, while visiting Olivia's parents in California, Harrison decided on the spur of the moment to stop by at the Krishna temple in Los Angeles and say hello to his old friend Mukunda. Rolling up in front of the massive pink stucco building in his gleaming silver BMW, George quietly hailed a young female devotee who was crossing the street. "Excuse me," Harrison called out shyly, "but I wanted to nip into the temple room for a sec and see if Mukunda is around. You don't think anyone will freak out, do you? The last thing in the world I want this afternoon is to be recognized by anyone."

"I'm sorry," said the confused and embarrassed teen, "but just who are you supposed to be, anyway?"

It was just what the world-weary Beatle had been waiting to hear for the last twenty years. "Create and preserve the image of your choice," he muttered to himself. "Hare Krishna!"

VII

SIR FRANK OF PARADISE ROAD

Finding a Home

It is impossible to imagine George without Friar Park and vice versa. As far as he's concerned, we Harrisons are little more than caretakers. To George, the Park will always belong strictly to old Sir Frank.

HARRY HARRISON, SR.

A bizarre folly in its own grounds behind the town hall.

FRIAR PARK, described in the BUILDINGS OF ENGLAND
series of the 1920s.

EVEN THE MOST CURSORY LOOK AT THE LIFE AND TIMES OF GEORGE Harrison must try to unknot the riddle of his unswerving devotion to Sir Frank Crisp and Friar Park. It is difficult to imagine how he feels about the place, having come himself from such humble beginnings: "Two rooms up and two down was all we ever had," he once told his chum Robbie Cain. Yet today he reigns as the great estate's second eccentric lord. Once more, George has submitted himself to yet another (albeit unlikely) guru. "Sir Frank helped my awareness," says Harrison. "Whatever it was I felt became stronger, or found more expression, by moving into that house. Everything stepped up or was heightened significantly."

Sir Frank Crisp, millionaire London solicitor and well-respected Oxfordshire justice of the peace, wrangled the sale of Friar Park from a Henley clergyman, the Reverend J. Collard, in 1899. A massive stone manor house on Paradise Road on the outskirts of Henley, Friar Park sat like a great sparkling diamond in the rough amidst acres of rambling grounds. Crisp's first order of business was to pull down all but a few of the original walls and start over. With the help of noted architect M. Clarke Edwards, Sir Frank began the laborious task of creating his very own quasi-gothic Disneyland.

The decorative theme of "Frank's folly," as some of Crisp's more conservative neighbors insisted on calling the mammoth project, reflects its original residents — humble friars. Friars, reasoned the philosophically inclined solicitor, "must be the hallmark of this home. God's most simple and yet keenly intellectual and spiritual of beings. Forsaking the push and shove of the world in search of a deeper understanding . . . . The ordinary man's most tangible link to the Great Unseen."

When the imposing stone manor house was nearly completed, Sir Frank went to work counseling sculptor T. Richardson on his vision of the Park's unique statuary. The result, a grotesquely beautiful array of stone gargoyles, statues of whimsical monks and quirky religious sayings carved over doors and windows, was beyond even Sir Frank's expectations. In his only known work, *The Friar Park Guide*, Crisp gives us a glimpse of the unique variety of stonework to be found on the property:

The heads of two "Grave" and "Gay" Friars cap the inner Pillars of the lower gates. The latter has a bloated and sensual face, while the former is thoughtful and intellectual.

Over the porch of the Lodge is a representation of a Fox, in the Cowl and Gown of a Friar, preaching. The hypocritical Fox turned ecclesiastic is preying upon his congregation.

The Leering Friar who is looking round the corner on the north side of the house with a broad grin on his face, is supposed to be watching the passing of the "remains" of the proprietor, and chuckling to himself that there are "Vestigia nulla retrorsum" (No footsteps backwards for you!).

Over the scullery is a Kitchen Friar engaged in washing up dishes, flanked by a pair of sculls on one side and a skull and cross-bones on the other.

Over the kitchen window is the culinary proverb: "God sends the meat, but the devil sends the cook."

The Verandah has representations of the Friars of the Winds. The North wind Friar with puffed-out cheeks as befits its blustering nature; the East wind with thin cheeks, representing its piercing character; the West wind tearful and watery, and the south wind with a smiling, sunny face.

Perhaps the most amusing of all the Park's many carved friars is one terribly dour-looking old acolyte stationed just outside the main entrance, holding a battered frying pan and captioned "Two holy friars." George Harrison was so captivated by this particular creation that he chose it to adorn the inside bi-fold cover of his *Thirty-Three & 1/3* album.

In addition to creating the estate's eyepopping statuary, Sir Frank saw fit to integrate his own peculiar philosophical statement inside the great house as well. He described the eccentric decor of his home in *The Friar Park Guide*:

Friars are met with throughout the interior. Thus the switches of the electric lights are the moveable noses of friars, which turn down and up as required. Friars also hold the electric lamps at various points. The capitals of the pillars supporting the Hall show friars engaged in sleeping, dreaming, snoring, yawning, and walking. There are friars with ordinary faces on one side and skulls on the other. Friars drinking, friars cooking, in fact, friars in all profusion that any lover of friars could wish.

In addition, a wry collection of what Crisp called "perverted proverbs" also decorate the interior of the manor house. Although mostly inscribed in Latin, Sir Frank's indomitable wit comes shining through in these original, quirky lines. The guide supplies a few examples:

> People who live in glass houses should dress in the dark.
> A bird in the bush is worth two in the bonnet.
> Punctuality is the thief of time.
> A rolling stone waits for no man.

It took a devoted team of local nurserymen more than twenty years to execute Sir Frank's grandiose plans for the acres of rolling gardens. Like his modern-day counterpart, George Harrison, Frank enjoyed an enduring love of flowering plants and shrubs.

In the August 5, 1905, edition of *Country Life* magazine, Friar Park's well-tended gardens were described as "a beautiful little paradise of flowers" nestled around "one of the most pleasant homes in Oxfordshire. Further, there is a superb topiary garden, charmingly natural colonies of old-fashioned flowers in the Elizabethan garden, walks of rambling roses, rosemary and lavendar to give effect in grey, and shades of crimson and purple from choice grounds of Japanese maples. Many profitable hours may be spent with Mr. Crisp in studying the rare collections which abound all over the unusual estate."

The property also featured many rare species of trees and flowers. One of a number of unusual attractions is a miniature Matterhorn — a mountain Crisp had always particularly admired — made of 20,000 tons of gravel. Sir Frank also had his very own caves constructed underneath the house. To make them even more exciting, he had them flooded so they could be enjoyed by boat; visitors therefore not having to exert themselves by a strenuous hike. Crisp loved taking his guests on an after-dinner cruise to wonder at the stalactite-covered caverns bathed in colored lights. In his 1981 book, *The Beatles After the Beatles*, John Blake provided a rare description of Sir Frank's fantasy caverns: "Each cave had its own extraordinary character: the skeleton cave contained countless skeletons and distorting mirrors, the vine cave huge bunches of illuminated glass 'grapes,' the gnome cave was filled with more gnomes than a row of Surbiton gardens. Sir Frank's favorite cave was the 'big cave,' where he had a wishing well installed. While one looked down, a servant swiveled a handle until four heads appeared in turn — two men and two women —

Sir Frank Crisp, the eccentric
founder of Friar Park.
COLLECTION OF GEOFFREY GIULIANO

The intricate tower of Friar Park's Lady David wing on the
outskirts of the mammoth estate. Note the three-headed horse
at the tower's base. Could this have been the genesis of
George's famous Dark Horse label logo? SKYBOOT PRODUCTIONS LTD.:
G. GIULIANO

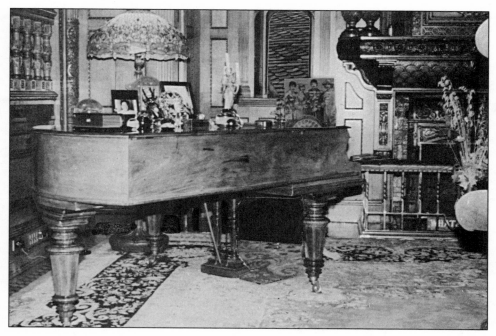

Friar Park's magnificent drawing room as it was in 1983. DELIBERATE ALCHEMY ARCHIVES

A view of Friar Park's well-manicured topiary gardens from old Sir Frank's day. A keen amateur botanist himself, George regularly employs the services of eleven full-time gardeners as well as two recognized experts on flowering shrubs and trees, just to keep the place looking tidy. COLLECTION OF GEOFFREY GIULIANO

Sir Frank's dream house, in 1969, shortly after the Harrisons moved in. DELIBERATE ALCHEMY ARCHIVES

from whom one could choose his or her future sweetheart."

In the early 1900s Sir Frank was called an eccentric. Today, he'd probably be chanting Hare Krishna and jetting back and forth to India. Crisp was a seeker. Maybe even a seer. Is it any wonder Harrison is so completely and inextricably captivated by the place? Friar Park is far more than stone and tiles, leaded glass and panoramic views. It is a signpost to the inner realm, rooted by its unusual founder in something far beyond the scope of this workaday world. Finally, it is old Sir Frank's own personal search sculpted in stone and carved in the face of every one of the estate's guardian monks.

Following Crisp's death in 1919, Friar Park was put up for sale by auction in five lots. Along with what a printed flyer hawked as the estate's "exceptional grounds and world famous rock gardens" went "the well appointed boat house with Summer rooms" and "three grand residential sites," as well as "the Oxford lodge," the main house and the majority of Sir Frank's exquisite furnishings.

By the early fifties, the Park was run as a convent, housing a strict order of Catholic nuns who later turned it into a private school for young ladies. Kirsten Grepne, a former high-fashion model in London and later "Legs" Larry Smith's erstwhile girlfriend, is an alumna of Friar Park School. She remembered her years there in a 1984 interview in Toronto:

My school days at Friar Park were wonderful. There was always a keen sense of adventure since we were generally allowed to make good use of the extensive grounds and vast, ornate buildings. We were often taken to play in the underground caves and went for long walks in the Swiss gardens.

The main building was delightfully decorated with humorous gargoyles and jolly friar lights . . . which always amused me. Since the nuns were from a very strict Roman Catholic order, the resident Mother Superior had miniature underwear painted onto some of the many lusty cherubs who were showing just a little bit more than she felt they ought to . . . .

Towards the end of the sixties the sisters tried to keep the school going but, due to a lack of funds, it was ultimately closed. By this time, of course, the estate needed a lot of work and the grounds, in particular, had become very run down. Everyone was thoroughly delighted, however, when we heard the news that George Harrison had purchased the Park and was planning to move in. It's been beautifully restored and looks today, one suspects, very much as it did in old Sir Frank's time.

After the decision was finally made to close the school, a group of local businessmen considered buying the estate with an eye to razing the manor and building a housing complex on the valuable real estate.

Meanwhile, George and Pattie had been house hunting for the past two years. Having outgrown their Esher bungalow, they were anxious for the added privacy and spaciousness of the countryside. And if Pattie were to become pregnant, it would be better for the baby, too. From the first day George saw Friar Park, he knew it must be his, despite the $336,000 price tag: "If Brian [Epstein] had been alive," George said in *I Me Mine*, "I probably wouldn't have ended up in this house because part of getting it meant that I was going beyond my means, completely. Karmically, the only way I could have done this was to have a manager who was going beyond his means, too. It was in [Allen Klein's] interest to keep us happy, so in a way he was doing the right thing. If I'd worried about whether or not to do it, well, I wouldn't have."

On moving day a few of the old sisters were still in residence and became visibly upset at the sight of Friar Park's trendy new owners. One of George's first official acts as lord of the manor was to tack up, over the ornate fireplace in the library, an oversized poster of Lord Vishnu slumbering transcendentally on the Ocean of Milk.

"What on earth?" shrieked the nuns.

"It's okay," George assured them. "God has many forms."

When Harrison first bought the estate in March 1970, he had no idea of Sir Frank's underground fantasy caves or even the full extent of the Park's original gardens. As George's friend Mukunda says, there turned out to be quite a few hidden treasures: "After the nuns moved in they covered a lot of the original stuff over. George actually excavated the whole thing after he found the plans to [Friar Park]. He discovered there was a whole waterfall system, underground caverns and a lot of things that the nuns didn't want, so they just had them buried."

George added to Crisp's eccentricities a few humble accouterments of his own, including a luxury swimming pool, a heliport, tennis court, a rustic playhouse overlooking a beautiful glade, an ornate fountain dedicated to Lord Shiva, and, most important of all, a state-of-the-art recording studio. Says George:

The studio was installed around '71, but there's been a few updates over the years because originally it was just sixteen tracks. After all that time at Abbey Road, EMI Studios, I just wanted to be able to tumble out of bed and get straight to work. No more running a gauntlet of fans on the way in, or paying by the hour. F.P.S.H.O.T. [Friar Park Studios Henley-on-Thames] was important to my creativity because it was the first place I could really relax while recording.

Originally Friar Park's upstairs ballroom, George's studio is an eclectic contrast of high-tech equipment set within an interior of polished wood and thick terra-cotta-colored carpets, decorated with several outrageously expensive Tiffany table lamps. A small bulletin board over the mixing board is crammed with snapshots of family and friends. Inside the control-room door a red-and-white sign reads simply "Silence."

Pattie and George both loved the easy, laid-back lifestyle they had created for themselves at Friar Park. Long, lazy summer days were spent just soaking up the sun or strolling through their gardens with old friends like Peter Sellers or Eric Clapton. Often she and George would pop into the local florist to buy fresh-cut flowers or be seen walking hand in hand along Henley's exclusive shopping district. Sometimes the Harrisons were spotted drinking quietly with friends at such places as the Angel Inn or the Row Barge Pub just off Paradise Road. On those rare occasions when they ate out, it was usually at one of the town's excellent Chinese or Indian restaurants. Only occasionally were they waylaid by Beatle fans.

Privacy was crucial to George, but that didn't stop him from sometimes trying to make friends with the locals. Kirsten Grepne tells of her first encounter with the naturally reclusive Harrison:

I was just sixteen and was standing near the entrance to Friar Park waiting for my father to pick me up from an outing in Henley. I soon became aware of a rustling in the bushes behind me, and suddenly out of nowhere pops this exceedingly strange-looking fellow wearing Wellington boots, an old brown felt hat with very, very long stringy hair and beard.

"Are you waiting for a bus, luv?" he said,

"No," I replied, "it's okay, I'm quite fine."

Grappling up over the top of the Park's stone wall, he then very politely asked if I'd fancy coming up to the house for a cup of tea.

"No," I said, trying for some strange reason not to actually look him in the face. "I'm waiting for my father."

"Some other time, then," he whispered, turning back to walk in through the main gates. Once inside he quickly pivoted and carefully latched the front gates. First one then the other. "Otherwise the swans will run off," he shouted. I didn't know what to say.

Eventually, George's two brothers, Harry and Peter, moved in along with their families. Harry was installed as estate manager and Peter put in charge of the Park's ten gardeners, plus one fill-time botanist. "I hardly ever see George," Peter said in the mid-eighties. "When we do talk, it's usually about the garden. He is a fanatic."

Fanatic is right. Like old Sir Frank, George is wild about gardening. He usually helps his small army of gardeners plant about 45,000 bulbs each fall. "Old Crisp could have done far worse than having George as the new custodian of Friar Park," Robbie Cain once commented. In a way it's as if Sir Frank is still somehow there, quietly inspiring George how to look after the place. "Once or twice he's even suggested he's actually seen him, striding confidently down the stairway, dressed in a smoking jacket, puffing away on a big cigar," says Cain.

"At Friar Park," says Robbie, "old Frank is everywhere."

For the first time, George Harrison had managed a real life away from the Beatles and the nonstop grind of the music business. Often he would climb the three long flights of stairs into one of the Park's rickety turrets to sit on the stone window sill and meditate. So far up above it all he felt at last free and at peace, the silence around him broken only by birdsong and the rustle of the manor's many colorful flags flapping carelessly in the breeze. Here George found time to reflect on his astounding career, his music and his marriage. Where was life taking him? Surely all this had happened for some good reason.

Sometimes he seemed more powerful than a king, so full was he of optimism and hope for the future. Other times, deep down, he felt unworthy and weak. Often it was almost too much for him to bear. Harrison's high-profile success also brought with it a heavy burden of worry and stress. Although Friar Park and the otherworldly philosophy of Sir Frank clearly meant a great deal to him, it still wasn't enough. Deep inside remained an emptiness no amount of comfort or money could ever hope to fill.

VIII

SPOT THE LOONY

Flying Solo

Pattie was just trying to get George's attention, get him jealous, and so she used me. The problem was that I soon fell madly in love with her. He'd been into . . . meditation for so long and yet couldn't keep his wife. All she wanted was for him to say "I love you," and all he was doing was meditating.

ERIC CLAPTON

AS GEORGE HARRISON SAT SERENELY AT THE FEET OF THE MAHARISHI at a Transcendental Meditation conference in Bangor, North Wales, many miles away in London Brian Epstein was struggling through his final agonizing moments of life. Inside the guru's comfortable, airy quarters at the local university, he spoke in glowing terms of the infinite possibilities of life lived in the fullness of cosmic consciousness. For Epstein, all such possibilities were finished. He died, a lonely victim of his own isolated lifestyle, on August 27, 1967. When the Beatles heard the news outside the lecture hall, they were stunned.

> REPORTER: (to George) Have you spoken to Brian since you've been here with the Maharishi this weekend?
> GEORGE: I spoke to him Wednesday evening. The evening before we first saw the Maharishi's lecture. He was in great spirits.
> REPORTER: And when did he tell you that he would like to become initiated?
> GEORGE: Well, when we arrived here on Friday we got a telephone call later that day to say that Brian would follow us up and be here Monday.
> REPORTER: Had the Maharishi ever met Mr. Epstein?
> JOHN: No, but he was looking forward to it.
> GEORGE: There is no such thing as death, only in the physical sense. We know he is okay now. He will return because he was striving for happiness and desired bliss so much.
> JOHN: Our meditation has given us the confidence to withstand such a shock.

Returning to London by car, the Beatles sank bank in their seats, absorbed in their tender thoughts for "Eppy." Meanwhile, back in London, the tragic events of the previous weekend were just beginning to be known. According to Peter Brown, Brian had invited him and NEMS associate Geoffrey Ellis to spend a quiet holiday weekend with Epstein at his lavish Sussex country home, Kingsley Hill. When they reached the rambling estate in the early evening, the two found Brian despondent over the last-minute cancellation of a date with a new male lover.

Following an elegant dinner, the three men consumed several bottles of expensive wine, which only darkened Epstein's already bleak mood.

A little after ten, Brian announced that he was going out for a drive, a decision questioned by Brown. Epstein, however, assured his friends that he was fine and sped off into the night. When he hadn't returned by midnight, Brown rang Brian's London home to see if perhaps he'd returned there. Epstein's butler, Antonio, confirmed that, yes, Mr. Epstein had indeed come in and was sleeping. At Brown's insistence he buzzed Epstein on the intercom, but there was no answer. "Let him sleep, then," said Brown. "Lord knows he could use the rest."

The next afternoon Brian rang Kingsley Hill and spoke briefly to Brown. He said that after breakfast he would be driving back to Sussex. Brown suggested that since he had taken several tranquilizers the night before and was presumably still a little groggy, it might be wiser to take the train. Brian agreed and promised to phone back later with his arrival time. He never did.

On Sunday Antonio and his wife Maria became concerned when they had heard nothing from their employer for almost twenty-four hours. When they tried to call him on the intercom, they got no response. After a few hasty phone calls, within half an hour Alistair Taylor, Epstein's chauffeur and a physician, Dr. John Gallway, had convened at Brian's London flat. Over the phone from Sussex, Peter Brown instructed them to break down the doors to Brian's bedroom. When they did, they found that the gracious, good-natured star-maker from Liverpool was dead.

"He was a very complex man," says Alistair Taylor, "and I think there was far more to him than simply being gay. He wasn't happy at that, you know. In fact he tried very hard not to be gay. Twice I had phone calls from him saying goodbye, he was committing suicide."

Brian Epstein died from a cumulative overdose of bromide mixed with large quantities of barbiturates and other antidepressants. An inquest found on September 8, 1967, that Brian's death was "accidental, due to repeated, incautious, self-administered doses of sleeping tablets."

But at the time, the widespread rumor was that Brian's death was no accident. Taylor remembers: "The times I've been asked the question, Why did he commit suicide? Well, I want someone to tell me where it says he committed suicide. The verdict by the coroner's court was accidental death, and the entire survey confirmed it. Remember, there were only a few people in that room, right? I've never said it was suicide. I've heard stories that there was a note found, but I certainly didn't find it."

Despite his controversial demise, it is clear that Brian Epstein had been that rarest of all show-business animals, a gentleman. Pattie Harrison remembers several times in the months preceding his death worrying with George over Brian's often intemperate pill-popping and boozing.

"Do you think you could talk to him?" she once asked.

"I'm afraid he's so far into it all that it wouldn't really do any good," George replied, shaking his head.

The Beatles lost in Brian Epstein not only a trusted adviser and ally but also a dear friend. Despite the tremendous difference between his and the group's lifestyles, the boys were still very aware of how much he had done for them, and they weren't about to forget.

After thirty-one years on the job, Harry Harrison was only too happy to permanently park his bus when, in 1965, George generously offered his dad an early retirement. "So how much are you making these days?" asked the junior Harrison during one of his now infrequent trips north on a weekend sabbatical from the band.

"Around ten quid," Harry replied.

"A day?" asked George incredulously.

When his father told him no, that was what he was taking home weekly, George was adamant. "I'll give you five times that for sitting around doing nothing."

"Son," Harry shot back, smiling broadly, "you've got yourself a deal!"

The next order of business for the Harrisons' upwardly mobile young son was to purchase for his parents a modern new home in the village of Appleton, a smart suburb near Warrington, in Cheshire.

"It was lovely," said Harry. "Very private on three splendid acres of gardens. I think George paid around £10,000, but it was worth every penny. Upstairs, there was a lovely, long room we used for entertaining. Pattie and Louise talked together quite a bit about the furniture as I recall. Eventually they settled on a modern look. I was lost to all that myself though, and mainly looked after the outdoor work with the gardener."

For the Harrisons their new home was a treat. Unfortunately, they spent only five happy years there together before Louise became seriously ill and died, on July 7, 1970. For everyone in George's family, it was a crushing blow.

"She'd got a tumor on the brain," George told journalist Timothy White in a 1986 issue of *Musician* magazine.

But the doctor was an idiot and was saying, "There's nothing wrong with her, she's having some psychological trouble." When I went up to see her, she didn't even know who I was. I had to punch the doctor out, because in England the family doctor has to be the one to get the specialist. So he got the guy to look at her and she ended up in the neurological hospital. The specialist said, "She could end up being a vegetable, but if it was my wife or mother, I'd do the operation" — which was a horrendous thing where they had to drill a hole in her skull. She recovered a little bit for about seven months. And during that period, my father, who'd taken care of her, had suddenly exploded with ulcers and was in the same hospital. I was pretending to both of them that the other one was okay. Then, running back and forth to do this record *All Things Must Pass*. I wrote the song ["Deep Blue"] . . . at home one exhausted morning with those major and minor chords. It's filled with the frustration and gloom of going to these hospitals, and the feeling of disease that permeated the atmosphere. Not being able to do anything for suffering family or loved ones is an awful experience.

Once Mrs. Harrison's passing was announced to the press, the genuine and immediate outpouring of love and affection for her from fans worldwide was overwhelming. Bouquets and cards of sympathy were sent by the hundreds, both to the Harrisons' home and to Apple. A group of concerned American fans soon established the Louise F. Harrison Memorial Cancer Fund, collecting money for cancer research in Britain. John, Paul and Ringo, as well as the Apple staff, all sent flowers but did not attend the private family funeral in Liverpool.

George was at his mother's bedside when she passed away. Naturally he was deeply troubled and upset by her death, but this was his Krishna conscious period and the teachings of Srila Prabhupada were of great comfort. Thumbing through his already well-worn copy of the guru's *Bhagavad Gita, As It Is*, he silently read and reread everything Sri Krishna had to say about the nature of death in this world. Two verses in particular stood out in his mind. Over the next few years he would be forced to seek the shelter of their wisdom on several other such occasions:

For the soul there is never birth or death. Nor, having once been, does he ever cease to be. He is unborn, eternal, ever-existing, undying, and primeval. He is not slain when the body is slain.

As a person puts on new garments, giving up old ones; similarly, the soul accepts new material bodies, giving up the old and useless ones.

Although Harry Harrison was devastated, he sought to continue his wife's correspondence with George's many fans. Alanna Nash was one of those who heard from Harry not long after the tragedy. Although the original letter was lost several years ago, she has constructed what she could from memory:

> Much has happened since you last saw Mrs. Harrison. She was taken very ill about July 1969, and after a 12-month illness, I am sorry to say she passed away in July. This no doubt will come as a shock to you, for having met her, you will remember how full of vitality she really was. Although I had been warned that nothing could be done for her, it was still a great blow to me when it happened. It is something I will never forget; we had been together for a long time, and my loss is immeasurable. Further to that, I was rushed into hospital with perforated ulcers and had three-fourths of my stomach removed.

Despite the tragedy, by late November of that year, George's marathon three-record set, *All Things Must Pass*, was released in the States and immediately began a steady climb to number one. It remained on the charts for an incredible thirty-eight weeks. The album, with its haunting melodies and sweeping, majestic production, was the culmination of months of painstakingly hard work by Harrison and producer Phil Spector. Having been continually shortchanged as a Beatle, George Harrison had finally come into his own. Not only was the album a gripping musical masterpiece but it was also imbued with an important spiritual message. Inspired by Harrison's homespun philosophy, young people everywhere began looking inside themselves for their own answers. The album spawned two popular singles, "What Is Life" and the international megahit, "My Sweet Lord." Almost overnight, Hare Krishna became a household word, and George Harrison was elevated, as a solo artist, to superstar status. John Lennon, as ever, was unguardedly cynical.

"I remember John was really negative at the time," George told Mitchell Glazer in *Crawdaddy* magazine. "I was away and he came round

Two of George's oldest and dearest friends, Peter Sellers and Ringo Starr, on location at Sotheby's in London filming *The Magic Christian*.
DELIBERATE ALCHEMY ARCHIVES

Harrison, circa 1969, with his longtime friend and musical colleague American soul singer Billy Preston.
DELIBERATE ALCHEMY ARCHIVES

George joins members of the Bonnie and Delaney troupe on the road in 1969. Old friend Eric Clapton is seated center. DELIBERATE ALCHEMY ARCHIVES

With sitar virtuoso Ravi Shankar in 1969.
DELIBERATE ALCHEMY ARCHIVES

In New York, 1967, with wife Pattie and sitar in hand. DELIBERATE ALCHEMY ARCHIVES

In the studio with members of the Hare Krishna movement. DELIBERATE ALCHEMY ARCHIVES

Chanting the Holy name of the Lord Sri
Krishna with members of London's Radha
Krishna Temple, 1969.
DELIBERATE ALCHEMY ARCHIVES

Pattie, George and Mal Evans leave the Isle of
Wight pop festival following Dylan's fabled
performance there in 1968.
DELIBERATE ALCHEMY ARCHIVES

On the rooftop at Apple with some friends.
DELIBERATE ALCHEMY ARCHIVES

At the London launch party for Apple's Radha
Krishna Temple LP, 1969.
DELIBERATE ALCHEMY ARCHIVES

MESSAGE FROM GEORGE HARRISON

Everybody is looking for Krishna.

Some don't realise that they are, but they are.

Krishna is GOD, the Source of all that exists, the Cause of all that is, was or ever will be.

As God is unlimited, HE has many Names.

Allah—Buddah—Jehova—Rama: All are Krishna, all are ONE.

God is not abstract, he has both the impersonal and the personal aspects to his personality which is SUPREME, ETERNAL, BLISSFUL, and full of knowledge. As a single drop of water has the same qualities as an ocean of water, so has our consciousness the qualities of GOD'S consciousness . . . but through our identification and attachment with material energy (physical body, sense pleasures, material possessions, ego etc.) our true TRANSCENDENTAL CONSCIOUSNESS has been polluted, and like a dirty mirror it is unable to reflect a pure image. With many lives our association with the temporary has grown. This impermanent body, a bag of bones and flesh, is mistaken for our true self, and we have accepted this temporary condition to be final.

Through all ages, great saints have remained as living proof that this non-temporary, permanent state of GOD CONSCIOUSNESS can be revived in all living souls. Each soul is potentially Divine.

Krishna says in BHAGAVAD GITA "Steady in the Self, being freed from all material contamination, the yogi achieves the highest perfectional stage of happiness in touch with the Supreme Consciousness. YOGA (a scientific method of GOD (SELF) realization) is the process by which we purify our consciousness, stop further pollution and arrive at the state of Perfection, full KNOWLEDGE full BLISS.

If there is a God, I want to see him. It's pointless to believe in something without proof, and Krishna Consciousness and meditation are methods where you can actually obtain GOD perception. You can actually see GOD, and hear him, play with HIM. It, might sound crazy but HE is actually there, actually with you.

There are many yogic paths Raja, Jnana, Hatha, Kriya, Karma, Bhakti which are all acclaimed by the MASTERS of each method.

SWAMI BHAKTIVEDANTA is as his title says a BHAKTI yogi following the path of DEVOTION. By serving GOD through each thought, word, and deed and by chanting of his holy names, the devotee quickly develops God-Consciousness. By chanting

HARE KRISHNA, HARE KRISHNA
KRISHNA KRISHNA, HARE HARE
HARE RAMA, HARE RAMA
RAMA RAMA, HARE HARE

One inevitably arrives at KRISHNA Consciousness. (The proof of the pudding is in the eating!)

GIVE PEACE A CHANCE.

ALL YOU NEED IS LOVE (KRISHNA) HARI BOL
GEORGE HARRISON 31/3/70

George Harrison

Apple Corps. Ltd.
3 Savile Row
London, W.1.
Tel: 01-734 8232

Radha Krishna Temple
7 Bury Place
London, W.C.1.
Tel: 01-242 0394

The official Apple press release for the Radha Krishna Temple from their benefactor, George Harrison. APPLE PRESS RELEASE

Srila Prabhupada, Pattie, George and
Dhananjaya Dasa stroll through the grounds of
Friar Park during the mid-seventies.
DELIBERATE ALCHEMY ARCHIVES

George with one of the many ladies in his life
arriving at Heathrow Airport following the
final collapse of his marriage to Pattie.
DELIBERATE ALCHEMY ARCHIVES

Harrison takes a morning meal in India with
Krishna guru Jayapataka Maharaj.
STEVEN ROSEN

Harrison sings his heart out for the war-torn
refugees from Pakistan and India at the
legendary Concert for Bangla Desh.
DELIBERATE ALCHEMY ARCHIVES

George and A&M co-founder Jerry
Moss celebrate Harrison's Dark
Horse Records' forthcoming
distribution deal with the label.
DELIBERATE ALCHEMY ARCHIVES

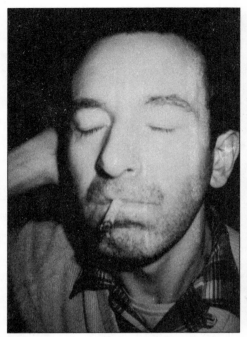

The author's revealing portrait of "Legs" Larry Smith at Jon Lord's rambling Oxfordshire estate, Yewden Lodge, 1983. Any guesses as to what he's smoking?
SKYBOOT PRODUCTIONS LTD.: G. GIULIANO

Robbie Cain, the big-hearted roadie for both Paul McCartney and George Harrison, breaks for tea at Reading Station, 1983.
SKYBOOT PRODUCTIONS LTD.: G. GIULIANO

George parties with former Wings guitarist Denny Laine and Mal Evans at a record industry party in L.A. DELIBERATE ALCHEMY ARCHIVES

An invitation to Eric and Pattie
Clapton's wedding reception 1979.
JO JO LAINE

HELLO

*Me and the Mrs. got married the other day, but that
was in America, so we've decided to have a bash in
my garden on Saturday May 19th about 3.00 p.m.
for all our mates here at home, if you are free, try
and make it, it's bound to be a laugh
......see you then.....*

Eric and Pattie Clapton

*P.S.
You don't have to
bring any presents
if you don't
want to*

A statue of the Virgin Mary, left behind at
Friar Park by the nuns who lived there prior
to George. It is said to be one of Harrison's
most prized works of art.
STEFANO CASTINO COLLECTION

The imposing wrought-iron gates to Friar Park, George's palatial Victorian manor in rural
Oxfordshire. SKYBOOT PRODUCTIONS LTD.: G. GIULIANO

A rare picture of Harrison in Maui in 1984, a period in his life in which he was seldom photographed. DELIBERATE ALCHEMY ARCHIVES

An exclusive view inside George's private quarters in Hana, on the exotic island of Maui, 1983. DELIBERATE ALCHEMY ARCHIVES

to my house and there was a friend of mine living there who was also a friend of John's. John just saw the album cover and said, 'He must be fucking mad, putting three records out. And look at the picture on the front, he looks like an asthmatic Leon Russell.' There was a lot of negativity going down . . . . I just felt that whatever happened, whether it was a flop or a success, I was gonna go on my own just to have a bit of peace of mind."

Happily, George's upfront attitude paid off in a big way. He was a force to be reckoned with now formally, and permanently, on his own — despite the many naysayers who wanted to see the Beatles back together, perpetually retracing their steps as pop's ever-smiling Fab Four.

His next public venture, the humanitarian Concert for Bangla Desh, showed the world that George Harrison was more than willing to go out on a limb for a cause in which he truly believed. It was the first example of the staggering philanthropic power of rock and roll. The historic concert was the benevolent precursor of events like Live Aid, the Prince's Trust annual shows and the Amnesty International tours. George Harrison and his three famous cohorts had already shown us that rock music had a mind; now he would prove to everyone that it had a heart as well.

The cause, a bloody vendetta of terror between West Pakistan and Bangladesh, came to the attention of George through his great friend Ravi Shankar. "When I talked with him," said Shankar in an interview conducted two days following the August 1971 concerts, "he was impressed by my sincerity, and I gave him lots to read and explained the situation."

Things started moving very fast then. George called Ringo in Spain where he was working on a film, and he talked to Leon Russell and all of these wonderful musicians from the west coast and east coast who came to play. And he contacted Mr. Klein, who has taken care of the business and administration. Everyone has shown such deep concern. And, of course, Bob Dylan, as luck would have it, was so wonderful to take part in this cause. In a period of only four or five weeks, all of this was done. To conceive, plan and execute such a large-scale program and do it successfully in such a short time must be setting a record in the history of world entertainment.

To say that George fully drew on his extensive web of show-business connections with almost unparalleled efficiency is an understatement. The truth is that from the first day he committed himself to the cause he acted like a man obsessed: writing, recording and promoting the superb single "Bangla Desh"; spending weeks on the phone calling lawyers, tax accountants, *sarod* players, program printers, disc jockeys, roadies, pop stars, travel agents and even his old Beatle buddies.

Right up until the eleventh hour, it was widely rumored and indeed anticipated that all four Beatles would reunite for the show. Ringo, for one, was definitely booked. John Lennon, too, had agreed tentatively to appear, but Paul McCartney was still playing hard to get. "I'd really love to come, *but* . . ." was all Harrison could get from the headstrong bass player, so after a while he simply gave up. Three Beatles, after all, was still nothing to sneeze at! As the date of the two big shows at New York's Madison Square Garden approached, however, John too began to entertain second thoughts. From the very moment Harrison approached Lennon, he had made it clear that there was no room on the bill for the somewhat questionable musical talents of Yoko Ono. Surprisingly, John hadn't seemed to mind at first, but as the day drew nearer, he began dropping little hints about how much more "comfortable" he would feel if "Mother" (Lennon's pathetic pet name for the anything but motherly Ono) were up there by his side. George, to his credit, stuck to his guns. This benefit was his baby, and as such, Ono wouldn't be emitting so much as a single conceptual squeak or squawk in his show! To no one's surprise, John bowed out at the last moment and the Lennons caught the next available flight out to Paris.

On July 27, George Harrison and Ravi Shankar staged a press conference in New York. Harrison held forth with the ever-attentive American media out in full force:

> Up until the time we decided to do the concert, there had been very little that I had actually read about it [Bangladesh]. I'd heard a little bit on television in England . . . . It's particularly a bad situation . . . . But it happens all the time. This is happening *everywhere*, like Biafra last year.
>
> I was asked by a friend to help, that's all. This was Ravi Shankar's idea. He wanted to do something about it . . . . Once I decided I was going to go on the show, then I organized the thing with a little help from my friends. Some of the musicians flew thousands of miles and didn't get paid for anything. They were really into the whole idea of helping the refugees.

One of those dozens of calls made by Harrison in preparation for the show went out to his buddy Shambu Das. The virtuoso sitarist was committed to introducing the serious study of the Indian classical arts into the mainstream of North America, and had moved to Canada in hopes of establishing such an institution. When Harrison's assistants finally got hold of him, he was in Montreal.

I got a call saying George wanted me in New York to help with the concert. The next day, I arrived and a big limousine was waiting to pick me up. I said to the driver, "Where am I going?" but he didn't answer, everything was very top secret. Eventually, I met up with George's road manager, Mal, who comes to my hotel room and says, "Shambu, you have to come quickly. We have to try and change the atmosphere in George's room because everyone is very nervous about the show." So I went up, and quite a few people were already there, Bob Dylan, George, his father, his sister and Pattie, among others. George didn't see me come in, though, so I sneaked up behind him, put my hands over his eyes and said, "Come on, tell me who it is!" And George says, "Hey, Shambu!" and everyone began to laugh and laugh.

Later that afternoon there was a final rehearsal at Madison Square Garden to which George insisted I tag along. Listening to his music in an empty house, of course, made the sound very, very loud. So George pulls out two bits of cotton and says, "Here, Shambu, put these in your ears."

"Okay," I said. "Now I'll hear your music really good!"

The roster of musicians slated to appear at the benefit read like a who's who of rock and roll. On drums were Ringo Starr and super sessionman Jim Keltner. Country rocker Leon Russell and Billy Preston took over on keyboards, while Eric Clapton, George Harrison and Jesse Ed Davis looked after most of the guitar work. In addition, the well-known Apple band, Badfinger, provided vocal harmonies and strummed along on acoustic guitars. Klaus Voormann played bass, and Jim Horn, as his name implies, led the electrifying horn section. On the Indian side of things, Ravi Shankar was on hand with his sitar, accompanied by his ever-present *tabla* man, the portly Alla Rakha. Phil Spector was in charge of recording the historic event, and Apple man Pete Bennett with promoting it. One notable name, however, was still missing. The big question on everybody's mind was, "What about Bob Dylan?"

Ever since word about the shows first spread, there was much speculation that the ultra-reclusive Dylan might turn up to trade licks with his old pal George. Behind the scenes, Harrison was doing everything he could to make that rumor a reality. At first Bob was skeptical, but willing to listen to what Harrison had to say. "I'll consider it, man," was about all George was able to pry out of their initial conversation, but it was enough to keep Harrison optimistic.

Dylan seemed to be tempted by Harrison's constant encouragement to leave the self-imposed isolation in which he had been living for the past five years. As the day drew near, he showed up more than once at Harrison's New York hotel to party. When the subject of the show would come up, however, the great tunesmith turned characteristically quiet. He eventually agreed to join Harrison for the final rehearsal and sound check at the Garden, and depending on how things went, would let him know if he "felt like" performing.

Huddled together on the gigantic cable-strewn stage, the two men looked surprisingly inconsequential for the rock legends that they were. Strumming first through the Harrison-Dylan composition "If Not for You," they conferred on chord changes, assisted the technical staff with their sound checks and meandered through a long list of numbers under consideration for the show. "We had a rehearsal the night before the concert," remembers Pete Bennett.

> Dylan and Ringo were both there, but Eric Clapton was not. He had not yet come into town and nobody knew where he was. We finally found him the next day at the Park Lane Hotel. It was time to go to the afternoon show, but he was spaced out in his hotel room. He was very sick. He had taken an overdose of pills or something. There was a doctor in the room with Clapton's girlfriend and they were trying to bring him around. "Hey, we have a concert here," I said, starting to pull Clapton out of bed, but nicely. He was spaced out, like a zombie, but luckily we got him into the car and to Madison Square Garden where he was on cloud nine through the whole Concert for Bangla Desh."

As the mammoth crowds slowly began making their way into the sold-out arena on August 1, Harrison was backstage in his dressing room, still wondering if Bob was going to turn up. "Harrison was all over me to make sure Bob was going to play," remembers Bennett. On his way through the busy backstage bustle, Pete stopped dead in his tracks when he heard the faint, echoing sounds of someone playing the harmonica in the men's room. Slowly inching open the door, he saw Dylan leaning in a corner against the cool tile walls, playing for a very select audience of one.

"Bob!" said Pete. "The show's starting. What the hell are you doing in the bathroom, for crying out loud?"

"I like it in here," replied Bob, pausing only momentarily from his zealous assault on his trusty harp. "How's George doin', Pete?"

"Fine. Fine. What do you mean, you like it here? It's a stinking toilet, Bob. You gotta get out there on stage, man."

"Maybe the people won't like me anymore, Pete," pouted Dylan, surprisingly insecure.

"Bob, shit, *Bob!*" screamed Bennett, throwing up his arms in amazement. "They'll *love* you, man. Everybody's waiting to see you!"

"Yeah, see me fuck it up, you mean."

"Look, Bob, what about George? He's your friend, isn't he? Do it for him," said Pete, unloading his big guns on the uncertain singer. "On second thought, fuck that, do it for *you!*"

Scuffing his big leather boots against a crack in the tiles, Dylan thought for a moment and then, looking the pudgy promo man right in the eyes, said, "Okay, I'll tell you what, I'll come if you come too."

Unable to contain himself, Bennett was so thrilled he grabbed Dylan and hugged him like a teddy bear. "You're priceless!" he said, grinning from ear to ear. "Let's go, man!"

Strolling out onto the stage into a shower of bright white light, Bennett presented his prize to George, nodding like a proud poppa at a high-school graduation. Harrison was beaming, too, almost skipping across the platform to embrace his superstar hero. "I'd like to introduce a friend of us all!" Harrison sang into the mike. Immediately the already keyed-up audience jumped to its feet, giving the heralded troubadour a solid ten-minute ovation.

In accordance with Harrison's plan to generate as much cash for the Bangladesh cause as possible, the shows were not only recorded for a later release as a live LP, but also filmed by Hollywood producer Saul Swimmer. Although both shows had completely sold out within six hours after the box office opened, the receipts from the gate were hardly enough to maintain a million and more refugees for any extended period. Still,

George reasoned, there were always the record royalties to look forward to, as well as the income from the film.

Unfortunately, Harrison's old foe, the ubiquitous tax man, had his eyes on that money as well and soon extended his hand directly into the idealistic Beatle's pocket. Learning that both American and British tax officials planned to carve off a generous slab of the pie for themselves, Harrison set up a meeting with England's chief financial undersecretary, Patric Jenkin, to try to convince the highly placed bureaucrat of the urgency of retaining as much of the proceeds as possible for his humanitarian quest. Throughout the two-hour meeting, Jenkin sat stiffly as George described the avalanche of human suffering unleashed upon the innocent people of Bangladesh by the bloody war. Finally, the impeccably groomed aristocrat confirmed George's worst fears. "Of course we are genuinely sympathetic, Mr. Harrison, however . . ." George felt his heart sink as Jenkin maintained the necessity of collecting all taxes due the government no matter how well-meaning the endeavor. "Have you ever heard the saying 'charity begins at home,' Mr. Harrison?"

"Thanks for your time," said George, rising to leave. "Perhaps you people would prefer it if I were to move out of England, like virtually every other major British pop star, and take my money with me?"

"That, sir, would, of course, be entirely up to you."

In the end, Harrison dutifully wrote out a check on all taxable monies earned through the concert. Yet that wasn't the only complication he had to face.

The three-record soundtrack from the event *The Concert for Bangla Desh* was released to the public on December 20, 1971, and immediately began selling well. Allen Klein, though, was having difficulties keeping the retail price consistently low (around nine dollars) in an effort to maximize the number of copies sold to bring in more money for the refugees. Initially, demand for the lavishly packaged album was so high that some unscrupulous record stores were charging anywhere from fifteen to eighteen dollars each — extra money that stayed with the retailer. To George, the spirit of the benefit was almost lost. "You can create the money," Harrison told American talk-show host Dick Cavett during an appearance on his program. "The problem is, who to give it to."

When all was said and done, the Concert for Bangla Desh raised a little more than $15 million. How much of that money actually translated into rice and medical supplies for that war-torn nation remains anybody's guess. Still, the historic concert and the spirit of cooperation that made them possible will long be remembered. For Harrison, the arduous mix of good and bad he was forced to endure was typical of the day-to-day duality of life in the material world, a life that despite the fervor of his religious beliefs seemed to be growing increasingly more problematic and less pleasurable by the hour.

It was around this time that George and Pattie began to admit that their marriage was steadily heading for trouble. A few days before the concert, a pretty twenty-year-old I'll call Marilyn was to find out first-hand just how bad things really were.

> I was basically just an intensely involved fan when George and I first met, though I tried very hard not to let him see it. I had been hanging around his hotel for days hoping to meet up with him, when suddenly his dad, Harry, passed by and then came back to talk. For his age Mr. Harrison was still a very attractive man, with his long silver hair and deep dark eyes. He was only recently widowed, but nevertheless was quite flirtatious. As we were standing in the lobby chatting, I told him how much I admired and cared for his son. He was charming. He listened intently as I went on and on about how I felt that beyond anyone else, George and I were meant to one day be together.
>
> "George is very, very difficult to get close to, you know," he told me softly, "but I know what you mean. Next to you, I'm probably his number-one fan."

A few minutes later, George came rushing through the lobby with several heavy-looking business types close on his heels. "Hold on a minute, son," Harry said loudly, collaring the obviously harried Beatle as he passed. I want you to meet your new mum!"

Jarred by this rather astounding introduction, George looked deeply into Marilyn's eyes and then shyly offered his hand. "Hello, luv."

"There was an instantaneous, almost electric, connection," says Marilyn. After chatting for a couple of minutes, George was hustled away by the other men, but left Marilyn with an especially warm and loving smile. "See ya soon," he said. "Why don't you hang out and maybe I'll see you later on?" He didn't bother to wait for an answer; he didn't have to. He *knew* she would be there.

Several hours later, Mal Evans approached Marilyn and said, "George wants to know if you'd like to come up to the room. He's alone now." Gathering up her courage, she silently followed as Evans cheerfully ushered her into the largest and most luxurious suite she had ever seen.

"Thanks, Mal," said George nonchalantly, as if the roadie had just delivered the evening paper. "We'll see you in the morning."

Alone at last with the object of her deepest, most sexual fantasies, the terrified young woman was amazed to see that George seemed to be far more uptight and shy than she was. "I remember thinking, 'My God, what's he got to feel weird about? After all, he's the Beatle!'" After a few minutes of strained small talk, Harrison made his move and almost immediately the two were on the bed making love. By Marilyn's account, George was a strong, considerate lover, and after several high-intensity interludes they both sank down into the huge bed, exhausted.

"He was very much into Krishna at the time," she remembers, "and after a quick nap and a shower he taught me how to chant."

I remember thinking, though, that he seemed so terribly sad and lonely that if it wasn't Krishna he was into then it might well have been smack or something else. He seemed to really need some sort of anchor to hold him down. He told me later that it was really a very bad period all around. Although he and Pattie made it a point of arriving and leaving together whenever they were in public, in between they both pretty much did as they liked.

One funny thing I remember from that night was George going on about how much he disliked being pounced upon by all the kids outside the hotel harassing him for photos and autographs. He never realized I had my trusty Brownie stashed in my purse not five feet away! He also talked a good bit about the Beatles, spending hours telling me old stories about their early days on the road and in Hamburg. I didn't have the heart to tell him that virtually every novice Beatle fan already knew most of them by heart.

After a while, Marilyn began to feel, for some reason, increasingly uncomfortable. She knew that she had to somehow make an excuse and get away from this painfully sad and lonely man. "It's hard to explain, but I suddenly just felt very awkward and out of place. As I was leaving, he kissed me softly and told me to be sure and hurry back. I guess maybe I just didn't want him to think that I was really that easy. I had to let him see that I was different from all the others, that I really did care."

Despite the evening's rather abrupt end, Marilyn did see Harrison again on several occasions. "We were together at the Record Plant once while he was working on the tapes of the concert. Another night we spent time together at the official opening of Ringo's spaghetti western, *Blindman*. I remember, too, going along to the after-show party for *Bangla Desh*, where my friend Jo Jo [later Mrs. Denny Laine] got up on stage with the house band and actually had the nerve to sing 'Something.'"

Marilyn and Harry Harrison too kept in regular touch through letters, getting together again in 1974 at the Boston Garden during George's Dark Horse tour. By this time, George had fallen deeply in love with Olivia Arias, so when the two ex-lovers met again backstage they simply exchanged a little hug, had a quick word together and parted.

After the show, Harry made arrangements with George's road crew for Marilyn to receive the star treatment when the tour rumbled into New York for its final December 19 and 20 shows at Madison Square Garden. Arriving in Manhattan, Marilyn looked up Harry at the Park Lane Hotel and was immediately invited to stay with him in his large, airy suite. At the time, both Marilyn and Mr. Harrison were severely under the weather, she with bronchitis, George's dad with the flu. Although the thought of an attractive young woman in such intimate circumstances with a vastly older, probably lonely widower does summon up some steamy images, Marilyn says that nothing physical occurred. Harry was far too much of a gentleman to ever make the first move. Instead, Marilyn says, the two of them sat up all night and talked about George, at one point even discussing the idea of collaborating on a book about the introspective ex-Beatle. Although that idea came to nothing, the two remained close friends until Mr. Harrison's death in 1978. Marilyn says that it is impossible to really understand George Harrison without first knowing what a large part Harry played in his life. "They were as close as a father and son could ever be. And I'm sure George must have been absolutely devastated when he passed away. He probably felt as though he'd had his arm hacked off with a dull blade. They were that close."

Harrison's next solo release, the philosophical *Living in the Material World* of 1973, was his last major attempt to promote his Krishna beliefs en masse. Although many reviewers saw the album as somewhat self-involved and even maudlin, Harrison remained confident that those who truly needed to would hear his God-centered message. Everybody else, as usual, would either ignore the work or, worse, see it simply as an old Beatle's newest trick.

Once again, Phil Spector acted as producer. "Phil worked on the second solo album," Harrison told Timothy White in *Musician* magazine.

> By that I mean he was around. Again, he kept falling over and breaking his ankles, wrists. The guy who was his helper was having heart attacks. Phil was never there. I literally used to have to go and break into the hotel to get him. I'd go along the roof at the Inn on the Park in London and climb in his window yelling, "Come on! We're supposed to be making a record!" He'd say, "Oh. Okay." And then he used to have eighteen cherry brandies before he could get himself down to the studio. I got so tired of that because I needed somebody to help. I was ending up with more work than if I'd just been doing it on my own.

As usual with any Harrison-directed work, the album contained the talents of a mighty array of session players including Ringo Starr, Nicky Hopkins, Gary Wright and Klaus Voormann, to name but a few. Inside the tastefully designed gatefold cover was a photograph of George hosting his own version of the Last Supper on the grounds of a lavish estate, dressed as a Catholic priest complete with a pair of very deadly looking six-shooters strapped to his waist. Nothing to get excited about, however — just George lampooning the established Western religious order with a parody of the materialism so prevalent in today's Christendom. The enclosed lyric sheet was illustrated with a fiery full-color painting of Krishna as the charioteer for his friend and disciple Arjuna on the battlefield of Kurukshetra, the original setting for the celestial *Bhagavad-gita*, Harrison's bible. Lyrically, the songs reflected the somber musical meanderings of a very straight Hare Krishna, which Harrison still was, in spirit if not in practice. Titles like "The Lord Loves the One Who Loves the Lord," "The Light That Has Lighted the World," "Be Here Now" and "Don't Let Me Wait Too Long," made it clear to everyone where the spiritually inclined ex-Beatle's head was at. Still for all its blatantly yogic overtones, the million-selling LP managed to produce one hit single in the mantra-like "Give Me Love (Give Me Peace on Earth)," which topped the charts in America for three months.

By late 1971, Harrison's home life at Friar Park was beginning to seriously unravel. After seven years of reasonably happy co-existence with Pattie, their relationship was now in trouble. Ironically, at the hub of their estrangement was their mutual interest in Hindu culture and philosophy. While intensely interested in yoga and all things Indian, Pattie was admittedly not as committed to the faith as George. The accouterments of the Eastern lifestyle were one thing. For years now, Pattie had sporadically meditated, was largely vegetarian, studied Indian dance, read volumes by George's favorite gurus, accompanied her husband on pilgrimages to India's holy places and even occasionally chanted Hare Krishna on the prayer beads presented to her by Srila Prabhupada. However, she fell short of actually calling herself a devotee of Krishna. Harrison, on the other hand, was intensely dedicated. Rumor has it that he even offered to "surrender" himself at the feet of Prabhupada by formally joining ISKCON. "No," his beloved master and friend was quoted as saying, "you can do far more for Krishna right where you are." By all accounts, Harrison took those words firmly to heart, even to the eventual detriment of his marriage.

To Pattie, one of the most troublesome tenets of Prabhupada's teachings was his strict ban on sex for pleasure. She just couldn't reconcile such an unyieldingly rigid attitude with the deep feelings of love she had for her husband. George, however, was convinced, at least philosophically, that until an individual had conquered the pleasures of the flesh, attaining true spiritual *gnosis* would remain just a distant dream. "No illicit sex means that you're not raving around knocking up everybody," explained George in 1969. "That then becomes a bit of discipline, as all these emotions like lust, anger and greed have got to be curbed."

"Sex life is meant for having nice children to raise in Krishna consciousness," said the guru, "that is all." Pattie would have loved nothing more than to have those "nice children" with George, but after two childless marriages, she seems unable to conceive. Sources close to Harrison speculate that this unhappy fact alone hammered a sizable wedge between the young couple. "He was a little embarrassed by it all," says an old business associate. "He apparently saw it as some kind of a slight on his manhood." Both of them went to doctors, but to no avail. George said the problem was probably his, but later, of course, he had a son by his second wife. At the time, Harrison's friends figured he was just taking the blame in an effort to shield Pattie from a potentially very embarrassing situation. Feeling those first faint tremors in her marriage, Pattie suggested that they consider adoption, but George apparently steadfastly refused. Pattie was heartbroken.

When they first got married, George insisted that Pattie give up her budding modeling career so she could shower her full attention upon their life together. Even charity work was out, as it might bring with it some unwanted publicity for George or the band. Consequently, Pattie found herself with little to do but sit at home looking stunning, waiting for her man to grace her with his presence. With George away on Beatle business so much of the time, Pattie did a lot of waiting.

On one occasion, Pattie was so desperate for something constructive to do that she responded to an unsolicited plea from a local do-gooder collecting bundles of used eyeglasses for distribution to the needy in Africa. Thinking it a suitably worthwhile cause, she rummaged through several London junk shops until she had amassed quite a number of the badly needed frames. Pattie then carefully smashed out the lenses with a hammer on her kitchen table, packaged up the glasses and phoned the old man to come and collect them. Within days a story heralding her generosity appeared in the London *Daily Mirror* — and George was furious. Needless to say, the career of Esher's newest patron saint of the poor was quickly cut short.

All this is not to say that George didn't love Pattie. He did, intensely. But his fairly straitlaced Liverpool upbringing and his espousal of right-wing Hinduism had apparently molded his views on women and family life in some rather peculiar ways.

So forlorn was Pattie about her idle existence that she even consulted a London clairvoyant to find some avocation that would be acceptable to her demanding husband. "Your grandmother, dear, was a very great natural musician," Pattie was told. "She still plays the violin beautifully on the other side. I'm sure she would love you to take it up as she did." Excited by the possibility of finally finding something to occupy and satisfy her, Pattie engaged a teacher to come to the house for lessons. After a few frustrating weeks, however, her enthusiasm began to wane, and the violin was consigned to an upstairs closet along with the forgotten piano exercise books from an earlier, similarly fruitless pursuit. After the Harrisons' Indian phase had begun, Pattie had even attempted to learn the immensely difficult *dillrube*, hoping that might help draw the two unfulfilled lovers closer together. It did not.

"I just don't want to be the little wife sitting at home," she told Hunter Davies in *The Beatles*. "I want to do something worthwhile." Around the house, Pattie did far more in the way of domestic chores than the other Beatle wives. Although in Esher the Harrisons retained a live-in

Apple promotion man Pete Bennett and George getting down during a listening party for Harrison's three-record set, *All Things Must Pass*, in 1970. PETE BENNETT INTERNATIONAL

Hanging out with the Dark Horse group, Jiva. DELIBERATE ALCHEMY ARCHIVES

housekeeper, Pattie did most of the cooking, shopping and tidying up. Still, it wasn't enough. Always extremely close to her sister Jenny, Pattie began making overnight visits to her London flat as her marriage came further apart. By the time the couple moved to Henley, Pattie and George were living fairly separate social lives.

Harrison's problems at home were aggravated by his basic inability to practice consistently what he so readily preached. "Prabhupada tells the story," says a former devotee and longtime friend of Harrison's, "of an elephant who, after taking a nice bath in the sacred Ganges, would dry himself off by rolling around in the soft, sandy dirt along the riverbank. In many ways this was George. Much of the good done by his devotion to chanting was then undone by his often less than spiritual behavior. Of course, it couldn't have been easy for George having so much facility available with which to enjoy the material world."

That, apparently, is one reason Srila Prabhupada didn't want Harrison initiated into ISKCON. He realized how difficult it would be for someone in Harrison's exalted position to adhere to the strict standards he set for his devotees. To Prabhupada, no sex meant exactly that. It was the same with intoxication of any kind. As long as one was engaged in any so-called illicit activity, there was no question of becoming truly Krishna conscious — which Harrison knew full well. It's one thing for an ordinary man to give up unrestricted sensual gratification; chances are his sphere of enjoyment isn't all that great to begin with. But George's was a different story altogether. Anything — and anyone — was his for the asking, and that was very difficult to give up. That's what Christ meant when He said that it is harder for a rich man to enter the kingdom of God than it is for a camel to pass through the eye of a needle. To his credit, though, that didn't stop George from *trying*. "He is perhaps one of the most divinely stubborn men I have ever known," says one of his devotee friends.

Perhaps George's biggest blunder in his attempt to attain that elusive spiritual status was his widely reported on-again, off-again romance with Ringo Starr's artistically talented first wife, Maureen. Such dangerous liaisons were reportedly nothing new for George, who didn't seem particularly troubled that the object of his affections was married to one of his pals. "How could you, with your best friend's wife?" he was asked some time later. "Incest, I guess," he replied, with a casual shrug of his shoulders.

Peter Brown, in his controversial 1983 book *Love You Make: An Insider's Story of the Beatles*, suggests that Pattie, too, fell from grace soon afterward with soon-to-be Rolling Stone guitarist Ron Wood, though the story remains unsubstantiated. What is clear, however, is that the Harrisons' marriage was by then essentially over. And though it is widely held that George's friend Eric Clapton had been carrying a heavy torch for the wide-eyed Pattie for some time, at least he kept from making any serious moves until he felt that the couple was finished. By that time, though, Clapton was battling some well-known demons of his own.

Clapton's long road to sobriety took the virtuoso rock guitarist on a slippery ride to hell and back for the better part of fifteen years. After becoming fed up with the paranoia and unpredictability of psychedelics and speed, around 1970 he started casually snorting coke with his show-business buddies and before long graduated to heroin. Terrified of needles, Eric preferred sniffing the deadly drug, a daily ritual that would eventually cost the musician as much as £1,000 a week. Toward the final days of Clapton's savage addiction, he even had to sell off one of his vintage guitars as well as a favorite car to help keep him in the devilish white powder. By that point, many of his friends and family doubted he'd live to see another year.

Perhaps George's first indication that Clapton was turned on by Pattie came the night of the London premiere of Kenneth Tynan's *Oh, Calcutta* in 1970. Peter Brown had taken Pattie to the play and to a VIP cast party later at the home of Robert Stigwood, the show's producer and Clapton's manager. George would have taken her himself, but he was finishing *All Things Must Pass* and was busy virtually every night in the studio. Following the late-night session, Harrison jumped into his Ferrari and drove to Stigwood's extravagant estate near Stanmore. At the party, he cornered Brown and asked where his wife was, only to be told that so far as anyone knew, she and Clapton had taken a stroll together some time before. Hopping mad, Harrison stormed back to his car and drove down the long, narrow driveway in search of Pattie. After only about a hundred yards, he came across his wife and Clapton walking arm in arm toward the house. George slammed on his brakes, skidding to a halt. "And just what the fuck is all this?" he screamed. Without waiting for an answer, Harrison grabbed Pattie by the arm and swung her into the car, speeding off toward Henley. Eric was left alone in the middle of the road, sadly watching his dreams disappear into the night. For everything the wealthy Clapton had, Pattie was apparently the one thing beyond his grasp. And it was tearing him apart.

Languishing in his rambling Surrey mansion, Hurtwood Edge,

Clapton rebounded into a relationship with Lady Alice Ormbsby-Gore, Lord Harlech's stunningly beautiful daughter, and continued to destroy himself with dangerously large doses of pure China White heroin. During this period he wrote the hauntingly beautiful "Layla," a tribute to his secret, unrequited love for Pattie. Based loosely on the Persian poem "Layla and Majnum," by Nazimi, it featured some revealing lyrics along with a memorable piano interlude and searing guitar intro.

Meanwhile, back at Friar Park, the situation wasn't at all improving between George and Pattie. By the fall of 1972, they were at odds with one another so much of the time that one day George, on the spur of the moment, climbed into his BMW and took off to stay with his friend Gary Wright at his home in Albufeira, Portugal. Driving nonstop from Henley, George kept himself awake by loudly chanting Hare Krishna. As it turned out, Portugal provided the perfect break he needed to realign his priorities and gather his thoughts. "I really do love Pattie," he told Wright. "But it's almost as though love alone isn't enough."

When he returned to England, George made a concerted effort to try to make things better between the two of them, but it was not to last. Bored with life at the cloistered Friar Park, Pattie defied George's wishes and resumed her modeling career, accepting an assignment from designer Ossie Clark for a Chelsea fashion show. Soon after, Harrison left for India, where he spent several weeks touring various holy places, constantly chanting on his *japa mala* beads and visiting with several well-known spiritual masters. Then once again he returned home ready to resume his career and salvage his floundering marriage. But this time it was too late. Pattie, in desperation, had flown to Los Angeles in June 1974 and was staying with her sister, Jenny, and her husband, Mick Fleetwood. Days later she linked up with Clapton in Miami, where he was recording his comeback hit album, *461 Ocean Boulevard*. For Pattie, there was no looking back. Maybe at first she had seen Eric's longing for her as a means to lure George back from his often dour, otherworldly pursuits, but now her affection for the sensitive, caring Clapton was real. Their love sprang full-grown from the disappointment and loneliness each had carried with them for so long. With Pattie's support, Clapton was finally able to control his addiction and began work at a furious pace, picking up the pieces of his broken career. By the summer of 1974 he was once again enjoying huge international success with a string of popular albums and a sold-out comeback tour.

For the first time in her life, Pattie Boyd Harrison had found real purpose in the reclamation of someone she dearly loved. Unlike the largely self-sustained and confident George, Eric needed Pattie desperately. Even the usually jaded Harrison could recognize it once he was able to overcome his initial anger and pain over the sloppy way they had parted. "There comes a time when splitting is for the best," he told reporters in September 1974. "It's no big deal. We've separated many times, but this time I don't know what will happen . . . . Eric is a fantastic guy. He's always been a close friend of mine; you always hurt the one you love. [Pattie and I] were getting on each other's nerves, and what with the pace of my work, splitting was the easiest thing to do. In this life, there is no time to lose in an uncomfortable situation."

After so many years of marriage, Harrison admittedly "went on a bit of a bender" after the breakup. "I wasn't ready to join Alcoholics Anonymous or anything; I don't think I was that far gone, but I could put back a bottle of brandy occasionally, plus all the other naughty things that fly around." For a time in 1974 he moved in with model Kathy Simmonds, Rod Stewart's former girlfriend, in a cozy villa near St. George's Bay, on the island of Grenada. As far as Harrison was concerned, though, the affair was just another quick fling, to be enjoyed for the moment and then casually cast away. But Kathy had convinced herself that this was the real thing. Several weeks later, Harrison flew alone to L.A. to begin making plans for his first solo concert tour, leaving without so much as a decent goodbye for the heartbroken twenty-four-year-old.

Added to the never-ending questions all the Beatles had to endure about whether the group might one day re-form, Harrison now had another big media cross to bear. "What about Pattie and Clapton?" he was continually asked. Perhaps his most complete answer was published in 1977 in a lengthy interview in *Crawdaddy*:

We both loved Eric, still do, but there were a few funny things. I pulled *his* chick once. That's happened, and now you'd think he was trying to get his own back on me . . . . Pattie and he got together after we'd really split, and actually we'd been splitting up for years. That was a funny thing, you know. I thought that was the best thing to do, for us to split, and we should've done it much sooner. I didn't have any problems about it; Eric had the problem. Every time I'd go and see him he'd really be hung up about it, and I'd be saying, "Fuck it, man, don't be apologizing," and he didn't believe me. I was saying, "I don't care."

In L.A., George's career began to sizzle. In the works was a twenty-seven-city tour with Ravi Shankar and Billy Preston, a multimillion-dollar deal with A&M Records to distribute his label, Dark Horse, as well as plans to record a new album.

Around this time, too, he met twenty-seven-year-old Mexican-born Olivia Trinidad Arias, originally an assistant in the merchandising department at A&M and later a secretary for Dark Horse Records. Deeply involved with setting up his new label, Harrison was often on the phone with the quiet, attractive Arias, discussing its day-to-day operation. Before long he realized that his brief encounters with the accommodating, unspoiled young woman were often the highlight of his day, and he began calling her all the way from Henley just to chat. Walking alone through the gardens of his estate, George found himself thinking about her more and more and soon telephoned a friend in California to have her checked out. After so many years of having people come on to him for all the wrong reasons, the world-weary Harrison knew full well what a great catch he had become for any enterprising female looking for a stepping-stone to the big time. Olivia, however, was found to have no ulterior motives for their telephone relationship, and George flew to Los Angeles to meet her face to face. It was indeed love at first sight, and from that moment on the two similar-looking lovers were inseparable.

The great event that made possible their meeting was, of course, Harrison's lucrative liaison between his newly formed Dark Horse label and Herb Alpert's and Jerry Moss's A&M. Legally incorporated in May of 1974, Dark Horse was Harrison's answer to the Beatles' ill-fated Apple, which sought to sign and then develop unknown talent in a gallant attempt to nudge open the often cliquish international recording industry. Apple, unfortunately, had lost sight of that dream around the time it turned over the reins to the notorious, fast-talking Allen Klein. Having personally presided over the inevitable Apple deathwatch, Harrison was not about to let the same thing happen twice. He was determined that Dark Horse would pick up where the Beatles and Apple had left off. One of the first acts he signed was his old mentor, Ravi Shankar, followed by former Apple prodigy Bill Elliott and his mate, Bob Purvis (known collectively as Splinter).

Harrison was asked in 1974 what his hopes were for Dark Horse: "I want it to be reasonably small. To tell you the truth, I've been over here [in Los Angeles] just over a week and if I signed all the people who gave me tapes, I'd be bigger than RCA, but fortunately, I don't have time to listen to them."

Harrison's original deal with A&M called for the singer to deliver not only several new artists to the company but also an LP of his own by July 1977 (following the expiration of his longstanding contract with Apple). In exchange, A&M put up $2.6 million to launch Harrison's dream company in hopes of reaping the rewards of the public's renewed interest in the former Beatle. George retained control over content, while A&M effectively acted as distributor.

One of the most eye-catching features of George's latest venture was the attractive Indian-influenced company logo, a seven-headed flying horse. As one story goes, Harrison was in India when he accidentally tripped over a paint can bearing a similar design, and was attracted by the symbolism of the spirited, soaring steed representing his own self-styled position as the Beatles' dark horse.

There are other theories, however. For instance, in 1984 I was wandering through the grounds of Friar Park one Sunday during a visit with "Legs" Larry Smith, and I noticed a bust of a beautifully carved three-headed horse at the base of a stone tower attached to a gate house. Despite being four heads short, the piece was virtually identical to Harrison's version. George must have passed the striking sculpture dozens of times over the years on his walks around the property. Still another possible answer can be found in the Hindu mythology, so much a part of Harrison's persona. According to legend, Vivasvan, the Sun God, is drawn across the morning sky in his blazing chariot by a seven-headed horse. The most likely possibility, however, is that George's creation was a subtle blend of all three influences.

Perhaps the best remembered event of 1974 for Harrison fans was his critically disastrous "George Harrison and Friends" world tour, which kicked off in Vancouver, British Columbia, on November 2. It included as its warm-up act a sixteen-piece Indian orchestra headed by Ravi Shankar. Nine days earlier, George met with representatives of the world press in Los Angeles to discuss his plans for the shows:

REPORTER: Why did you decide to return to America?
GEORGE: I've been back here, many times. This the first time I've been back to work, though. It's also the first time I've had an H-1 visa since '71.
REPORTER: What was the reason for your not having the H-1?

GEORGE: I had the same problem as John Lennon. I was busted for marijuana way back in '67 . . .

REPORTER: Would you ever consider touring Mexico?

GEORGE: I wouldn't mind. I mean, I would go anywhere. This is really a test. I either finish this tour ecstatically happy and want to go on tour everywhere, or I'll end up just going back to my cave again for another five years.

REPORTER: Could you tell us your feelings and expectations for the upcoming tour?

GEORGE: I think if I had more time I'd be panic-stricken, but I don't really have the time to get worried about it.

REPORTER: Are you getting divorced from Pattie?

GEORGE: No. I mean, that's as silly as marriage.

REPORTER: Can you foresee a time when you'll give up your musical objectives?

GEORGE: I can see a time when I'd give up this sort of madness, but music — I mean, *everything* is based upon music. I'll never stop my music.

REPORTER: What direction is your music going in now?

GEORGE: Haven't got a clue. I mean it's getting a bit funkier, especially with Willy Weeks and all them.

REPORTER: What's your attitude about drugs now?

GEORGE: Drugs? What drugs? Aspirins or what are you talking about? I mean, I think it's awful when it ruins people. What do you define as a drug? Like whisky? I don't want to advocate anything because it's so difficult to get into America these days.

Working with Harrison and the Indian musicians were bassist Willie Weeks, Robben Ford on guitar, drummer Andy Newmark, percussionist Emil Richards, Billy Preston on keyboards, saxophonist Tom Scott and Chuck Findley, trumpet. Despite the heavy artillery, however, none of the extravagantly staged shows was particularly well received by either audiences or the music media.

The complaints were numerous. First, a lot of fans were extremely disappointed that Harrison refused to perform any but four classic Beatle hits. Even then, in his new, *improved* versions of "In My Life," "While My Guitar Gently Weeps," "For You Blue" and "Something," George had altered some of the lyrics to reflect his current outlook on the past — a sacrilege in the eyes of Beatle fans. For George to sing, "Something in the way she moves 'it'" did seem a little disrespectful of a tune Frank Sinatra once called, "the most beautiful love song ever written." Another bone of contention among the fans was Harrison's decision to devote the entire first set of the show to the twangy, unfamiliar sounds of his many Indian buddies. Ravi Shankar is beyond doubt a great artist, and Harrison's idea to concoct an all-Indian orchestra was a North American first. But weaving Indian classical music into what people had expected to be purely a rock concert may have asked too much of American audiences. Sensing the crowd's lack of enthusiasm one evening during Shankar's introduction, George pointed to the embarrassed band of middle-aged musicians and said, "I'd die for this," and tapping on the side of his airbrushed Stratocaster, he added, "but not for this!"

Clearly, from that first night in Vancouver, the cultural battle lines had been drawn. "George says people expect him to be exactly what he was ten years ago," Shankar commented in a 1974 *Rolling Stone* cover story by Ben Fong-Torres. "He's matured so much in so many ways. That's the problem with *all* the artists, I suppose. People like to hear the old nostalgia." Also scrambling to Harrison's defense in the somewhat scathing article was Harrison's sidekick Tom Scott. "George is one of the few guys with the prestige and the resources to do something good and is willing to do it and put his neck on the line," he said. "By that I mean presenting a show with so much new material when people are expecting him to do a Beatles." The press, however, was not so ready to rationalize, or to forgive. "Never a strong singer," said the *San Francisco Examiner*, "but a moving one, Harrison found that he had virtually no voice left and had to croak his way through even the delicate 'Something.'"

Never one to take much notice of what the press had to say, George came back with a characteristically tough retort:

I know ten people who say the show sucks every night. And we get a hundred who, when we ask them did they like the show say, "We got much more than we ever hoped for." I don't care if nobody comes to see me, nobody ever buys another record of mine. I don't give a shit, it doesn't matter to me, but I'm going to do what I feel within myself. Gandhi says create and preserve the image of your choice. The image of my choice is *not* Beatle George. Why live in the past? *Be here now*, and now, whether you like me or not, is where I am.

Fuck my life belongs to me. It actually doesn't. It belongs to Him. My life belongs to the Lord Krishna and there's my dog collar to prove it. I'm just a dog and I'm led around by my dog collar by Krishna. That's how I feel. I've never been so humble in all my life, and I feel great.

As if this wasn't enough for one tour, there was also a lot of criticism leveled at the God-conscious guitarist to lighten up on the religious content of the shows. Breaking into the thundering rhythm guitar intro to "My Sweet Lord," Harrison would soon begin to invite the cheering, largely stoned crowd to "chant the holy name of the Lord." Few responded. Switching messiahs midstream, he would then rocket into the famous Krishna Hallelujah chorus and begin singing, "Om Christ, Om Christ, Om Christ" over and over, adding, "I know a lot of you out there think that's swearing, but it's not! If we all chant together purely for one minute, we'll blow the roof off this place." Suffice it to say, not so much as a single shingle was ever disturbed during one of the ex-Beatle's fifty performances.

Not everyone, though, found Harrison's high-flown tirades objectionable. At the time, I was on retainer from Apple Corps to investigate the possible illegal taping of George's concerts and the bootlegging of the Beatles' marathon *Let It Be* sessions. Sent to the Atlanta show under the direction of Apple's Los Angeles attorney, Bruce Graykal, I was making my way through a crowd of long-haired teenagers who were hanging around the arena's backstage entrance when I noticed a gaunt young man, with a rather faraway look in his eyes, furiously but quietly chanting a mantra I couldn't quite make out. Dressed in the standard hippie-issue faded bell-bottom jeans, he also wore a long Indian *kirta* over which was an old army jacket plastered with Oms and other Hindu signs. I paused for a moment to say hello. "Hare Krishna," I said, nodding my head slightly in a sign of respect.

"Screw you, man," replied the kid, suddenly ultra aggressive. "It's not Hare Krishna, it's *Hare Harrison!*" It seems the old Dark Horse had his dedicated disciples as well.

Altogether, the ill-fated tour grossed somewhere in the neighborhood of $4 million. And despite the often lukewarm audience reception and bad press, the shows were generally good, if certainly not great, entertainment. Most rock stars usually scoot into the safety of their chauffeur-driven limos immediately after the last note has been struck, yet on one or two occasions during the tour, Harrison hung back in his dressing room until almost the entire stadium was deserted. In a 1987 issue of *Rolling Stone*, he tells of the experience:

> I was just hanging around the stadium, and I watched them bull-dozing. They had a bulldozer in the middle — you know, that "festival seating" situation, where everybody's standing up; . . . and they were bulldozing all of the rubble left by the audience. There were mountains of empty bottles of gin and bourbon and tequila and brassieres and shoes and coats and trash. I mean, it was unbelievable. Another thing, you know, that rock band I was in, they were some pretty heavy-duty people. We had been known in the past to smoke some reefer ourselves. But I'd go on out there, and you'd just get stoned, there was so much reefer going about. And, I don't know, I just thought, "Do I actually have anything in common with these people?" Even now, after the Prince's Trust [Prince Charles's personal charitable organization] people said "Oh, doesn't it make you want to go on the road?" I said, "No. It doesn't." It doesn't because it's tiring, and just being stuck in some crummy motel in Philadelphia is not my idea of having fun. I mean, I wouldn't mind doing shows here and there, but it's tiring. It is very tiring.

Keeping in mind that touring without an album in the stores leaves nothing for an audience to run out to buy the next day, Harrison tried to release his next offering, *Dark Horse*, to coincide with the shows. He didn't quite make it, but did manage to get it out in England just ten days after his final American gig in Boston.

Harrison wrote the title track while in the studio with a little help from Ringo and drummer Jim Keltner, but he never got a chance to finish vocals on the bouncy, tongue-in-cheek number. Rushing off to rehearsals for the tour, he packed the multitrack masters with an eye to finishing the album in L.A. After the strain of so many long hours spent running through the music he wanted to perform on the road, George's basically untrained voice was just about shot before he'd even begun serious work on the project. It was a frustrating experience to try to record anything when he sounded, in his words, "like Louis Armstrong." Still, Harrison had an obligation not only to his fans but to the record company as well, and therefore had no choice but to proceed. Rehearsing and recording by day, he held late-night mixing sessions at A&M right up until a few days before the tour. Harrison remembers: "I suppose I made the mistake of doing too many concerts at a time when I was tired and wiped out anyhow. I'd been in the studio and made three albums [*Shankar Family & Friends, Splinter* and *Dark Horse*] before I went on the road, and I was still trying to finish my album, and then I went into rehearsals, and although I enjoyed a lot of that tour, I physically became run-down."

Out of the gate like a bullet with *All Things Must Pass*, Harrison's *Living in the Material World* and the subsequent *Dark Horse* failed to catch fire with the majority of the record-buying public. While Harrison maintained that the negative reaction to the tour didn't bother him, he was, in fact, badly bruised by it. Discouraged, as well, over *Dark Horse*'s poor sales and still quietly brooding over Pattie's embarrassing departure, George soon sank into a deep, seemingly irreversible depression. He would not see friends, rarely went out and became verbally abusive to those around him. He also all but abandoned his spiritual practice, although there was still the heavy Krishna conscious rap. *Always the rap.*

Things really got bad in early 1976, when his health started to decline, partly because of his increased drinking. One day, looking into that same magnificent peer-glass in which old Sir Frank used to primp prior to seeing his clients, Harrison noticed that his eyes had turned a deep, sickly yellow. He was also rapidly losing weight, looking more and more like one of the refugees he had worked so hard to save just five years earlier. Thumbing through Paramahansa Yogananda's *Scientific Healing Affirmations*, he even began chanting translated Kriya Yoga mantras aimed at restoring lost health. Eventually, though, he gave in to Olivia's insistence that he consult a physician, and was diagnosed as having serum hepatitis. He had suffered some liver damage, for which he was prescribed large doses of vitamins. Unfortunately, Harrison didn't respond to treatment. The only positive outcome of this nightmare was that at least now he was scared, scared enough to make an effort to truly become well.

Toward that end, Olivia contacted the well-known acupuncturist to the stars, Dr. Zion Yu in California. She had first heard of the doctor after her younger brother Peter sought treatment with him following a near-fatal motorcycle accident. After several visits to Dr. Yu, Harrison's condition began to steadily improve, and within a few months he seemed to be completely cured.

Following the disastrous *Dark Horse*, George recorded another marginally successful album with the rather inscrutable title of *Extra Texture — Read All About It*. Released in Britain on September 22, 1975, the LP contained several very listenable but rather depressing cuts, among them "Grey Cloudy Lies," "This Guitar Can't Keep From Crying," "World of Stone" and "Tired of Midnight Blue." The album's real gem, however, lay buried at the very end of the record. Entitled "Ladies and Gentlemen His Name Is Legs," in its own decidedly offbeat, Monty-Pythonesque way, it accomplished two very important things. First, it reassured everyone who either didn't know or had simply forgotten that George Harrison definitely had a highly developed sense of the absurd, and second, it introduced to the world at large the incomparable "Legs" Larry Smith.

"If there were no Mr. Smith," a close friend of the two once said, "it would have been necessary for George Harrison to invent one." Smith, who has for years been George's unofficial comic relief and part-time court jester, has virtually fashioned a career out of entertaining the often grumpy laird of Friar Park. As the drummer of the late Bonzo Dog Do Dah Band, Smith is the undisputed master of the quick quip and the upside down pun. Described in song by his former bandmate and Bonzo Dog headmaster Vivian Stanshall as the "serpent of the perfumed parlor," "Legs" Larry may well be the most interesting and unknowable of all Harrison's close friends. As my literary partner on a highly unlikely 1983 screenplay, "Half of Larry's Lunch," the canny Smith taught me a great deal — very little of which had anything remotely to do with writing.

Harrison's next album, the infinitely more accessible *Thirty-Three & 1/3*, seemed to indicate that he was now squarely back on musical track. Behind the scenes, however, things were still fairly tangled up. Harrison had missed his July 26, 1976, deadline by two months and when he finally arrived in L.A. to deliver the master tapes to A&M, he discovered that Jerry Moss was preparing to sue him for the delay — to the tune of a staggering $10 million.

George's response was to ring the brass at Warner Brothers and offer the album to them on the condition that they immediately buy out his contract with A&M. Warner agreed and made plans to promptly release the LP. In appreciation, Harrison consented (for the first time in several records) to actively promote the album by traveling with Olivia to several major American cities, meeting freely with the media at each stop.

"Some of the songs," Harrison commented, "are closer to the songs and spirit of *All Things Must Pass*. This new one has a more focused production, though, and it's very positive, very up, and most of the songs are love songs and happy songs. It doesn't compare at all to the last album, *Extra Texture*. That one caught me in a less than happy mood."

Harrison, eager to please his new distributor, shot a film at his home in Henley for the tune "Crackerbox Palace," to aid in the promotion of the album. Featuring a whole gang of his closest friends, including ex-Rutle Neil Innes, the film was masterfully directed by Eric Idle (as was another promo for the song "True Love"). Recalls George:

> In the song, when I say I met someone called Mr. Grief, it isn't just a clever rhyme with *life* as most people would think. There is a real person, and I met him in southern France. He was talking to me, and the way he was talking really struck me. So I told him, "I don't know if this is an insult or not, but you remind me of Lord Buckley. He's my favorite comedian." He's dead now, but he was one of the first real hip comics. And the guy nearly fell over. He said, "Hey, I managed him for eighteen years!"
>
> So we were talking about Lord Buckley, and Mr. Grief said he lived in a little shack, which he called Crackerbox Palace . . . . I loved the way "Crackerbox Palace" sounded. I loved the whole idea of it, so I wrote a song and turned it from that shack into a phrase for the physical world. The world is very serious and at times such a very sad place. But at the same time, it's such a joke. It's *all* Crackerbox Palace.

It was a good thing Harrison was becoming so open to the humor behind the hassles of the material world, as he was then up to his ears in litigation brought against him by the proprietors of Bright Tunes Music Corporation, who were alleging that George had lifted the tune for his "My Sweet Lord" from the Chiffons' "He's So Fine," the 1963 classic to which they owned the rights.

The controversial case went to court in January 1976 and garnered international headlines with each and every bump and grind of the slowly moving wheels of justice. Represented by an army of high-powered copyright lawyers, Harrison sat quietly in the crowded New York City court as a barrage of nasty accusations and innuendos flew back and forth. In a detailed summary of the proceedings, West Key Number Systems, a microfilm publisher of legal cases, issued an interesting account of the case that described the genesis of the popular tune:

> Harrison and his group, which include an American black gospel singer named Billy Preston, were in Copenhagen, Denmark, on a singing engagement. There was a press conference involving the group going on backstage. Harrison slipped away from the press conference and went to a room upstairs and began "vamping" some guitar chords, fitting on to the chords he was playing the words "Hallelujah" and "Hare Krishna" in various ways. During the course of this vamping, he was alternating between what musicians call a Minor II chord and a Major V chord. At some point he went down to meet with others of the group, asking them to listen, which they did, and everyone began to join in, taking first "Hallelujah" and then "Hare Krishna" and putting them into four-part harmony . . . . In any event, from this very free-flowing exchange of ideas, with Harrison playing his two chords and everybody singing "Hallelujah" and "Hare Krishna," there began to emerge the "My Sweet Lord" text idea, which Harrison sought to develop a little bit further during the following week as he was playing it on his guitar.
>
> Approximately one week later the entire group flew back to London because they had earlier booked time to go to a recording studio with Billy Preston to make an album. In the studio, Preston was the principal musician. Harrison did not play on the session. He had given Preston his basic motif with the idea that it be turned into a song, and went back and forth from the studio to the engineer's recording booth, supervising the recording "takes." Under circumstances that Harrison was utterly unable to recall, while everybody was working toward a finished song, in the recording studio, somehow or other the essential three notes of motif A reached polished form.

Though Harrison may not have been aware of the distinct similarities between the two hit tunes, somewhere along the way either he or Billy Preston inserted the critical three notes that later convinced District Judge Owen that George had indeed committed an act of plagiarism against Bright Tunes. In his final statement before the court, Owen pronounced his judgment: "Did Harrison deliberately use the music of 'He's So Fine?' I do not believe he did so *deliberately*. Nevertheless, it is clear that 'My Sweet Lord' is the very same song as 'He's So Fine' with different words, and Harrison had access to 'He's So Fine.' This is, under the law, infringement of copyright, and is no less so even though subconsciously accomplished."

Harrison's former manager, Allen Klein, had in 1978 — after the trial — purchased the rights to "He's So Fine" and was therefore the direct beneficiary of George's grief. The court took note of this, considering it interference by Klein, and limited the damages to what he had paid for the song — $587,000, which Harrison paid as ordered in 1981.

While promoting *Thirty-Three & 1/3*, Harrison reflected:

I'd be willing every time I write a song if somebody will have a computer and I can just go up to the thing and sing my new song into it and the computer will say *sorry* or *yes*, *ok*. I'm willing to do that, because the last thing I want to do is keep spending the rest of my life in court, or being faced with that problem. Once you get people thinking, "Oh, well, they beat Harrison on 'My Sweet Lord,' let's sue" . . . they can sue the world! It made me so paranoid about writing. And I thought, "God, I don't even want to touch the guitar or the piano, in case I'm touching somebody's note." Somebody might own that note, so you'd better watch out!

Probably the only good thing to come out of the Bright Tunes ordeal for Harrison was that it gave him the inspiration to compose "This Song," a biting satire of the whole sordid affair, and the biggest tune on *Thirty-Three & 1/3*. "All in all," said a Warner Brothers official as "This Song" started its steady climb up the American charts, "Harrison picked a mighty tough way to get a hit record."

IX

ENTER THE FRENCHMAN

Harrison Lost and Found

One time George and Olivia came over to my place and after a very pleasant evening of just sitting around watching the telly and drinking a little red wine, he took me aside and said, "You know, Robbie, if you and I stay friends you'll never have to really worry about anything again. I take care of my pals, believe me."

"Look, George," I said, "can't you understand that perhaps anyone just likes you for you? I couldn't care less about your money, or who you are."

He said, "Great," he understood and appreciated it. But to be honest, something about the way he looked told me that either he didn't really believe it or worse, just couldn't comprehend anyone really able to treat him like an everyday person.

ROBBIE CAIN

GEORGE HARRISON WAS AT HOME IN HENLEY-ON-THAMES ON JANUARY 5, 1976, when he received the news. Mal Evans, the Beatles' ever-faithful roadie and friend, was dead. Since the group split, Mal had been employed at various times by all the Fabs, but he worked the most for George. He had been at Bangla Desh, overseen the day-to-day goings-on at Friar Park for a time and traveled to the States to assist on recording sessions. He was someone the inherently skeptical George could trust.

When the Beatles' bubble finally burst in 1970, all four were financially set for life. Between record royalties, music publishing and a galaxy of outside investments, they had no money worries. The same could not be said, though, for many of the people who had helped to make them what they were. By late 1975, Evans was having a very rough time. With his marriage finished, Evans took refuge in Los Angeles, where he hoped to find work as a free-lance record producer. Although only George Martin had spent more time in the studio assisting the Beatles in the production of their work, that didn't make Mal a musician, nor did it give him the meticulous skills necessary to be a successful producer. One would think that Evans, having worked so intimately with the greatest show-business phenomenon of our time, would have had plenty of opportunities. But instead, after having been at the pinnacle of the record industry for so long, he found everything that followed rather a giant step down. You just don't go from fifteen years with the Beatles to working with basement bands from Encino. And, if you're as proud a man as Mal Evans, you don't hit up your millionaire pals, either. Had any of the Beatles known how perilously close he was to the edge, there is little doubt someone would have come to his aid. But the great bear of a man didn't ask for help. Instead, he turned to pills and drink.

Mal was then living with a woman and her daughter in a modest West Hollywood apartment. He was out of work, but still felt he had to play the big man anytime one of his show-biz buddies happened to breeze through Los Angeles. People always looked to Mal for a party, a ride to the airport or a night on the town, but no one bothered to make sure that he was all right. Surely the man once in charge of looking after all of them could see to himself.

Despondent over the deteriorating relationship with his girlfriend and agonizing over money, Evans barricaded himself in the bedroom of his apartment and threatened suicide. The young woman phoned the police, who dispatched several officers to the scene. Although Mal's only weapon was an air pistol, it was enough to convince the police that Evans was serious. As they burst through the door, Mal turned and swung the harmless weapon in their direction. He was caught in the chest with a barrage of bullets and died instantly. That's one way to handle a suicide call, I guess.

In the bitterest irony of all, back in the turbulent heyday of Beatlemania, Mal was made an honorary sheriff of Los Angeles County in recognition of his efforts in helping to keep the peace during the Beatles' frantic assault on the City of Angels.

"I was horrified when I heard about the accident," says Apple songstress Mary Hopkin. "It was awful. I think it was unforgivable. They should have just shot him in the knees or something . . . . They didn't have to kill him. He was the gentlest person I've ever known. My sister and I used to go out for drinks with him in the evening and to clubs. He was a darling. I got to know him and his family very well."

When Mal died, the diaries he had kept religiously since first coming to work for the Beatles disappeared. In 1983, Harrison hinted to me that even if they were found, due to legal entanglements they would probably never be published.

In the 1988 limited-edition book *Songs by George Harrison*, George, with a little help from master illustrator Keith West, concocted a clever centerfold painting in which a summer garden party at Friar Park is attended by a host of George's closest friends. Evans is in the picture. Despite his sometimes gruff exterior, Harrison is actually quite sentimental. Author John Blake, in his 1981 book *The Beatles After the Beatles*, says that when Harrison and the other Beatles heard of Mal's death, they broke down and cried. Although it makes a good tale, it doesn't really seem very likely. The Beatles just aren't the crying kind.

For George Harrison, the next two years were eventful and productive. On June 9, 1977, he and Pattie were granted a divorce in London on the grounds of irreconcilable differences. For Olivia and George and Pattie and Eric, it was a chance to finally cut loose from the past and begin again. In a rare 1985 comment to the press, Pattie said of her days as the first Mrs. Harrison: "They were good times, with so many laughs. I don't regret a thing. I still try on an old miniskirt once in a while. I just cannot believe we really wore them that short."

After his wife, Louise, died, Harry Harrison often went to visit his sons at Friar Park. Growing his striking silver hair well past his shoulders, the sixty-five-year-old began spending a lot of time with George and his friends, even joining his son on the road for the 1974 Dark Horse tour.

The elder Harrison was happier and more fulfilled than he had ever dreamed possible. Although he missed Louise terribly, he had made a good life for himself at Appleton and seemed quite content to putter about in the garden, or take a stroll down to his local pub for a friendly pint or two with his mates.

One evening in May 1978, George and Olivia went to bed early after a particularly exhausting day. Sometime during the night George became aware of a dull blue and gold light ringing the darkened room. Suddenly, there was his father, standing solemnly in the middle of the large room looking lovingly down at his astonished son. After a moment or two, Harry quietly bade George and his brothers farewell and then disappeared. That same day, at his home in Cheshire, Harry Harrison died of emphysema, related to a lifetime of very heavy smoking. Although everyone was saddened and upset, George was comforted somewhat by what he considered to be his father's spiritually auspicious passing.

On August 1, 1978, George and Olivia's only child, Dhani, was born at the Princess Christian Nursing Home in Windsor, just a short hop down the highway from Friar Park. *Dhani* is the Sanskrit word for "wealthy," but Harrison insists he was only aware of its significance as a term relating to his beloved Indian music. So excited was George by the birth of his son and heir that he rushed down to his friend Rodney Turner's in Henley to pick up a new baby-blue Rolls-Royce he had ordered in celebration of the great event. Harrison was like a man reborn. So concerned and possessive was he that, for the next few months, only he and Olivia were allowed to touch young Dhani. Like John Lennon after his son Sean was born, George was frantic that the baby might "pick up" something if handled by anyone. These Beatles, it seems, take their babies very seriously.

George and Olivia invited her parents to fly over from California to be the sole guests at their secret wedding on September 2 at the Henley Registry Office. Sometime later, the happy couple treated themselves to a luxurious honeymoon in Tunisia. By the time they returned, George was anxious to get back to work.

Harrison's first musical project following his father's passing and Dhani's arrival was the masterfully conceived and lyrically brilliant *George Harrison*, issued in England on February 23, 1979. The LP featured ten thoughtful new tracks and was once again infused with Harrison's familiar Krishna-conscious philosophy, only this time presented in a far more palatable manner, sandwiched as it was between a lot of genuinely great music. "It's the first time I've done a birth, a marriage and a death during making a record," says George. "We had a lot of stoppages, but I don't think it really took any longer than any other album to record. The other night Mick Ralphs from Bad Company said to me, 'Do you feel like you're in the after-the-album lull?' And I said, 'I'm in that while I'm making it.'"

Two tunes in particular, the bouncy "Blow Away" and "Faster," seemed to capture the imagination of George's fans, and both singles sold well. Of the genesis of "Blow Away," Harrison had this to say: "I hadn't written anything for a year, since *Thirty-Three & 1/3*. Fuck, what happens if I can't write anymore? So one day it's pissing with rain, just coming down in buckets, and I wrote this song. Actually I was a bit embarrassed because it was so catchy and simple . . . but in the end everyone said, 'Wow, that's a good one,' because people tend to like things simple. Anyway, it turned into 'Blow Away.'"

With "Faster," Harrison celebrated his lifelong love of auto racing with a song that even the sport's detractors were likely to enjoy. Harrison explained: "Jackie Stewart had written a book years ago called *Faster*, so that was my starting point. I nicked the title from his book, and then I went to work on it . . . . I wanted it to be a song that people who weren't the slightest bit interested in motor racing could listen to, and it still has a story."

Perhaps the most lyrically intriguing cut is a funky, good-natured guitar boogie called "Soft Hearted Hana," based on a bad trip Harrison experienced while cruising on magic mushrooms in his Hawaiian hideaway, Hana, on the exclusive island of Maui. It is interesting to note that so many years after George had supposedly given up drugs for good, he was still occasionally communing with the universe pharmacologically.

Said Harrison: "I hadn't had any psychedelic drugs for almost ten years since the sixties when we were all loonies, so I thought maybe I should have it again just to see . . . if it reminds me of anything." Unfortunately, the only thing he was reminded of was why he had quit taking hallucinogens in the first place. Although the trip started out peacefully enough, four- or five-thousand brain cells later Harrison was under the distinct impression that he was about to die a scandalous, untimely death. "You have to be a bit careful [with mushrooms] because they're so good," warned Harrison. "That stuff is very organic, you know. You feel great, and everything's in perfect focus, even the physical body feels good. But because I felt so good, I just kept on eating them all day. I nearly did myself in; I had too many. I fell over and left my body, hit my head on a piece of concrete — but they were great!"

Meanwhile, the year 1979 brought with it some interesting developments. On March 27, Eric Clapton, dressed in an off-white cowboy hat, white tux and black vest, tied the knot with Pattie Harrison at the Temple Bethel in Tucson, Arizona, in front of forty of the couple's closest friends. Clapton was reportedly two hours late for the brief twenty-minute ceremony, and in the end didn't have the eight-dollar fee for the pastor. Fortunately a friend quickly stepped in and settled the tab. As close as George and the new Mrs. Harrison supposedly still were to the bride and groom, they chose not to attend the ceremony.

On May 19, however, almost all of rock's upper echelon dropped what they were doing to attend a grand reception for the happy couple held in Clapton's sprawling back garden, at Hurtwood Edge, his baronial estate in the tiny village of Ewehurst.

One of the guests, Jo Jo Laine, Denny Laine's former wife, remembers being stunned by the sea of famous faces in attendance. Mick Jagger was there, as were Paul McCartney, Ringo Starr, David Bowie, skiffle king Lonnie Donegan and Elton John, among others. Clapton had personally invited George and Olivia, who happily turned up.

"I remember all of us sitting around cross-legged on the grass and me saying to George that it reminded me of the time the Beatles and their ladies posed outside with the Maharishi in India," remembers Laine. "George and I sat together for some time, just chatting about this and that, when suddenly he looked me straight in the eyes and said, 'Jo Jo, you look so beautiful today.' I was wearing a long white cotton dress, which he also remarked upon. With George everything is straight from the heart."

Clapton had hired a local building firm to erect a large wooden stage at one end of the garden in case anyone felt like playing. All afternoon the kids climbed up and down like monkeys. They hammered on the drums, screeched into the mikes, zapped the controls on several concert-size amps and strummed on the exotic assortment of guitars. Finally, as day turned to night, the assembled superstars were sufficiently loose to have a go themselves. First on stage was Paul McCartney, followed by George, Eric, drummer Ginger Baker and Mick Jagger. Jo Jo, who, by her own admission, was frolicking in the shrubbery smoking a huge joint with Ringo Starr, remembers:

So there we were, Ringo and I quite happily getting loaded on this joint and maybe even a little line or two when he says to me, "Come on, Jo, let's go up and join in."

"Are you crazy?" I said. "There's not one woman up there. You go, I'll stay here."

So Ringo starts giving me these big eyes and says, "Be a sport," so in the end we jumped up on the stage together.

Taking his place on the drums, Ringo did a big thumbs-up to the cheering, tipsy guests. Before long, it dawned on everyone that this was no run-of-the-mill pop-star jam session, but rather three-fourths of a bona fide off-the-cuff Beatles reunion. "I was on a mike trying to do harmonies and backup," Jo Jo continues. "After 'Magical Mystery Tour' and one or two old Chuck Berry things, the band whips in to 'Get Back,' and Paul turns around and gives me this really dirty look when he gets to the line 'Get back, Jo Jo.' Everybody else, though, was great. It was a super day. After all, how many couples get to have the Beatles play at their wedding reception?"

Her former husband Denny, however, doesn't remember being quite so impressed with the musical portion of the all-star evening: "I played with them, and I think it's lucky nobody made a tape. The music was terrible, absolute rubbish."

By 1980, George was beginning to feel that the time was right to record another album. Gathering together an array of old friends — Ringo, Alla Rakha, Ray Cooper, Herbie Flowers, Willie Weeks, Al Kooper, Jim Keltner and Tom Scott— Harrison began sessions at Friar Park for what would later become *Somewhere in England*. The album Harrison submitted to Warner Brothers records in Los Angeles consisted of eight new tracks as well as two old standards, "Baltimore Oriole" and "Hong Kong Blues." It also included a suitably slick, sophisticated cover photo of George's profile merged with a satellite shot of a cloudy Great Britain. Warner Brothers unfortunately was not particularly impressed with either the music or art and tersely rejected the album. In the end, four tracks were cut — "Flying Hour," "Lay His Head," "Sat Singing" and "Tears of the World" — and in their place, four new "Harrisongs" were added, "Tear Drops," "Blood From a Clone," "That Which I Have Lost" and "All Those Years Ago." A new cover was also put together by Ray Cooper and photographer Caroline Irwin. The album, released in June 1981, spawned two singles, "Tear Drops" and "All Those Years Ago," Harrison's touching tribute to his late partner, John Lennon.

Recorded at Friar Park studios, "All Those Years Ago" was originally intended as a vehicle for Ringo. But following Lennon's murder in December 1980, it was rewritten by George to include specific references to the tragedy. On the spur of the moment, Harrison decided it would be fitting if he were joined on the session by Ringo and Paul. Happily, they agreed, thus making it the first and only Beatles' reunion of the new decade. Produced with the help of George Martin, the song included backup vocals by Linda McCartney and Denny Laine, who tells me he has yet to be paid for the session! Although it was a pretty bleak circumstance under which to record a new "Beatle" song, it was nevertheless a touching gesture. The tune rose to number two on the charts and remains a popular jukebox hit in North America to this day.

One subject interviewed for this book revealed that even in death John Lennon shared an unbreakable bond with his musical colleague, George. As Lennon was wheeled into the emergency room of Roosevelt Hospital the night of the shooting, the blood-soaked stretcher was left for a moment while the staff prepared a special room in which to work on the mortally wounded singer. Among the other patients in the ward that evening was a young father and his slightly injured toddler son. Gruesome as the sight of the gasping, rapidly fading man on the gurney was, several patients recognized him. Slowly rising to his feet, the young father dropped his son's hand, stepped up to Lennon and began to softly chant "Hare Krishna" into his ear. Just then the hospital staff pushed him out of the way in a vain attempt to resuscitate the dying man.

According to Hindu belief, however, he who hears the holy, transcendental vibration of the Hare Krishna mantra at the time of death is forgiven for all accumulated sins and is immediately transferred to Krishna's timeless heaven, Goloka Vrndavana, in the anti-material spiritual sky.

George Harrison was at home sleeping when the phone rang. The jarring noise startled him, and left him shaking. Before he even touched the receiver he felt that something must be wrong. The wavering, crackling line told him instantly that the call was from overseas — it was Louise, Harrison's eldest sister, who had lived stateside for many years. George quickly began to prepare himself for what he was sure must be bad news.

That afternoon in London, the Beatles' former promo man, Derek

Taylor, wandered over to Apple's last sorry incarnation on St. James Street to sit with the company's managing director, Neil Aspinall, and wait for the calls to start flooding in. John Lennon had been shot dead by a maniac at point-blank range on December 8, 1980, as he and Yoko were returning from a late-night mixing session for a tune called "Walking on Thin Ice." After a couple of awkward hours spent painfully reminiscing, Taylor and Aspinall said goodbye. Derek walked into the street and caught a cab to George Harrison's London office. A short time later, he summoned up the courage to finally ring George. After a decade spent on the phone, this was one call he dreaded. "George, maybe you should make some sort of statement, just to get the bastards off your back."

"I can't now," Harrison replied. There was a long pause. "Later, maybe."

The line suddenly clicked off. Taylor replaced the receiver and lit a cigaret. He didn't want to push the issue, but his better judgment told him that the longer George waited to speak, the worse it would ultimately be. Less than an hour later he was back on the line to the Park. This time George agreed to help the misty-eyed PR man formulate a statement for the press:

> After all we went through together I had and still have great love and respect for him [John Lennon].
>
> I am shocked and stunned. To rob life is the ultimate robbery in life. This perpetual encroachment on other people's space is taken to the limit with the use of a gun. It is an outrage that people can take other people's lives when they obviously haven't got their own lives in order.

After phoning the copy through to all the major London news agencies, Taylor caught the train home to Brundon Mills, his elegant country house in Suffolk, bought by a lifetime of carefully chosen words. He wept softly as he stared out the train window and, like millions of other people around the world, asked himself, "Why?"

Pete Shotton was a boyhood friend of all the Beatles, especially John, though he and George had spent a lot of time together over the years. After hearing of the murder, Pete only knew he didn't want to be alone. Jumping into his car, he drove straight to Friar Park early that afternoon. Harrison met him at the front door, and arm-in-arm they walked into the Park's mammoth kitchen for a large dose of tea and sympathy. Within a few minutes, George received a transatlantic call from Ringo, who was in the Bahamas. A little later, several musicians arrived for a session at George's home studio. Outside, one of Harrison's estate managers rummaged in an old shed for a length of chain. Hurrying to the bottom of the estate's long winding drive, he slammed the tall wrought-iron gates shut and then carefully wrapped the chain around the two inside posts. A few feet away, a small crowd of locals began to gather in front of the former Beatle's estate. There wasn't much talk. It wasn't that kind of occasion. After a few minutes, several police cars arrived, and the grim-faced bobbies linked arms, forming a human chain to hold back the steadily swelling crowd. Inside, George stood alone at a window, staring blankly at the sky. Under his breath, he chanted a mantra once or twice, then walked slowly to the studio. Like his old mate, Pete, he didn't want to be alone.

The front gates of Friar Park have never been left open since.

Lennon's death wasn't the only sadness Harrison experienced that year. On July 24, 1980, at age fifty-four, Peter Sellers, one of his oldest and dearest friends, died of a massive heart attack in the intensive-care unit of a London hospital. The comedic actor managed to survive for thirty-six hours before finally succumbing. At his bedside were his fourth wife, Lynne Fredrick, and two of his three children, Victoria and Michael. Harrison, by now no stranger to such unhappy news, was shaken but not terribly shocked. It had been the actor's fourth heart attack in sixteen years. In 1977, doctors had fitted him with a pacemaker after another near-fatal attack, and Peter had resigned himself to the possibility of an early death. Through George, Sellers had become interested in Krishna consciousness and yogic philosophy, and had even met Srila Prabhupada several times in the mid-seventies. Reportedly, toward the end of his life he no longer even thought of himself as an actor, but rather as an aspiring yogi. Although Peter's life had always been rather turbulent, his moments with George were particularly precious to both men. Harrison spoke to *Musician* magazine about their friendship:

> Long before I met him I was a fan of "The Goon Show," and then I used to see him at parties. I got to spend a lot of time with him in the sixties when I was with Ravi Shankar, because Peter liked Ravi a lot. Peter, Ravi and I all went to Disneyland in 1971. Can you imagine all of us going on the Pirate and the Haunted Mansion rides together?

Peter was a devoted hippie, a free soul. He came on tour with me in 1974, flew on the plane with us. When Peter was up, he was the funniest person you could ever imagine; so many voices and characters. But that was his problem: when he wasn't up, he didn't know who he was supposed to be. He was a considerable influence on my getting into the film world. Peter used to come to my Henley house with all these sixteen-millimeter films and we'd sit round and have dinner and watch. His favorite picture — which has been mine ever since Peter showed it to me — was Mel Brooks's *The Producers.* He kept saying, "You've got to see this movie!" Eventually we put it on, and I've never taken it off.

During the ups and downs of Harrison's post-Beatle recording career, he frequently jetted off to warmer climes, like Hawaii and Australia. In Hawaii, he would hole up in a rambling ranch-style, two-story mansion overlooking the ocean in Hana. Here he would spend his days wrestling happily with Dhani, walking along Maui's long, sandy beaches with Olivia or exploring the island paradise by helicopter with such friends as Eric and Tania Idle. There, George was almost completely unencumbered by the restraints of duty and responsibility. He was intent on making the very most of every glorious moment of freedom his vast wealth had afforded him. Sometimes, if things became a little too laid back in sleepy Hana, the Harrisons would charter a chopper to Honolulu and check into one of the big island's plush hotels for a week or two of partying, shopping or just hanging out by the pool sipping George's favorite red wine.

A frequent houseguest at the Harrisons' Hawaiian hacienda was "Legs" Larry Smith, or Mr. Smith, as George prefers. It's not surprising that the often solemn guitarist enjoyed the company of the zany Smith so much. He is unendingly witty, impeccably charming and, in the nicest possible way, crazier than a bedbug. Although Larry was often out of work, his lack of ready cash was of no concern to the often extravagant Harrison. If Smith needed a ticket to fly from England to join the happy threesome, George would be happy to provide it. If Smith lacked a telly for his bedsitter, Olivia could just run out and pick one up. For a time in the early eighties, the two friends even wore identical wristwatches, presents from Olivia, and on more than one occasion, Smith has been surprised with several very chic and expensive suits from some of London's smartest boutiques. To top it off, his small flat is furnished almost entirely with leftover odds and ends from Friar Park. "Legs'" long-time friendship is clearly one of George's greatest private pleasures. He and Olivia go to great lengths to preserve and protect the eccentric artist's fragile psyche.

For more than two years in the mid-eighties, I lived off and on with Larry in Hambleden, just a stone's throw from Friar Park and the often wonderfully unreal world of George and his friends. I drank at the same pubs, ordered Chinese from the same seedy take-out restaurants, rode in the same cabs and choked back the same gooey black Afghan hash favored by Oxfordshire's rock elite. There is nowhere else in the world like Henley. Rod Stewart can often be seen shopping for tea biscuits at Waitrose. Mary Hopkin might be motoring past in an old auto left over from her marriage to millionaire record producer Tony Visconti. Living within a ten-mile radius are David Gilmour; Alvin Lee; sixties crooner Joe Brown; half of Deep Purple; and more old roadies, big-time groupies and part-time dope dealers than you can shake a Thai stick at.

To the faithful, George Harrison reigns supreme as the peaceful valley's mystical, feudal lord. In Henley, a late-night invitation to Friar Park is like a summons to court in the bygone days of Camelot. Harrison is more a living icon to these people than a man, the exiled Dalai Lama of rock and roll holding forth in his walled city of pleasure. His calls are carefully screened, first by the Park's office personnel, then by Olivia. Even the message on Harrison's answering machine was recorded by his wife, in her uniquely American twang. George's sultry voice is not heard by anyone outside the inner circle. One wrong number, and his carefully manicured cover might be forever blown.

My entrée into this topsy-turvy world of show-biz elitism was, of course, Larry, perhaps George's best friend. After a while, the day-to-day goings-on at Friar Park became rather a daily topic of conversation between us. Larry was always very guarded, however, and I got the feeling that his relationship with Harrison was definitely the one bright spot in his otherwise rather dreary existence. More than once he has tantalized me with some juicy tidbit of Harrison gossip, only to immediately pull back the very moment I began to respond. One time in Toronto, he waved a private letter George had written him from Hawaii under my nose, only to snap it back into his coat pocket as soon as I was able to make out who it was from.

Kirsten Grepne is also a regular visitor to the Park. "We have had some very happy times up there," says Kirsten. "George is into car racing,

"Legs" Larry Smith *(right)*, Olivia, George and London gallery owner Mary Tambini at the Park. Note the photo of Adolf Hitler on the wall just behind Harrison. For years now the former Beatle and his buddies Derek Taylor and Smith have shared a kind of comical fixation with the führer.
DELIBERATE ALCHEMY ARCHIVES

George and Paul Simon perform on the American television show "Saturday Night Live" during the mid-seventies. NATIONAL BROADCASTING CORPORATION

so he has numerous videos of different international events. He loves it. Actually, he's very unaffected and genuine. He has a great sense of humor and is very much a gentleman. If you didn't know he was in show business, he might be a gardener or a nursery worker. Occasionally, he has the odd expensive jacket on, but in general, he could be anybody." Kirsten also reports that George enjoys a good old-fashioned sing-along with his friends from time to time. She remembers him once singing Culture Club's "Black Dog." He is, she says, quite fond of the music of Boy George.

Olivia does most of the cooking — with her specialty being Mexican vegetarian fare — but occasionally Harrison has been known to rustle up a pretty mean cheese and mushroom omelet. The Harrisons' drink of choice is often French champagne, though just as regularly George likes a cold bottle of ale, just like any other working gardener at the end of the day.

According to just about everyone who knows the family, young Dhani is the light of George's life. Rumor has it that a long-time aide and close friend of Harrison's was dismissed in the mid-eighties after twenty years of loyal service, because he was overtly homosexual and Olivia felt he might be a bad influence on their young son. In spite of the Harrisons' devotion to their son, one or two people once close to George say they often feel quite sorry for Dhani. "When I used to go up there he always rushed out the door like mad to get me to play with him. He'd hang on me practically the whole time I was there. It was like he was somehow isolated in that big, drafty house. It seemed as though he wasn't getting the male companionship he apparently needed and therefore was often quite starved for attention. When I knew him, George and Olivia didn't generally get up until two or three in the afternoon anyway, so what is the kid supposed to do?"

By all accounts Olivia would love to have another child, as she is concerned about the effect that so much inherited wealth and power will have on an only child. Still, for the moment anyway, Dhani remains reasonably unspoiled by the milieu in which he lives. "He's very nice-looking," says Kirsten. "I'd put it down to him just being a nice boy, well-mannered and polite. He goes to a local primary school, which is their choice. They obviously feel that they would like him to be brought up to be just as normal as possible."

"I stopped being as crazy as I used to be because I want this child to have a father a bit longer," George has said. "Also, with a child around I can realize what it was like to be my father. At the same time, you can relive certain aspects of being a child. You watch them and have all these flashbacks of when you were the kid. It somehow completes the generation thing."

He also wants very much to teach his son the proper values. "I try to make him realize that not everyone lives in such a big house or has as much money as we do. That's a very difficult lesson to teach someone in his position, but we think we do a good job."

By all accounts, George's second marriage has worked out far better than his first. Old friend Mukunda also feels that the atmosphere at the Park is very much improved since 1974, when Olivia first moved in. "I think people change one another when they become husband and wife. He certainly seems happier than he was before. George and Olivia are very domesticated. They really vibrate on the same wavelength."

There is controversy, however, about the relationship. "Sometimes when I'm up there I can *feel* George looking at me in a very strange way," says one young woman friend. "I have no doubt that if I gave him any positive signals at all he wouldn't hesitate to make the best use of them." There have been numerous rumors of Harrison's amorous adventures over the years. One of the most scandalous of all — next to his alleged affair with Ringo's first wife — concerns the wife of a member of one of the sixties' most popular bands. Around Henley, the scuttlebutt is that Olivia once walked in on George and the vivacious young woman making love at a friend's home. A mutual acquaintance mentioned the story to a few people around town; it got back to George, and he was subsequently banned from Friar Park. However, the incident remains largely unsubstantiated and might turn out to be just another ugly rumor.

There were other strains on the marriage as well. For a brief time in the early eighties, George reportedly became rather too fond of staying up all night snorting cocaine with the neighborhood lads. Back in 1983 and 1984 when I was in Henley, the dreaded white powder was everywhere. More than once I've heard the phone ring at Larry's in the middle of the night and heard Smith talking to George about taking "the Frenchman" to the Park right away. "The Frenchman" being their code word for coke when speaking over the telephone. Grabbing a small green hand-painted suitcase, Larry would rush around the tiny flat gathering up his stash for the late-night rendezvous with Harrison. And it didn't much matter if one of Larry's many girlfriends happened to be staying over, either. When George beckoned, Smith invariably went running.

Perhaps the best quip I've heard about the infamous "devil's dandruff" comes from Derek Taylor, who has said, "Coke makes you feel like a new man. Then the new man wants a line!" This, apparently, was what happened to George and his friends. One internationally famous rock star close to Harrison told me that he used to get so desperate for a toot that, to stop himself, he would hide his stash under the nanny's mattress every evening. Once the rather innocent young lady went to bed, there was no way he could get to it.

Sources close to the Harrisons have suggested that at first George went out of his way to hide his recreational drug use from Olivia, which served to erect a wall of secrecy between the normally close couple. After a time, though, he finally confided in her but the naturally conservative young woman found it very difficult to either accept or undestand.

One episode I was made aware of in 1983 illustrates the intensity of the Henley-on-Thames cocaine connection. One evening, a well-known bisexual piano player arrived unexpectedly at the Park with a lovely young lady in tow, with the intention of spending a rollicking evening partying with Mr. and Mrs. Harrison. George, however, was fresh out of blow, so politely excused himself to call a local dealer who might be able to help. Not having anything to party with would have been a serious lapse of pop-star etiquette. But luckily, the diminutive superstar hadn't come empty-handed and with a flourish produced a small plastic bag containing five grams of fluffy Peruvian flake. Pouring the entire contents onto a small mirror, he gestured to George to take the first hit. Acting under the old doper's axiom that the first line is always the best, Harrison bent over and deeply inhaled the oily powder through a thin glass straw. "Go on, mate, have another."

"Give us a minute," said Harrison. "I've just had a huge one. Let me enjoy it."

Harrison's appetite for coke was allegedly so strong during this time that when he went on holiday to Hawaii or Australia, the joke goes, Henley's many dealers had to go on the dole until he returned.

This is not to say, however, that all George did during the early eighties was sit on his ass hoovering up cocaine. He also found time to record one disastrous album. *Gone Troppo*, released on October 27, 1982, was Harrison's most disappointing LP since the abysmal Zapple release, *Electronic Sound*, in May 1969 (Zapple being the experimental-music subsidiary of Apple). Although both the performance and the production were quite competent, the songs were contrived and, even worse, uninteresting. "You can't imagine how many mixes I heard of that thing," says

Robbie Cain. "It seems like every time I dropped by the Park [George] was running to the stereo with a new cassette. Especially the song 'That's the Way It Goes.' He was intent on getting it all just as good as possible."

Despite such efforts, though, the album sold so poorly it failed to even make the charts and within a couple of weeks, retailers began reluctantly shipping it back to the warehouses. Said Harrison at the time:

> It's one thing writing a song, taping it and then making a record, but I wasn't interested in promoting myself after all that had happened with the Beatles. I'm not into myself in that manner, and I think you have to be quite a bit of an egomaniac to go touring and promoting yourself all the time. There was a bit of pressure once I got started making my own records, because everyone expected each of us to be as powerful as the Beatles, which was an impossibility.
>
> Sometimes, you release an album and the record company just about ignores it, and so many people don't even know it's out. And I'm not about to jump up and down shouting, "Hey, folks, look at me! I'm cool and groovy!" That's not what George Harrison is all about.

George soon discovered that the record business of the early eighties was far different from what it had been a decade earlier. "They all started to cut corners; and a lot of artists as well. The radio stations, at least in America, seemed to me to be going crazy; they didn't have direction. There was a general confusion going on . . . . Why did *Gone Troppo* fail? Because I was fed up with people saying, 'Oh, maybe you should do this kind of song, or that kind of song.' It's time to give up when you're not allowed or expected to be yourself. My music is like me. It's a reflection of me. And if you don't like that, or if it doesn't fit in, I'm not going to come out there and pretend I'm Michael Jackson, because I'm not."

About the only good thing to be said about the album was that it sported what was perhaps the most original and inventive cover art since *Sgt. Pepper*. "Legs" Larry Smith was the illustrator. In a 1983 interview he spoke about the unique project:

> I go through periods of being absolutely drunk and periods of great sobriety, and this, happily is my sober period coming up. I always do

174

things in tens, so I spent ten years drinking, and now I'm on my second year of being sober. I'm beginning to work a bit more these days, and last year I was offered the chance to design an album cover for George. In fact, design the entire campaign, which included a lot of things: the songbook, two posters and basically overseeing the whole *Gone Troppo* campaign. Actually I should say it in an Australian accent because "gone troppo" literally means "gone a bit loony." It was a wonderful thing to do, it was a great few months working on it. I kept whizzing over to George's every couple of weeks. As the album tracks were forming, so were the designs and stuff in my head. George took a real interest in the process. Of course, he already knew a lot about the process of making album covers, obviously, because he's done so many. But he was very involved in this particular one.

In September 1983 Larry and George teamed up once again, this time with Harrison's company, Hand Made Films, for work on the movie *Bullshot!* Unfortunately, it was another creative bomb. But the involvement of Smith was one of the highlights of the otherwise obtuse British comedy.

On *Bullshot!*, Larry continues: "Well, I'm singing the theme song of the film, the last Hand Made production to come out . . . and George is yodeling as well . . . I also play a little bit in the film itself . . . . I [tap danced] with a crazy band of ruffians, rapscallions and ragamuffins, but we didn't exactly have a name . . . There was Zoot Money, Ray Cooper, myself and two other wonderful gentlemen who were in this band of street urchins and buskers with us. Why, we spent half the day wanking and the other half dancing!"

Following the commercial failure of *Gone Troppo* and a rather rough patch finding audiences for the various Hand Made epics, Harrison all but dropped from sight for the next few months. He spent his time shuttling between Friar Park, Maui and Hamilton Island, Australia. Sometimes he took along Dhani and Olivia, and sometimes he didn't. Gone were his pristine spiritual aspirations. When long-time Krishna devotee and old friend Dhananjaya Dasa dropped by the Park one rainy, windswept evening late in 1983, Harrison entertained him only briefly, then showed him the door, saying gruffly, "Why don't you go out and get a couple of beers down you? You're boring!" When the astounded devotee reminded

George that it had been almost ten years since they had last seen each other, Harrison responded, "So? We're not lovers. Why are you here, anyway?" The embarrassed young man didn't bother to contact him again. "Poor George is really in *maya* [illusion]," he told me over the phone later that week. "I've never seen him looking so bad."

Part of the problem, of course, was Harrison's enduring paranoia over the assassination of John Lennon. At a rare public appearance with Olivia at the famous Chelsea Flower Show in May 1984, he commented briefly after being stalked by reporters all afternoon. "After what happened to John, I'm absolutely terrified. I don't like being seen in public. I never know who might be around, and I don't like being photographed." The musician was then hustled away to a waiting car by two very menacing-looking private bodyguards.

"George is a man of great dignity," commented Deep Purple keyboard player Jon Lord in 1984, "and does not swing around saying that he is an ex-Beatle . . . . He has a great sense of humor. I, however, do not agree with his policy of not talking to the outside world, and have told him so. George just feels he has said all there is to say about himself."

Clearly, the once-dynamic musician and poet was adrift on a sea of inner turmoil and hopelessness. "All this stuff about the Beatles being able to save the world was rubbish," George told me in 1983. "I can't even save *myself*. It was just people trying to put the responsibility on our shoulders. The thing about the Beatles is that they saved the world from boredom. I mean, even when we got to America the first time, everybody was running around with Bermuda shorts on, brush cuts, and braces on their teeth. But we didn't really create any great change, we just heralded that change of consciousness that happened in the sixties. We went along with it, that's all. The whole Beatles thing is a nightmare. I don't even like to talk about it. I just hate it."

"The simple fact of the matter is that with George, the hunger is not there as it was in the old days," says Harrison's hometown acquaintance, Barrymore Barlow, the former Jethro Tull drummer. "He's not huddled in the back of the van anymore scrambling to get to a gig. Of course you can't blame him for it. You have to look at the lifestyles of these artists, the extravagant way they live and what they do from day to day. It's all part and parcel of what they ultimately create."

Olivia, meanwhile, worked out with Henley's other trendy wives at a local aerobics studio run by a woman from California, attended art openings and became a familiar face at the most exclusive couturiers in

London. Her life with George seemed to be on hold as she waited for her dangerously depressed husband to come around.

All that beautiful music, it seemed, had somehow spiraled its way right out of his world-weary soul. Looking ages older than his forty years, George Harrison confronted an unknown future. "You can walk away from it all at any time," he told Jon and Vicki Lord one evening in 1983 over drinks. But not even he looked as if he believed it.

X

DEUS NON FORTUNA*

Forging a Life

Past is gone, thou canst not that recall
Future is not, may not be at all
Present is, improve the flying hour
Present only is within thy power.

SIR FRANK CRISP

Heaven is made for us
Eternity draws near
And this false world
Consumes our desires.

MEDIEVAL PROVERB

* "God Not Fortune," the ancient Harrison family motto

GEORGE HARRISON IS PRETTY STINGY WHEN IT COMES TO ACCEPTING
as real anything he feels is born of the ego, whether it's his or anyone else's.
Even the things he seems to genuinely love, like auto racing, producing
movies and his music, are not exempt. In this, Harrison keeps true to his
covenant to try to eliminate the tricky I, me and mine that have vexed
him all his life. It is a measure of the man's dogged integrity that he simply
refuses to compromise when it comes to playing out the tired role of Beatle
George. All he wants these days is to be himself, which, of course, is pretty
much a full-time job for anyone.

By the early eighties, one of the few areas of George's life for which
he had not yet lost enthusiasm was car racing. "I've liked it since I was a
kid," he has said. "It's a bit more interesting for me now because of having
friends like Jackie Stewart. I know all the back-room stuff that goes on.
Perhaps a bit too much of it!"

In late 1977, George traded his beloved BMW for a souped-up
Porsche Turbo. He and Olivia then broke the car in by driving it up and
down the twisting country roads of France, eventually meeting up with
Ringo and a lady friend to take in the Monte Carlo Grand Prix.

Like Hare Krishna and the mind-expanding hallucinogens of yes-
teryear, fast cars were becoming George's new obsession. At Friar Park,
the garage was soon filled with several customized Porsches, as well as an
awesome Ferarri Dino Spyder. Eventually, Harrison's passion for racing
extended beyond simply adoring the monster machines of racing and
began to focus on the daredevil lifestyles of the men who drove them.

One of Harrison's closest friends during this period was Scotsman
Jackie Stewart, though soon Harrison also began palling around with such
racing greats as Ronnie Petersen, Mario Andretti, Barry Sheene and James
Hunt.

Stewart, who was at his peak as a driver during the heyday of the
Fab Four, was an unabashed Beatles fan. Harrison impressed Stewart with
his encyclopedic knowledge of racing and of Stewart's celebrated career.
Whenever he spoke publicly of his interest in racing, George never missed
an opportunity to praise the diminutive driver. "Jackie did a lot for the
sport and was criticized for it," he told England's *Motor* magazine in the
mid-eighties. "People moaned and groaned when he wore fireproof suits
and talked safety, things which are so obvious and practical now, but at
that time were being put down. Another thing was, he always projected
the sport beyond just the racing enthusiast, which I think is very important."

One of Harrison's favorite racing tales involves his good friend Barry Sheene, a former world motorcycle champ. Sheene was considering moving into car racing, and he took George along for a ride one morning when he tried out a supercharged Surtees TS19. As Harrison told *Motor*:

> Barry persuaded John Surtees to let me have a go. But John said, he's got no gear. So Barry rips off his fireproof vest and says to me, "Here y'are, you can wear this." I just slipped on this sweaty old thing and borrowed John's crash helmet, got in the car and said, "I'm not going to go fast because I haven't even walked around Brands Hatch, let alone driven around!" So he said, "Oh, shit, you had better get in the road car."
>
> Well, we went bombing off round the track in his Mercedes and he was saying things like, "Keep it over to the left here; make sure the tail doesn't flick out too much here, fourth here," and so on. I was just hanging on for dear life. I got in the F1 car and thought, "Now, what did he say?" Then, while I was pulling away in the pit lane, trying not to stall it, I was thinking, "God, it's windy in the car." I hadn't even remembered to close my visor . . . . It was like, wow . . . those wheels just dig in round the corners. I didn't go very fast. I just signed the chitty saying that if I killed myself, it wasn't John's fault.

As time went on, Harrison, no longer content to remain on the sidelines, financed Grand Prix motorcyclist Steve Parrish to the tune of more than $25,000. Eventually he even summoned up the nerve to climb behind the wheel of a Lotus 18 at a much-publicized charity event at Britain's Donington Racetrack.

All things considered, Harrison's motor racing involvement may have been fun for the singer, but it did nothing to help put him back on track either musically or spiritually. Even George had to acknowledge that, compared with his former high-flown philosophical and humanitarian ideals, watching a load of grown men racing around in a circle for hours on end was little more than a mildly stimulating diversion. Clearly, George Harrison had traveled a long way from the days when he said he considered work to be the single most important thing in his life.

Perhaps one of the most bizarre aspects of George's personality is the fascination he shares with friends Derek Taylor and "Legs" Larry Smith regarding Adolf Hitler. Harrison and his pals are not Nazi sympathizers, but they still find something undeniably fascinating about the Führer. "It's just that they appreciate the unparalleled degree of his absolute madness," says a friend.

> Old Adolf was so incredibly off his rocker that he eventually con-vinced himself that only his version of reality was the right one. What's even more surreal was his ability to convince so many others, as well. While there have certainly been a lot of loony leaders throughout history, none so far as George and his mates are con-cerned possessed the same magical ability to drag so many other so-called sane people into his desperate psychosis along with him.
>
> They only dig him in a silly Monty Pythonesque way, like a crazy character from some mad movie. As far as the horrible things he actually did, they, of course, are certainly just as appalled as anyone else.

Such tidy rationalizations fall short of explaining why Harrison keeps so many photos of Hitler around his house. Allegedly, he even displays a huge German swastika at times. Although Hitler borrowed the symbol of eternal life from Harrison's beloved Hindus, it is still difficult to imagine just how the normally peace-loving ex-Beatle justifies his attraction to such evil.

It may be that Smith and Taylor are the real instigators of this rather sick fantasy. Larry has been working for years now on a zany musical based on the life of the silver-tongued Austrian, entitled *Call Me Adolf*. With such song titles as "I've Got a Braun New Girl" and "The Führer Burger," it is doubtful that any legitimate producer would consider bringing it to the stage, no matter how clever or catchy the ex-Bonzo Dog man's calypso-inspired rhythms. When I was living in Henley, I answered a telephone call one evening from Derek Taylor. For fifteen minutes the semiretired publicist talked about which photographer had taken the most charismatic shots of the Führer. Strange indeed.

While most of the world thinks of George as a fine musician and a dedicated part-time philanthropist, in 1978 the mercurial minstrel star-tled everyone by changing hats to become the spiritual powerhouse behind Hand Made Film Productions Ltd., a London-based partnership put together by Harrison and his personal manager, Denis O'Brien, an American investment banker and attorney. The infant company's first project was to bail out the controversial Monty Python parody, *The Life of Brian.* The twisted spoof of Brian, a reluctant and immensely unqualified messiah, has grossed more than $24 million in the United States since its release in October 1979. "I'm not a businessman," Harrison hastened to remind the media at the time.

> I hate business and all that wheeling and dealing . . . I go to the set and I'm meant to be the big cheese, but I'm not really.
>
> Making films is sort of a hobby for me. I can't let it become too serious, otherwise it'd become work. And once I'd got myself out of that star rat race, I promised myself I'd never work again. Well, I do work, but I want it to be enjoyable, not just a slog.
>
> We make the sort of films that I want to see, which means we pick up a lot of films the other companies don't want. We're not looking for enormous success: we're just lads mucking about making interesting films that wouldn't normally get made. You see, you've got to take chances to make something worthwhile.

A prime example of George's desire to produce "small" films that might otherwise have been overlooked was Hand Made's compelling *Mona Lisa*, the bittersweet love story about an ex-con from London who becomes infatuated with a high-priced bisexual hooker. Starring ace character man Bob Hoskins, the film captured the best-actor award at the 1986 Cannes Film Festival and an Academy Award nomination in the same category. George was delighted.

"In the midst of all these *Rambo*-type films that are just crash, bang, wallop, there's a shortage of films that touch the human side," he has said. "Although *Mona Lisa* is about the seedy side of life, it's funny, and the characters are very real. It allows the audience to use their intelligence. That's pretty rare; most of those American films treat the audience as if they were idiots."

All things considered, Hand Made was doing quite well until rock singer Madonna and her hot-tempered actor husband, Sean Penn, entered the scene in 1986. George put up more than $15 million to film the dismally predictable screenplay by John Kohn and Robert Bentley called *Shanghai Surprise*, a romantic adventure comedy starring the naughty Penns. The story was set in the 1930s with pop goddess Madonna cast as a missionary, of all things, with Sean, a fast-talking soldier of fortune. Not surprisingly, the hokey film was universally maligned by critics and became the laughingstock of Hollywood. Most of the real action, however, occurred offscreen, and the saucy British tabloids had a field day reporting it all in minute detail.

Day by day, the accusations by cast members against the media flew. The crew claimed the press had somehow gained admission to the strictly closed set and bugged the ladies' washroom. Madonna reportedly had her purse stolen, and the film's beleaguered director complained that a set of Polaroids important to the filming were nicked by some overzealous reporter. Sean clashed with the *paparazzi*, and at least one lawsuit was filed in the London courts. Receiving word of this madness at Friar Park, Harrison concluded that the only way the media would ever back off and allow them to carry on filming was to immediately call a press conference, in hopes that, once given full access to the troublesome couple, Fleet Street would call off its dogs. Before the frantic afternoon was over, however, Harrison found himself more of a referee than a moderator.

"You're all so busy creating a fuss, then writing all about it as if *we* staged it for publicity," Harrison lectured the assembled press as the petite Madonna looked on innocently. "Stars are just people who become famous. They are just human beings. After a while, the only thing left is to knock them . . . I think it's fortunate that I'm able to relate to Sean and Madonna because of my past."

Matters were made worse when, at the last moment, Sean backed out of the press conference. "Where is Penn?" shouted several reporters, to which Harrison tersely replied, "He's busy working."

Another journalist asked Madonna whether she fought with her husband. "Do you row with your wife?" Harrison retorted. When asked what the obviously ticked-off Harrison expected from the media, George stated simply, "*non*-animals." To which a reporter shot back, "Speaking of animals, is it true Sean was giving orders to everyone on the set?"

"Sean was an actor chosen as a feisty young guy," said George. "Apart from all the bullshit, he's a nice talented actor. You have to separate the two things, his job and his ability to do that job, and the sensationalism because he happens to be married to Madonna."

When asked what she thought of her Beatle boss, Madonna replied, "He's great, very understanding and sympathetic. He's given me more advice on how to deal with the press, though, than how to make movies."

Harrison tried to protect his young stars, but after the movie was finished and had flopped, he was characteristically blunt in his appraisal. "Penn is a pain in the ass," he complained to the *Hollywood Reporter*. Of

Madonna, he was quoted in *Cleo* magazine as saying, "All this aloofness and star stuff . . . it's just bullshit. I'm not trying to be nasty. She's probably got a lot in her that she hasn't even discovered yet, but she has to realize that you can be a fabulous person and be humble as well."

And how did Harrison compare the hoopla surrounding the Penns with the global madness of Beatlemania? "In the sixties and seventies you couldn't have a decent life because you were always being persecuted by the media. Fame does make relationships difficult; the difference is, we never lost our sense of humor. I think that's why people liked us, not just because of our music, but because we said funny and outrageous things and were real people."

The only redeeming aspect of *Shanghai Surprise* was its brilliant soundtrack, which was arranged chiefly by George. Although unreleased on record, the movie's title track — an exotic otherworldly duet between Harrison and Vicki Brown, singer Joe's wife — indicated that George Harrison was still a musical force to be reckoned with.

During the eighties, the smooth operation of Hand Made Films kept Harrison as busy as he cared to be, but he still longed to top the international charts once again with a hit album. After the *Gone Troppo* disaster, he wasn't so quick to release his musical creations on record, but he was still recording. Having the luxury of a state-of-the-art studio in his home, George often wandered into the pastel-colored control room to lay down demos of recently written songs, or to jam with friends. Among the tunes recorded about this time were the proposed title track for Terry Gilliam's wonderfully bizarre film *Brazil*, several versions of a wild instrumental called "Sooty Goes to Hawaii" and a Mexican folk song—with his father-in-law, of all people.

These few tunes represent only the recorded material *known* to exist from this period in George Harrison's musical life. There are no doubt dozens more demos and even finished recordings that have yet to be released. Even at Harrison's lowest, professionally and perhaps personally, it was his music that held him aloft. For years the stubborn singer steadfastly refused to play the role of pop star, and it angered people that he would dare shun the worldwide audience that had given him so much. Harrison, however, disagreed. "Everyone creates their own destiny," he has said. "If the karma isn't there, no one can really do anything for, or even against, another person. The responsibility rests with each individual alone. I am what I am because of me, not you."

As intent as George was to lie low musically during the latter half of the decade, by January 1986 he experienced a head-on collision with his intentions for an early retirement.

The unlikely harbinger of Harrison's renewed enthusiasm for his art came in the person of affable country rocker Carl Perkins, one of George's earliest and most important musical influences. Perkins, fifty-three, was musically as sharp as ever, but in the past few years had experienced a serious slump in his remarkable career. How ironic that the musician who helped inspire Harrison to pick up the guitar in the first place would be responsible for bringing him back into the fold. Seriously considering retirement himself, Perkins and his manager cooked up the idea of a star-studded rockabilly extravaganza featuring the crème de la crème of the pop world in a concert designed to showcase Perkins's exceptional talents.

To that end, he videotaped personalized invitations to Ringo Starr, Eric Clapton, Dave Edmunds and George Harrison, among others. Within ten days, Perkins had received notes of acceptance from everyone he contacted, with the exception of George. "I thought I was wasting my time," Perkins told *People* magazine, "because I read that [George] would never go before a live audience again." Several days later, however, Harrison enthusiastically accepted, and the big show was on. Perkins's people engineered a lucrative deal with the Cinemax cable network in the United States to air the one-hour special, entitled "Blue Suede Shoes."

Perkins wasn't the first of his peers to try to coax George onstage after his unhappy tour of America in 1974. New York promoter Sid Bernstein attempted to get the Beatles together for an internationally televised benefit in 1979 to aid Cambodia's boat people, as did United Nations secretary general Kurt Waldheim for another concert later that year. Both efforts, unfortunately, failed to convince Harrison to perform, as did Bob Geldof, Live Aid's patron saint, in his bid for the guitarist to participate in his star-studded extravaganza. Until Carl Perkins ambled onto the scene in late 1985, most observers doubted whether Harrison would ever perform onstage again.

The evening of the taping on October 21 at Limehouse Studios in London, Harrison was a bundle of nerves. He paced anxiously around his dressing room, chain-smoking. Then, balancing on the arm of a sofa, he tuned and retuned his vintage Gibson. Onstage, sensing George's butter-flies, Perkins immediately eased the situation by inviting the studio audience to clap along to "Everybody's Trying to Be My Baby." Even before the end of that first song, Harrison had regained his confidence and was relishing the spotlight after so many years spent in self-imposed exile. "George Harrison, everybody!" yelled Perkins as the audience exploded with applause. "Don't he look good?" By the time Perkins, George and Dave Edmunds ripped into the classic "Your True Love," it was obvious to everyone that Harrison was having the time of his life.

Meanwhile, Olivia stood watching in the wings, not caring that the large tears streaming down her face were making a mess of her makeup. George was back! Not just for his old buddies and the fans, but for her and Dhani and, best of all, for himself. It was perhaps the single happiest night of their married life. "I haven't seen him so happy in years," she commented later to the press. "That's my old George!"

From that moment on, Harrison was suddenly wild about sharing his music with the world once again. When he wasn't in the studio writing or recording, he was jamming with friends at any one of a number of exotic locations. In February 1987, he and Bob Dylan went along to see guitarist Jesse Ed Davis play with the Graffiti Band at the Palomino Club in North Hollywood. Before the night was out, both of them were up onstage playing their hearts out. Overnight, it seemed, George Harrison was one of the hottest things going, and this time he was ready for action.

George's next major public appearance came four months later on June 5 and 6. The occasion was the Prince's Trust annual charity concerts at Wembley Stadium, just outside London. As usual, rumors of an impending Beatles reunion were rife, but came to nothing. When the lights went down and Eric Clapton stepped up to the mike to introduce George and Ringo, the audience was ecstatic. Even half a loaf, when it came to the Beatles, was something to shout about. Harrison and Clapton traded lead licks on a stinging version of "While My Guitar Gently Weeps," followed by a remarkably touching rendition of "Here Comes the Sun," which also featured George's new musical colleague, Jeff Lynne, formerly of the "Beatlesque" Electric Light Orchestra.

And why did George finally decide to do the shows? "Well, it's for a good cause, and I happen to like Prince Charles and his Trust," he told reporters backstage. Once again, though, playing for a live audience did tend to make him rather tense. "It's nerve-racking," he said. "I haven't done a show in England since 1966, and the last time I did a concert tour was 1974. So it makes you nervous when you don't perform all the time."

Another big night for George Harrison came on January 20, 1988, when the Beatles were inducted into the Rock 'n' Roll Hall of Fame at the Waldorf Astoria Hotel in Manhattan. "They had long hair, scruffy clothes, but they had a record contract," joked presenter Mick Jagger at the official ceremony. "I was almost sick! I'm really proud to be the one who leads them into the Hall of Fame." It was a fabulous night. George, Ringo, and Julian and Sean Lennon took the stage with an unusually frumpy-looking Yoko Ono. The only damper on the splendid evening came when word leaked out that Paul McCartney would *not* be making the trip.

"I was keen to go and pick up my award," said McCartney in a brief statement later issued to the press, "but after twenty years the Beatles still have some business differences, which I had hoped would have been settled by now. Unfortunately they haven't, so I would feel like a hypocrite waving and smiling with them at a fake reunion." This was a difficult period in Paul's life. His latest album, *Press to Play*, was selling poorly, with the single, "Press," finding only limited airplay in the United States and abroad. Some observers, including Harrison, wondered whether George's recent success had made Paul somehow uneasy. At the time of the Hall of Fame induction, Harrison's single, "Got My Mind Set on You," was securely in the Top Ten and was rapidly heading for number one. For once, Beatle Paul was dramatically overshadowed by his introspective mate from Wavertree.

Despite the controversy over Paul's absence, George was enthusiastic when the time came for him to say a few words on behalf of the group. "I don't have much to say," he began, "because I'm the quiet Beatle. We all know why John can't be here, and I'm sure he would be, and it's really hard to stand here supposedly representing the Beatles . . . what's left, I'm afraid. But we all loved him so much . . . . It's unfortunate that Paul's not here, because he was the one who had the speech in his pocket!"

Later, at the award's all-star jam session, George and Ringo were joined by Mick Jagger, Bob Dylan, Little Richard, Bruce Springsteen, Elton John and several other big names in a raucous version of "I Saw Her Standing There." One can only imagine how badly McCartney must have felt watching the great event on the telly back home in England. Even one of his infamous killer joints would not be able to obliterate the hurt and depression he must surely have felt.

George's next album release following the *Troppo* fiasco took place on November 2, 1987 with the issuance of *Cloud Nine*. This time, however, George was fully committed to the album's promotion and made himself available to the media. George had wanted to call the album *Fab* as a joke on his Beatle past, but changed his mind after seeing pictures of

George on a tour of ISKCON's mammoth temple building project in Mayapur, India, in 1982.
STEVEN ROSEN

"Legs" Larry Smith and Dhani in Maui, 1983. Deliberate Alchemy Archives

himself standing with his guitar in front of a panorama of puffy clouds. "I racked my brains for weeks and months to try to think of a title because I was trying not to have a song title," Harrison explained. "In the end, I just had to have a title; otherwise the album would never come out, so as it was clouds on the cover, we called it *Cloud Nine.*"

Among the talents assembled for the album were Harrison's usual stable of superstar musicians, including Ringo, Jim Keltner, Gary Wright, Ray Cooper and Eric Clapton. Two relative newcomers to Friar Park Studios were Elton John and Jeff Lynne. Lynne, who had been an especially enthusiastic Beatles fan, was thrilled to have the chance to work with one of his long-time heroes.

Lynne and Harrison were originally brought together by well-known British rocker Dave Edmunds. For years Harrison had been an ardent admirer of Lynne's extravagant Electric Light Orchestra. He explains his reasons for finally settling on Jeff as his musical cohort and producer:

> Choosing Jeff to produce was part of a long process. I tried to think of someone who could complement my music without overpowering it . . . and also somebody I had respect for as a producer or as a songwriter. Then I thought, well, Jeff has a lot in common with me. I mean, a lot of his songs sound like the old pop songs or even like some old Beatle songs . . . .
>
> I spent a year calling him and talking to him and hanging out with him. When it seemed like we were getting to be good buddies, I said, "Well, actually, I'm going to make an album." He said, "I'll help you a bit."

The album contains ten balanced and well-crafted tunes written by Harrison or Harrison and Lynne with one tune by veteran rocker Rudy Clark called "Got My Mind Set on You." "The tune's been stuck in my head for twenty years, although this version is quite different from the original," said George at the time. "It rocks along quite nicely."

He was right. Within three months it was the number-one single in America, with the LP comfortably situated in the Top Ten as well. It was the first time George had been blessed with a number-one hit since 1971 with "My Sweet Lord."

Although many people think of *Cloud Nine* as Harrison's comeback album, he bristles at the description. "People think in terms of a comeback, but I really haven't been anywhere," he said. "I've been here the whole time. And this record is very much the music I wanted to make. I don't think it's right to try to mold what you do to the current market. It's like the old song says, 'Take me as I am or let me go.' This is me; I hope I fit in, but I'm not going to lose any sleep over it."

The sweeping success of *Cloud Nine* went a long way toward helping to reestablish Harrison as the major artist his many fans always knew he was. For the first time in several years, the name George Harrison once again translated into big ratings on radio and television. The album opened up a whole new audience of young people to the life and work of this reluctant world legend.

Harrison was also part of the magnificent Traveling Wilburys. It was the first time George had been a member of a bona fide band in eighteen years. The inception of the big-name group, consisting of Bob Dylan, Roy Orbison, Tom Petty, Jeff Lynne and George, came about rather casually as an outgrowth of the *Cloud Nine* project. In April 1988, Harrison was in Los Angeles tying up some loose ends regarding the hit album when Warner Brothers asked him to consider recording a new tune to back the twelve-inch extended-play version of the popular "This Is Love." George, however, couldn't really think of anything he had back at Friar Park that would be suitable, and so mentioned his dilemma to Lynne and Orbison during dinner at a swanky L.A. eatery. George suggested that the three of them book some studio time and record something together. Orbison and Lynne readily agreed. Bearing in mind the time restraints placed upon the trio by the record company, Lynne suggested asking Bob Dylan if they might use his private studio, located in the garage of his luxurious Malibu home. A few days later, Harrison dropped by Tom Petty's house to pick up a guitar for the session and on the spur of the moment invited Petty to join them. George and Jeff wrote the tune together the next day in the studio and then persuaded Dylan to sit in as well.

After the five old pros layed down the musical tracks for the upbeat folksy number, they sat together in Dylan's garden on a lunch break and wrote the words. "Okay, you guys," said Harrison, smiling broadly. "We're all supposed to be such hot stuff, how about some lyrics, then?" Spying a discarded cardboard box sporting a bright orange sticker that said "Handle With Care," they had their title, and by the time it was over a major hit as well.

So pleased were they with the finished track that Harrison decided it was far too good to simply be stuck on the B side of one of his singles. He suggested they do an album together. The sessions went on for about two weeks, with some additional work done in England at Friar Park. The group's sidemen, dubbed "The Sideburys" by Harrison, included Jim Keltner, percussionist Ray Cooper, Ian Wallace playing the tom-toms and Jim Horn wailing away on sax.

Lynne and Harrison came up with the name Traveling Wilburys from a joke bandied about during the long, eight-month sessions for *Cloud Nine*. Apparently, someone coined the phrase "tremblin' willburys" to describe the unwelcome little screwups and glitches that occurred while they were recording the multitrack masters, and the name stuck. A full year before he even thought of putting a group together, Harrison had some custom guitar picks made up that had "Traveling Wilburys" printed along the top.

In keeping with the zany spirit of the album, the five co-conspirators decided to adopt bizarre new Wilbury names. Harrison took the alias Nelson Wilbury, while Dylan assumed the name Lucky; Petty was Charlie T., while Orbison was called Lefty. The album, entitled *The Traveling Wilburys: Volume One*, was released on October 25, 1988, on the newly formed Wilbury Records label. Distributed by Warner Brothers, it contained ten tracks and a tongue-in-cheek history lesson on the origins of the Wilbury clan penned by one Hugh Hampton E. F. Norti-Blitz, better known as Monty Python's brilliant Michael Palin.

MTV in America premiered the classy "Handle With Care" video with much fanfare on October 25, and within a few short weeks the album was selling like hotcakes on both sides of the Atlantic. There was talk of a Wilbury tour, scheduled for sometime in the new year, while Volume Two was eagerly awaited by a whole new breed of Wilburymaniacs.

The staggering success of the band was a boon to George after so many years of brooding over the musical malaise of the record industry. But it was the energizing effect on Roy Orbison's career that secretly pleased Harrison the most. In his final interview, Orbison praised Harrison for persuading him to join the Wilburys at a time when his solo career had taken a turn for the worse.

The Wilburys' curtain however came crashing to the ground with the sudden death of Orbison on December 6, 1988, from a massive heart attack. Upon hearing the tragic news, George told reporters that Roy was "a sweet, sweet man. We loved Roy, and still do. He's out there, really, his spirit. You know, life flows on within you and without you. He's around."

No matter how high any of the surviving Beatles fly in their solo careers, there will always be the inevitable push for them to get back together just one more time. Ringo has bitterly joked that even when there's only one Beatle left, people will still be asking, "When are you getting back together?"

The public's endless fascination with the Beatles is a frustrating mystery to George. "The Beatles can't save the world — we'll be lucky if we can even save ourselves," he once said. Still, he knows the fans will always dream of a reunion, even if it includes only three-fourths of the original group. "I have a problem, I must admit, when people try to get the Beatles together," George told *Rolling Stone* in 1988. "They're still suggesting it even though John is dead . . . . I suppose the three of us could get back together, but it was such a struggle to find our individual identities after the Beatles."

Harrison says that although things are far better than they were in the past, he still finds Paul McCartney rather "too moody" for his liking, and admits he is "more friendly now with other musicians. Our relationship is quite good but there's no reunion of any Beatles," he told the Associated Press in 1989.

We have been having dinner together. We are friends now; it's the first time we have been this close for a long time. But it doesn't mean to say that we are going to make another group or anything. You know, I could go out and try to become a superstar, and I tell you, if I went to an agent and a manager and checked myself out and practiced a bit, I could do it. But I don't really want to do that. That's being a kamikaze pop star, the tours and everything. I don't have to prove anything . . . . I don't want to be in the business full-time because I'm a gardener: I plant flowers and watch them grow.

Although he has lived most of his life in the never-ending scrutiny of the media, George Harrison has always managed to be very much his own man. Whereas most people tended to see the Beatles as public property, Harrison has remained aloof. Like a lotus flower growing in an oily, polluted river, its delicate petals never getting wet, George Harrison with few exceptions has emerged unscathed from a potentially lethal dose of fame and fortune. Even when he fell — and fall he did, many times — he never surrendered his ideals or his stubbornly held right to live out his life the way *he* wanted to. Often down, but so far never out, his steadfast allegiance to his unique vision of truth has served him well. In a brief, dark world, George's faith has been a beacon of reflected light for himself and countless others, too. "For the forest to be green, each tree must be green," Harrison has often quoted the Maharishi as saying. "The movement you need is on your shoulders," said another old friend.

Still, no matter how you say it, or which way you choose to look, Harrison's truth belongs to all of *us* as well. And maybe that's what we admire most about the man after all these years. Like the simple Chauncey Gardener in the film *Being There*, George Harrison is carefully cultivating his own small garden of truth, season after season. Which, of course, is really just about all any of us can do.

APPENDICES

GEORGE HARRISON'S FAMILY TREE

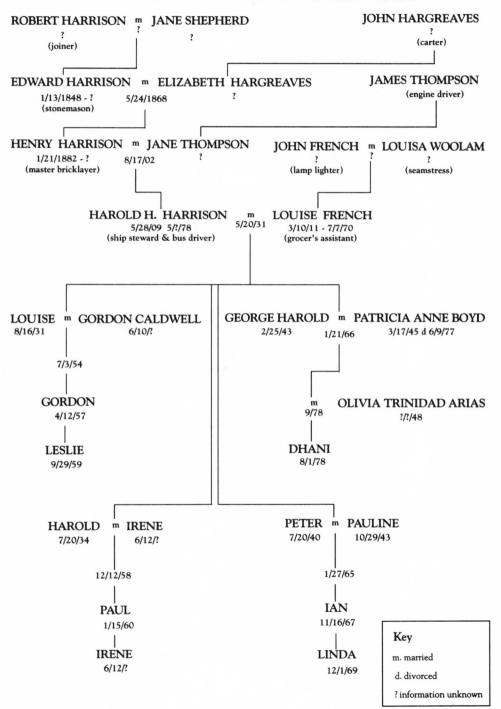

ROBERT HARRISON m JANE SHEPHERD
?   ?   ?
(joiner)

JOHN HARGREAVES
?
(carter)

EDWARD HARRISON m ELIZABETH HARGREAVES
1/13/1848 - ?   5/24/1868   ?
(stonemason)

JAMES THOMPSON
(engine driver)

HENRY HARRISON m JANE THOMPSON
1/21/1882 - ?   8/17/02   ?
(master bricklayer)

JOHN FRENCH m LOUISA WOOLAM
?   ?   ?
(lamp lighter)   (seamstress)

HAROLD H. HARRISON   m   LOUISE FRENCH
5/28/09 5/?/78   5/20/31   3/10/11 - 7/7/70
(ship steward & bus driver)   (grocer's assistant)

LOUISE m GORDON CALDWELL
8/16/31   6/10/?

GEORGE HAROLD m PATRICIA ANNE BOYD
2/25/43   1/21/66   3/17/45 d 6/9/77

7/3/54

GORDON
4/12/57

m   OLIVIA TRINIDAD ARIAS
9/78   ?/?/48

LESLIE
9/29/59

DHANI
8/1/78

HAROLD m IRENE
7/20/34   6/12/?

PETER m PAULINE
7/20/40   10/29/43

12/12/58

1/27/65

PAUL
1/15/60

IAN
11/16/67

IRENE
6/12/?

LINDA
12/1/69

Key

m. married

d. divorced

? information unknown

197

A Conversation, 1988

The following is from a tape recording of George Harrison's Toronto press conference in February 1988 at the Sutton Place Hotel, held to mark the release of *Cloud Nine*:

QUESTION: You've said that you aren't especially taken with today's music, and that the spirit doesn't seem to be there as it was in earlier years. When you were getting ready to record *Cloud Nine*, what did you do to get away from that?

GEORGE HARRISON: Well, I set out not to use drum computers and midi-keyboards for a start, because most things these days are done like that. I wanted to make records like in the past, basically, and just have things a bit more human.

QUESTION: George, how did you and Jeff Lynne meet and come to work together on this project?

GEORGE: I thought that he'd make a good producer for me, and Dave Edmunds, who was a neighbor of mine, had worked with him before, so I asked if he ever saw Jeff to tell him I'd like to meet. That was back in about 1985. So then he came over and had dinner and we just kept in touch and by the end of '86 I said, "Well, I'm going to make a record soon, do you want to do it?"

QUESTION: Were you familiar with his work with the Electric Light Orchestra?

GEORGE: Oh, yeah, that's why I wanted to call him up and meet him. I thought he'd be perfect for me, which he was.

QUESTION: George, I had a dream last night that you and everybody on your new record decided to go on tour. (*Laughter*) Is there any chance that dream is going to come true?

GEORGE: Possibly. But I don't fancy being the star of the show. I wouldn't mind being part of a show doing some of my tunes, but I wouldn't like the responsibility of being out there all on my own . . . If I'm going to do anything at all I had better do it pretty soon, otherwise I'll be on crutches or something. (*Laughter*)

QUESTION: You've said that you weren't that crazy about doing a big video, but "Got My Mind Set on You," I think, is hilarious. I wondered how much of your own sense of humor was actually a part of that, and do you feel better now about the possibility of doing more videos?

GEORGE: You mean the video where I did the back flip? (*Laughter*) Well, you know, my humor is such that I have to be able to have something funny happening around me so I can be deadpan, as I'm not really into acting. I think that works very well for me. The director was a guy called Gary Weiss, who incidentally directed *The Rutles*, so he's a very funny fellow himself. He thought of having a simple setting like that room and making it move so I could just sing straight, play straight and everything else would be the joke.

QUESTION: What gave you the idea to do the video for "When We Was Fab?"
GEORGE: Well, basically I just thought it would be nice to write a song with the sound of the '67 or '68 period. It was just a whim, really. Especially since at that time I was with Jeff Lynne in Australia and I know how much he likes the old stuff, so I started out to write it. I didn't have any lyrics at the time, so it was tentatively called "Aussie Fab" because it was reminiscent of the Fabs and written in Australia. So it was purely a trip down memory lane.

QUESTION: I read where your song "Just for Today" came to being after you saw a pamphlet from Alcoholics Anonymous, which is kind of a different way of getting a song, isn't it?
GEORGE: Well, really, if you're into the songwriting mood, then anything can trigger it. I had these three friends who were all in AA at my house one night back in 1983, and this guy showed me a brochure that was called "Just for Today." It seemed so nice, you know, a nice idea, to try and live through this day only. I mean, it's not just for alcoholism. It's good for everybody to remember that we can only live today and the only thing that really exists is now. The past is gone, the future we don't know about. So it's like an extension of the "be here now" idea. I thought it would make a nice song, so I wrote it. But it's good also for AA, I think. Maybe we could make it into a TV commercial.

QUESTION: George, at one time you considered calling your latest album "Fab" and then you changed it to *Cloud Nine*. Why?
GEORGE: If you know about the connotations of the past, of the sixties and the Fab Four and all those things, then it's a good little joke. But if you don't know about all that, it sounds a bit pretentious. Also, when I looked at the photograph on the album sleeve with me and all these clouds, it looked more like Cloud Nine.

QUESTION: Now that you're a solo performer, how different is it for you?
GEORGE: Well, it's totally different, really. In those days, it was the four of us. We just went into the studios and made some records, went out on tour, then went back in the studio to make some more records. That was it, really. Nowadays, it's a big business and it has to be coordinated. With the Beatles, after around 1964, we just had to put the records out and people rushed out to buy them. It's not like that these days. You have to work with the record labels and coordinate releases and do a lot of promotion work. I'm on my own, whereas in the past I had three other smartasses with me all cracking jokes. (*Laughter*)

QUESTION: Do you miss that?
GEORGE: I miss that side of it, yes. We used to have good fun at press conferences. They used to be really great because there would always be somebody with a wisecrack. I do miss that side of the Fab Four, I admit.

QUESTION: George, do people treat you as some sort of religious icon these days?
GEORGE: No, not really. I think people seem to give me some respect, however, which is quite nice.

QUESTION: The last couple of years you seem to have had some reservations about getting too involved with the record business.
GEORGE: Yeah, I got a bit tired of it back around about 1980. I just felt there was no point. The way the music was going, I couldn't relate to it. I just thought, "Well, I've got a lot of other things to do so I might as well have a rest." Nowadays, I never consider that I'm going to be out there with this record and people may not buy it or whatever. I didn't even think about that. I mean, if you have a flop, it's a flop. I think you have to just make something that you enjoy yourself and see what happens. And I've had enough success in my life that if I fail, it's okay.

QUESTION: What's more difficult, being a Beatle or an ex-Beatle?
GEORGE: I think being one was much more difficult. I mean, it was fun for a long time, but there was so much pressure on us. It became really tiresome and it was good, in a way, to dissipate that energy that there was with the four of us together. You know, let it go away so that we could have some semblance of a life. Otherwise, it would have just been madness continually.

QUESTION: Has your attitude about today's music changed?
GEORGE: Yeah, I think the main reason for the problem, you know, was the recession. It went through all kinds of businesses, through radio, the music industry, and people didn't seem to know what was happening. They were confused about what was supposed to be good. I think they lost all direction, and I just didn't want to be a part of that. Maybe the only change was that I've changed, and I just felt it would be fun to do an album and see what happens.

QUESTION: Do you hear anything today that you like, any artists that capture your imagination?
GEORGE: Bob Dylan! (*Laughter*) I do, but unfortunately not so much in pop music or Top Forty. My favorite music at the moment is this Bulgarian choir. It's called the "Mysterious Voices of Bulgaria" and it's the most brilliant vocals, it's quite beautiful.

QUESTION: How did you get involved with [Monty Python] in the first place?
GEORGE: Well, I've just been friendly with them for a long time and when they were beginning *Life of Brian*, the original film company backed out as they were right into pre-production. A friend of mine asked if I could think of any way to help. I asked my business manager and he thought about it for a few days, then he came back and said, "Yeah, okay, we'll be the producers." So we borrowed the money from the bank and formed Hand Made Films. I did it because I wanted to see the film. I couldn't stand the idea of it never being made.

QUESTION: Could you tell me what a typical day in the life of George Harrison is like?

GEORGE: It's different all the time . . . . Like last week I've been just getting up, going for a run around my garden, eat a bowl of Scotts porridge oats, and then right into the recording studio. Go out for dinner, finish off what I was doing, and go to bed. That kind of thing. Or get up, go to London to the office. Varied things, you know. There's no typical day, really. Get on the Concorde and fly to New York!

QUESTION: Paul McCartney is currently working with Elvis Costello. When I heard the news I was very surprised and I thought, what a combination, to have the intelligence of a Costello with a great pop songwriter like McCartney. Do you think that Paul was in a bit of a rut and was looking for someone, I dare say, to work with similar to John Lennon?

GEORGE: I wouldn't say that Elvis Costello is like John Lennon at all. Personally, I don't think he is. I don't think he even comes close, anywhere near John. I mean, Elvis Costello is pretty good *but* . . .

QUESTION: I just meant that he was a very thoughtful writer.

GEORGE: Well, he wears glasses! (*Laughter*) But I think Paul definitely was in a rut. In a "Rutle." (*Laughter*) And yeah, I think it's good. He should work with various people and hopefully he'll find somebody who will actually tell him something because most people who work with Paul are afraid to say anything to him. And I think that's no good. You need to have somebody you can work with who'll tell you you're no good when you're no good. Otherwise, it's no help at all. So I look forward to hearing what they come up with. It may be good, I don't know.

QUESTION: That brings us to the inevitable question. I read something a couple of weeks ago where you said that there was a possibility that you, Paul and Ringo might do some work together.

GEORGE: Yeah, well, Paul has asked, you know. Suggested maybe the chance of me and him writing something together and, I mean, it's pretty funny really because I've only been there about thirty years in Paul's life and now he wants to write with me. But I think it's maybe quite interesting sometime to do that.

QUESTION: Would you tell him if he was no good?

GEORGE: Sure. For the last few years I've spoken my mind to him. Whenever I felt something, like [Paul's film] *Broad Street*, which I thought was a big mistake. Not making the film, because I quite enjoyed it myself, but the idea of trying to write and do everything yourself. That's the mistake. I think the only barrier between us now is our astrological signs. Some of the time we get on pretty well and the rest of the time I find that I don't really have anything in common with him.

QUESTION: Does that surprise you, after all these years together?

GEORGE: Well, I think if you have a relationship with somebody else, you have to be able to trust each other, and to do that you have to be able to talk to each other straight. The thing with Paul is one minute he says one thing and he's really charming, and the next minute, you know, he's all uptight. Now we all go through that, good and bad stuff, but I think by now that we've got to find somewhere in the center. Anyway, he's getting better. *Broad Street*, I think, humbled him a bit. (*Laughter*) You know, he's going to be okay.

QUESTION: What about pop's so-called new social conscience?

GEORGE: I haven't heard it yet. (*Laughter*)

QUESTION: Like Live Aid . . .

GEORGE: Oh, yeah, well all that's good. I like anything like that. Sometimes I feel it's a shame that it's down to musicians to go around saving the world, however. I think some of the politicians should get their fingers out occasionally.

QUESTION: Can you tell us about your son, Dhani? Is he a budding musician?

GEORGE: Yeah, he's nine and a half and he's got a pretty good ear for music. He enjoys all kinds of music. From Mozart to Ravi Shankar to Little Richard and Chuck Berry. He's playing the piano a little bit and I think he's going to be okay. I'm not saying that's what he's going to be in his life, but he's hopefully got a good musical ability for his age.

QUESTION: Does he understand that his father was a Beatle?

GEORGE: Now he does. You can't turn on the television without seeing something to do with the Beatles, can you? As I was just saying to somebody earlier, kids pick up on the Beatles through the old movie *Yellow Submarine*. See, I made a point of not saying anything about them to him. But by the time he was five he wanted to know how the piano part to "Hey Bulldog" went, which completely threw me because I didn't understand where he'd heard a song like that. I haven't heard that myself really. Then I realized it was in *Yellow Submarine*.

QUESTION: If you did go on tour, how much of a consideration would your feelings about being out in public bother you?

GEORGE: I'm not really worried about being in public. I'm not crazy about being in crowds, though. This is even just walking in an airport or being in a football match or something. It's nothing to do with people looking for me or threatening me. I just don't like crowds. I don't like traffic jams either. I don't like that situation. I prefer peace and quiet. But I don't really worry about anything like that. The only time is if you get a mob of people who know you're going to be somewhere. I mean, there's always fanatics at rock concerts. But to do a tour wouldn't be any trouble because you have all the security and you know the way in and the way out and it's no bother, really. I don't fear for my life like some people try to suggest. They've said, since John Lennon got killed, I would go and hide and I've had a big fence built around my property. I had a fence around my property back in 1965, so there's no change, really.

QUESTION: So you don't have any bodyguards?
GEORGE: No. Absolutely, on my honor. I don't even have a roadie!

QUESTION: When you have jam sessions at your home studio, do you do Beatle tunes and do you remember all the words?
GEORGE: No, I don't know *any* of the words. (*Laughter*) Occasionally I can remember one or two, but we don't do Beatle tunes. More likely to do Everly Brothers or Chuck Berry tunes.

QUESTION: You've proven yourself to be an astute businessman away from the music business. Do you feel that you have rounded out your life more at this point in your career? Do you feel satisfied with what you've done?
GEORGE: Having done the film company and the various things we're talking about, I think they impress everybody else more, so their *concept of me* is now more rounded out. They all think, "He's smarter than we thought," but it doesn't impress me.

QUESTION: I'd like to know about your religious philosophy. Are you still promoting it or do you keep it to yourself these days?
GEORGE: Well, I keep it to myself unless somebody asks me about it. But I still feel the same as I felt back in the sixties. I lost touch with the Krishnas when Prabhupada died, maybe ten years ago or something. I know one or two of them, but I don't really hang out with them anymore. I used to go and see the old master, you know, A.C. Bhaktivedanta, quite a lot. He was real good. I'm still involved but it's something which is more like a thing you do inside yourself. You don't actually do it in the road. It's a way of just trying to get in touch with yourself . . . I still write songs with it in there in little bits and pieces, but lots of songs that are unfinished say various things but maybe I say it in different ways now. There's a song on this album which is straight out of Yogananda, "Fish on the Sand" it's called.

QUESTION: Do you think that you were underused during the Beatle years?
GEORGE: Yeah, possibly, but the Beatle producer, George Martin, said recently how he always felt sorry because he concentrated more on them and he should have paid more attention to me. He said, "I hope you'll forgive me." But I'm quite happy with my role in the Beatles. You know, it split up because of all those problems, there were too many songs. Because we got too close to each other, but I'm quite happy with the way things went. I feel that whatever I am now, I always have been that, you know. Maybe different things have taken longer to reach the surface or whatever, but I'm who I am and I am not really that much different to how I was then. Maybe I'm more able to express it or maybe people are more interested now in what I have to say. Because in the sixties and the early seventies they thought I was a loony. Because I just went to India, did all that bit.

QUESTION: George, you seem like such a modest person despite the incredible events of your life.

GEORGE: I'm not a fanatical person. About astrology or anything, really. I don't want you to get me wrong, but I'm a Pisces, and Pisces is like that. One-half going where the other half's just been. I tend to be more withdrawn or whatever. If you look at Pisces, they're the spiritual ones who often get pushed around, but these days it's really mostly clear sailing.

A Diary of Events
1926–1988

1926 — Harry Harrison goes to sea as a steward with the White Star Fleet.

1929 — While on shore leave in Liverpool, Harry meets his future wife, Louise French.

May 20, 1930 — Harry and Louise marry in a quiet civil ceremony in Liverpool.

1931 — The Harrisons' first child is born. She is named Louise after her mother.

1934 — The Harrisons' second child is born. This time they name the little boy Harold, after his father.

September 19, 1934 — The Beatles' future manager and mentor, Brian Epstein, is born in suburban Liverpool.

1936 — Harry Harrison comes ashore after ten years at sea. Following months of sporadic unemployment, he lands a job as a bus conductor.

1937 — Harry Harrison is proudly promoted to the position of driver.

1940 — The Harrisons' third child, Peter, is born.

July 7, 1940 — Richard Starkey, later Ringo Starr, is born just after midnight at 9 Madryn Street, the Dingle, Liverpool.

October 9, 1940 — The future founder and leader of the Beatles, John Winston Lennon, is born at the Oxford Street Maternity Hospital during a particularly vicious German air attack.

1941 — Peter Randolph Best, the Beatles' first real drummer, is born in Madras, India.

June 18, 1942 — James Paul McCartney is born at Walton Hospital, Liverpool. He is the first child of James and Mary.

February 25, 1943 — George Harold Harrison, the Harrisons' fourth and final child, is born at 12 Arnold Grove, Wavertree, Liverpool.

March 17, 1945 — Patricia Ann Boyd, George's future first wife, is born.

1949 — The Harrison family moves into a roomy council house in the Liverpool suburb of Speke. They had made their application some eighteen years earlier.

1950 — The Maharishi Mahesh Yogi arrives in Hawaii, where he forms the first Western chapter of his Spiritual Regeneration Movement.

1954 — After attending Dovedale Primary School, George is enrolled at the Liverpool Institute also attended by Paul McCartney and his younger brother, Michael.

1954–55 — George and schoolmate Paul McCartney get together for the first time and begin bashing out Lonnie Donegan material in the front room of the Harrisons' home at 25 Upton Green, Speke.

1956 — Young George wangles the purchase of a cheap box guitar from a school chum for three pounds ten shillings. After bashing away for several months, George, his brother Peter and some friends form the Rebels, playing their first gig at the Speke British Legion Club.

January 16, 1957 — A former wine cellar on Matthew Street in Liverpool is opened under the name of the Cavern Club as a showcase for local jazz and skiffle groups. The playing of rock and roll is strictly forbidden by order of the management.

Late 1957 — Through McCartney, George is introduced to John Lennon at Wilson Hall in Garston.

February 6, 1958 — George is accepted as a member of the Quarrymen.

June 19, 1959 — George leaves school without graduating. His plan is to look for a solid full-time job while playing in the Quarrymen part-time.

November 1959 — The Quarrymen disband only to immediately reform as Johnny and the Moondogs and then later as the Silver Beatles. George briefly adopts the professional name of Carl Harrison as a tribute to his long-time rock and roll idol, the great Carl Perkins.

Spring 1960 — The Silver Beatles tour Scotland as a backing group for singer Johnny Gentle. By this time, Lennon's schoolfriend Stuart Sutcliffe has joined the group. All the fledgling quartet needs now is a full-time drummer.

August 1960 — Paul McCartney invites Pete Best to accompany the band on a tour of Hamburg's notorious Reeperbahn as their new drummer.

August 18, 1960 — The Beatles begin performing at Hamburg's Indra Club, owned by German businessman Bruno Koschmider.

October 1960 — The band makes its first professional recording with members of rival Liverpool group, Rory Storm and the Hurricanes, at Akustik Studios in Hamburg.

November 21, 1960 — The Beatles' stay in Germany is interrupted after George is found to be underage by German immigration officials and is unceremoniously deported. The other Beatles soon follow and end up back in Liverpool feeling beaten and dejected.

January 1961 — The Beatles begin appearing regularly at the Cavern Club, which has since undergone a change of heart about rock and roll music.

March 1, 1961 — Allan Williams, the Beatles' first manager, writes a letter to the German consulate in Liverpool requesting that the group be allowed to return to Germany now that Harrison has finally come of age.

April 1961 — The boys return to Hamburg to appear at the Top Ten Club.

July 1961 — The group returns home to Liverpool minus Stuart Sutcliffe, who has fallen in love with German photographer Astrid Kirchherr. Paul generously takes over Stu's duties on the bass.

October 29, 1961 — Raymond Jones walks into the NEMS record store in Liverpool's Whitechapel shopping district and asks proprietor Brian Epstein for a copy of "My Bonnie" by a group called the Beatles.

November 9, 1961 — Intrigued that a local Liverpool group has actually cut a record, Epstein and his personal assistant, Alistair Taylor, attend a lunchtime session at the Cavern, where they witness the Beatles in action for the very first time.

December 3, 1961 — Epstein and the Beatles meet at NEMS to discuss the possibility of his taking over management of the group.

January 1, 1962 — The Beatles travel to London for an audition at Decca Records, during which George sings "The Sheik of Araby." Recording manager Dick Rowe subsequently turns down the group, confiding to Brian that "groups with guitars are on the way out."

April 10, 1962 — Stuart Sutcliffe dies at the age of twenty-one of an apparent brain hemorrhage.

April 11, 1962 — The Beatles fly to Hamburg to begin a seven-week engagement at the Star Club.

June 4, 1962 — George Martin signs the Beatles to Parlophone Records, a small offshoot of the vast EMI empire.

August 16, 1962 — Brian Epstein summons Pete Best to his office, where he is rather unceremoniously given the sack. He is told that Ringo Starr will replace him as the Beatles' drummer.

December 18, 1962 — The Beatles begin their final engagement at the Star Club.

February 22, 1963 — The Beatles' first major record, "Please Please Me," hits the coveted number-one position on the British pop charts.

November 4, 1963 — The Beatles play a royal command performance.

February 7, 1964 — The Beatles and their entourage land at Kennedy Airport in New York, where they experience their first taste of the intensity of American Beatlemania.

March 2, 1964 — George Harrison meets model Pattie Boyd during the first day's filming for *A Hard Day's Night*.

March 27–29, 1964 — John and Cynthia Lennon are joined by George and Pattie aboard a private plane bound for a vacation in the Irish countryside.

April 4, 1964 — The Beatles hold the top four positions on the American pop charts.

August 1964 — The Beatles make their second trek to the U.S. to begin a rigorous twenty-five-city tour.

September 11, 1964 — George forms his own music publishing company, Mornyork Ltd., later called Harrisongs.

January 27, 1965 — George Harrison acts as best man at his brother Peter's wedding.

August 15, 1965 — While in the States on yet another tour, the Beatles are visited by Bob Dylan in their suite at the Warwick Hotel.

October 26, 1965 — The Beatles are awarded MBEs by Her Majesty Queen Elizabeth.

December 23, 1965 — George proposes to Pattie Boyd while driving into London for a party at Brian Epstein's home.

January 21, 1966 — George and Pattie marry at the Epson Registry Office in Surrey. Paul McCartney is the only Beatle in attendance.

June 1966 — George Harrison meets his musical guru, Ravi Shankar, for the first time during a dinner party at actor Peter Sellers's home. A few days later, Ravi and his portly *tabla* player, Alla Rakah, give a private performance for George, the other Beatles and a few select friends.

August 29, 1966 — The Beatles perform their final North American concert at Candlestick Park in San Francisco.

September 14-October 22, 1966 — The Harrisons travel to India, where George begins a period of intensive training on the sitar. Though George is under the direct tutelage of Ravi Shankar, it is Shankar's young protégé, Shambu Das, who sees to Harrison's day-to-day instruction.

January 1, 1967 — Brian Epstein, Eric Clapton and the Harrisons are asked to leave Annabol's nightclub in London because George is not wearing a tie.

February, 1967 — Pattie becomes a member of the Maharishi's Spiritual Regeneration Movement and thereby introduces the Beatles to Transcendental Meditation.

August 7, 1967 — The Harrisons visit San Francisco's infamous Haight-Ashbury district with Beatle crony Derek Taylor but George comes away disillusioned, commenting that the hippies seem to him more like "Bowery bums."

August 26, 1967 — The Beatles, their wives, Mick Jagger and Marianne Faithfull, among others, are formally initiated into the Maharishi's International Meditation Society in Bangor, North Wales.

August 27, 1967 — Beatles' manager Brian Epstein is found dead in his Belgravia townhouse from a suspected drug overdose.

December 10, 1967 — George Harrison and Ravi Shankar appear on a broadcast taped at the United Nations buildings in New York and in London.

January 7, 1968 — George Harrison flies to Bombay, India, where he commences work on the recording of tracks for the *Wonderwall* album. The sessions take the better part of ten days to complete.

February 16, 1968 — The Harrisons, along with John and Cynthia Lennon, return to India to begin their teacher's training course in Transcendental Meditation with the Maharishi. Paul and Ringo arrive on February 19.

March 1968 — Harrison disposes of his shares of Northern Songs when his contract expires.

May 22, 1968 — George and John attend the opening of a shop with designer John Crittle in Chelsea called Apple Tailoring (Civil and Theatrical).

December 4, 1968 — Harrison informs the staff at Apple that several members of the California Hell's Angels may be visiting Apple in the near future.

January 10, 1969 — Following a bitter row among all four Beatles, George walks off the *Let It Be* movie set over plans for a new Beatle tour.

January 21, 1969 — Harrison is fined £100 for assaulting a French photographer the previous spring.

February 7, 1969 — Harrison is admitted to a London hospital in order to have his infected tonsils removed. He's out of commission for about ten days.

March 12, 1969 — Sgt. Norman Pilcher and members of Scotland Yard's drug squad raid the Harrisons' Esher home. Both Pattie and George are arrested. They are later released from the Esher Jail after posting a £500 bond.

March 31, 1969 — The Harrisons are fined £250 each for the possession charge after pleading guilty on the advice of counsel.

April 7, 1969 — George is quoted in a London paper as saying he will never again keep any drugs in his home.

July 11, 1969 — Harrison records vocal tracks for the Beatles' international hit "Something."

July 26, 1969—Harrison plugs the Hare Krishna movement's world-famous *Rathayatra* Festival in a series of radio spots paid for by Apple.

August 22, 1969 — Apple's unlikely new singing discovery, the Radha Krishna Temple, has their first record, *The Hare Krishna Mantra*, released in the U.S.

September 1969 — His Divine Grace A. C. Bhaktivedanta Swami Prabhupada arrives in London to meet with his disciples. He is picked up at Heathrow Airport in John Lennon's chauffeur-driven Rolls-Royce and immediately spirited away to Tittenhurst Park. There he meets privately for several hours with George, Yoko and John. For Harrison, the deeply moving experience helps to intensify his devotion to the practice of Bhakti Yoga.

Mid-September 1969 — Louise Harrison is hospitalized in Liverpool with a cancerous brain tumor.

September 1969–January 1970 — George Harrison produces an album's worth of Vedic mantras for Apple's Radha Krishna Temple.

May 1, 1970 — While in New York, George Harrison and Bob Dylan record enough tracks together to fill an album. For some reason the project is scrapped and the material never officially released.

November 1970 — George's triple solo album *All Things Must Pass* receives worldwide critical acclaim.

November 25, 1970 — The Harrisons fly to New York to introduce the Apple group Badfinger to the New York press.

December 26, 1970 — George's "My Sweet Lord" becomes the number-one tune on the *Billboard* singles chart, remaining on top for four weeks.

December 31, 1970 — Paul McCartney files suit against the Beatles and Company seeking legal dissolution of their partnership.

February 23, 1971 — During a series of unpleasant encounters with London traffic cops, George loses his license and is banned from driving for a year.

March 12, 1971 — An official Receiver is appointed in the Beatles' pending litigation.

July 27, 1971 — George announces plans for the Concert for Bangla Desh and releases a single named for the war-torn country.

August 1, 1971 — Harrison and a galaxy of stars including Ringo Starr, Bob Dylan, Eric Clapton, Ravi Shankar, Billy Preston, Leon Russell and Badfinger play two shows at Madison Square Garden in New York in aid of the refugees of the Bangladesh-Pakistani war.

February 8, 1972 — The Official Beatle Fan Club closes up shop forever.

February 28, 1972 — Only days after the return of George's driving license, George and Pattie wreck their car near Maidenhead.

October 1972 — Scotland Yard's Sgt. Pilcher is jailed for six years, found guilty of planting dope on several innocent people.

April 1973 — John, Ringo and George terminate their contract with Allen Klein's ABKCO.

April 26, 1973 — The Material World Charitable Foundation is founded in England as Harrison's official charity, receiving portions of royalties from his music publishing and records.

May 1973 — George releases the popular single "Give Me Love."

May 30, 1973 — George's LP *Living in the Material World* is released.

November 2, 1973 — George, Ringo and John sue Allen Klein, who in turn sues George, Ringo and John.

February 1974 — At a Paris press conference, George announces the formation of his own label, Dark Horse Records, to be distributed by the American company A&M.

September 16, 1974 — Official announcement of George's forthcoming international tour with Ravi Shankar.

September 23, 1974 — Ravi Shankar's Music Festival From India, sponsored by the Material World Charitable Foundation (and produced by George), commences a series of shows in London. The concert is filmed by Dark Horse Records, although it is never released.

November 2, 1974 — George plays the first date of his solo tour at the Pacific Coliseum in Vancouver. A total of fifty shows in twenty-seven cities are included on the tour.

December 13, 1974 — Thanks to a chance backstage encounter with Jack Ford, son of the American president, George, his father Harry, Billy Preston and Ravi Shankar are invited to the White House for an afternoon visit with the president.

October 3, 1975 — George's *Extra Texture* LP is released in England (September 22 in the U.S.). On it is a song entitled "Ladies and Gentlemen His Name Is Legs," George's musical ode to his long-time crony, "Legs" Larry Smith.

November 20, 1976 — George appears on "Saturday Night Live," performing a duet with singer Paul Simon.

June 7, 1977 — In celebration of the Queen's Silver Jubilee, George attends an outdoor children's party in Henley.

June 9, 1977 — George and Pattie Harrison are divorced in a London court.

November 18, 1977 — Srila Prabhupada dies in Vrndavana, India, at the age of eighty-one.

December 17, 1977 — George plays unannounced at the Row Barge Pub in Henley, just around the corner from Friar Park.

August 1, 1978 — George and his new companion, Olivia, celebrate the birth of their first child, Dhani, born at the Princess Christian Nursing Home in Windsor.

September 2, 1978 — George marries his long-time live-in lover, Olivia Trinidad Arias, in a private civil ceremony in Henley. Only the bride's parents are invited to attend.

May 19, 1979 — Ringo, Paul and George perform an impromptu concert in the back garden of Eric Clapton's home in Ewehurst, Surrey. The occasion: Clapton's marriage to George's first wife, Pattie.

August 22, 1979 — George's limited-edition leatherbound autobiography, I ME MINE, is published by Genesis Publications.

August 1, 1980 — George and business partner Denis O'Brien form Hand Made Film Productions Limited.

December 8, 1980 — John Lennon is cut down by a barrage of bullets outside his home in Manhattan by a deranged "fan." He is pronounced dead on arrival at Roosevelt Hospital. The world mourns his loss. George is reportedly in a state of shock.

February 26, 1981 — A New York judge orders Harrison to pay $587,000 in damages to Bright Tunes, copyright holders of the song "He's So Fine," from which the proprietors allege that the ex-Beatle has plagiarized portions of his megahit, "My Sweet Lord."

June 5, 1981 — George's *Somewhere in England* is released in Great Britain (June 1 in the U.S.).

November 5, 1982 — George's *Gone Troppo* LP is released in England (October 27 in the U.S.). For the cover, Harrison commissions "Legs" Larry Smith to produce one of his bizarre surreal collages, which works beautifully. The record, however, is a certified flop.

July 25, 1983 — The three remaining Beatles have a few drinks together in a London hotel.

December 1, 1983 — George, Ringo and Paul meet with Yoko Ono at the Dorchester Hotel in London, trading strategies for the business of their jointly owned company, Apple Corps Limited.

November 30, 1984 — Derek Taylor and George Harrison attend a literary party in Sydney, Australia, for Taylor's limited-edition autobiography, *Fifty Years Adrift*.

December 14, 1984 — George joins Deep Purple on stage during one of their concerts on the Australian leg of their world tour.

October 21, 1985 — Ringo and George appear in a television special called "Blue Suede Shoes," a musical tribute to their boyhood idol, Carl Perkins.

March 6, 1986 — Hand Made Films holds a press conference in London following a particularly troubled shooting for the film *Shanghai Surprise*. George and pop singer Madonna meet the press in an effort to defuse the bad publicity.

June 19, 1986 — George is one of thousands in attendance at an anti-nuclear rally at Trafalgar Square.

July 18, 1986 — George writes an article in the *Henley Standard* admonishing the local planning board, which has approved the destruction of the city's only cinema to make way for a supermarket.

December 4, 1986 — George and his fellow protesters win their fight to save the Regal Cinema.

February 19, 1987 — George jams with Bob Dylan, John Fogerty and Taj Mahal at the Palomino Club in Hollywood.

March 15, 1987 — The Harrisons attend the BAFTA Awards at a swanky London Hotel.

March 27, 1987 — Ringo and second wife Barbara, along with George and Olivia, attend Elton John's birthday party.

November 2, 1987 — George's *Cloud Nine* is released in the United States.

January 20, 1988 — George, Ringo, Yoko Ono and Sean and Julian Lennon attend the Beatles' induction into the Rock 'n' Roll Hall of Fame at the Waldorf Astoria Hotel in New York.

March 5, 1988 — George and Ringo are guests on the British TV show "Aspel and Company."

October 25, 1988 — The album *The Traveling Wilburys: Volume One* by the Traveling Wilburys is released.

George Harrison
Solo Discography

Title	Artist	Release Date America/Britain	Label
ALBUMS			
WONDERWALL MUSIC (original soundtrack)	George Harrison	12/2/68 11/1/68	Apple

This was the first album issued on the Beatles' Apple Records label.

| GOODBYE | Cream | 2/5/69 2/28/69 | ATCO Polydor |

The Harrison/Clapton song "Badge" is included.

| JAMES TAYLOR | James Taylor | 2/17/69 12/6/68 | Apple |

George performed backup vocals and miscellaneous instrumentation.

| IS THIS WHAT YOU WANT? | Jackie Lomax | 5/19/69 5/21/69 | Apple |

Produced by George Harrison, who also played guitar and wrote the track "Sour Milk Sea."

| ELECTRONIC SOUND | George Harrison | 5/26/69 5/9/69 | Zapple |

| THAT'S THE WAY GOD PLANNED IT | Billy Preston | 9/10/69 8/22/69 | Apple |

Harrison produced.

| SONGS FOR A TAILOR | Jack Bruce | 10/6/69 8/29/69 | ATCO Polydor |

George plays guitar on the track "Never Tell Your Mother She's Out of Tune." Due to the contractual difficulties of playing on artists' records not signed to EMI, Harrison appears as L'Angelo Misterioso.

| LEON RUSSELL | Leon Russell | 3/23/70 4/24/70 | Shelter |

Harrison plays guitar on several tunes.

THE WORST OF ASHTON, GARDNER AND DUKE	Ashton, Gardner and Duke	9/28/70 2/5/71	Capitol

George appears as George O'Hara Smith on "I'm Your Spiritual Breadman."

DORIS TROY	Doris Troy	11/9/70 9/11/70	Apple

George had a hand in composing the songs "Ain't That Cute," "Give Me Back My Dynamite," "Gonna Get My Baby Back," "You Give My Joy Joy" as well as arranging "Jacob's Ladder." In addition, he produced several tracks and played guitar.

ENCOURAGING WORDS	Billy Preston	11/9/70 9/11/70	Apple

The album was produced by Billy Preston and George Harrison. Billy also performed Harrison's "My Sweet Lord," "Sing One for the Lord" and "All Things Must Pass." George played guitar and sang backup.

ALL THINGS MUST PASS	George Harrison	11/27/70 11/30/70	Apple

THE RADHA KRISHNA TEMPLE	Radha Krishna Temple	5/21/71 5/28/71	Apple

George produced, as well as arranging and performing on guitar.

IMAGINE	John Lennon	9/9/71 10/8/71	Apple

Harrison played slide guitar and dobro.

FOOTPRINT	Gary Wright	11/1/71 1/21/71	A&M

Playing slide guitar and lead, Harrison shows up as George O'Hara.

I WROTE A SIMPLE SONG	Billy Preston	11/8/71 1/14/72	A&M

Harrison plays lead as George H.

RAGA (original soundtrack)	Ravi Shankar	12/7/71	Apple

Harrison produced.

STRAIGHT UP	Badfinger	12/13/71 2/11/72	Apple

George produced four tracks and played lead guitar on "Day After Day."

THE CONCERT FOR BANGLA DESH	George Harrison & Friends	12/20/71 1/10/72	Apple

DAVID BROMBERG	David Bromberg	2/16/72 6/2/72	Columbia CBS

Bromberg and Harrison co-wrote the song "The Holdup."

ULULU	Jesse Ed Davis	3/6/72	ATCO
		5/19/72	Atlantic

Davis performs George's "Sue Me Sue You Blues."

HISTORY OF	Eric Clapton	4/10/72	ATCO
ERIC CLAPTON		7/7/72	Polydor

The tune "Badge" appears, and Harrison plays guitar on "Tell the Truth."

SOMETIME IN	John & Yoko	6/12/72	Apple
NEW YORK CITY	Lennon	9/15/72	

Harrison appears as part of the Plastic Ono Supergroup on a live recording of a gig at the London Lyceum Ballroom, December 15, 1969.

BOBBY KEYS	Bobby Keys	No Amer. rel.	Warner
		7/7/72	Bros.

George and Ringo play on this album throughout.

SON OF SCHMILSSON	Harry Nilsson	7/10/72	RCA
		7/28/72	

George plays slide as George Harrysong.

BROTHER	Lon & Derrek	9/22/72	Apple
	Van Eaton	2/9/73	

Produced by Harrison.

IN CONCERT 1972	Ravi Shankar &	1/22/73	Apple
	Ali Akbar Khan	4/13/73	

George helped with the mixing and editing.

THE TIN MAN WAS	Nicky Hopkins	4/23/73	Columbia
A DREAMER		7/27/73	CBS

Harrison plays guitar as George O'Hara.

LIVING IN THE	George Harrison	5/30/73	Apple
MATERIAL WORLD		6/22/73	

LOS COCHINOS	Cheech and Chong	8/27/73	Ode
		9/28/73	

George plays guitar on the tune "Basketball Jones Featuring Tyrone Shoelaces."

ON THE ROAD	Alvin Lee	10/2/73	Chrysalis
TO FREEDOM		12/7/73	Columbia

Lee records the Harrisong "So Sad (No Love of His Own")."

IT'S LIKE YOU NEVER LEFT	Dave Mason	10/29/73	Columbia
		2/8/74	CBS

George appears as Son of Harry on the track "If You've Got Love."

RINGO	Ringo Starr	11/2/73	Apple
		11/9/73	

Harrison penned the tune "Sunshine Life for Me (Sail Away Raymond)" and assisted on the composition of "Photograph" and "You and Me (Babe)." He also played guitar on "I'm the Greatest" and the other songs listed above. In addition, he did vocal harmonies on "Photograph" and "Sunshine Life for Me."

WANTED DEAD OR ALIVE	David Bromberg	1/7/74	Columbia
		No Brit. rel.	

George performs.

I'VE GOT MY OWN	Ron Wood	9/23/74	Warner
ALBUM TO DO		9/27/74	Brothers

George's song "Far East Man" is included.

THE PLACE I LOVE	Splinter	9/25/74	Dark
		9/20/74	Horse

George produced and performed on all the tracks listed either as Jai Raj Harisein, Hari Georgeson or P. Roducer.

SHANKAR FAMILY	Ravi Shankar	10/7/74	Dark
& FRIENDS	& Friends	9/20/74	Horse

Produced by Harrison.

DARK HORSE	George Harrison	12/9/74	Apple
		12/20/74	

IT'S MY PLEASURE	Billy Preston	7/20/75	A&M
		7/19/75	

George plays guitar as Hari Georgeson on the song "That's Life."

EXTRA TEXTURE	George Harrison	9/22/75	Apple
(Read All About It)		10/3/75	

HARDER TO LIVE	Splinter	10/6/75	Dark
		10/24/75	Horse

Harrison acted as co-producer and played guitar on the song "Lonely Man."

BLAST FROM YOUR PAST	Ringo Starr	11/20/75	Apple
		12/12/75	

George and Ringo's song "Photograph" is included in this, the last LP ever issued on the Apple label.

RAVI SHANKAR'S MUSIC	Ravi Shankar	2/6/76	Dark
FESTIVAL FROM INDIA	& Friends	3/19/76	Horse

George produced.

THIRTY-THREE & 1/3	George Harrison	11/24/76	Dark
		11/19/76	Horse

THE BEST OF GEORGE HARRISON	George Harrison	11/8/76 11/20/76	Capitol EMI
TWO MAN BAND	Splinter	10/3/77 10/7/77	Dark Horse

Harrison is listed on the album as executive producer; he also plays guitar on all tracks.

GEORGE HARRISON	George Harrison	2/14/79 2/16/79	Dark Horse
UNDERSIDE (bootleg)	George Harrison	1979 No Brit. rel.	Underside Programmers
SOMEWHERE IN ENGLAND (original first cover)	George Harrison	unreleased unreleased	Dark Horse
SOMEWHERE IN ENGLAND	George Harrison	6/1/81 6/5/81	Dark Horse
BY GEORGE (bootleg)	George Harrison	1981 No Brit. rel.	Hand Made Records
GONE TROPPO	George Harrison	10/27/82 11/8/82	Dark Horse
PORKY'S REVENGE Soundtrack	Various artists	3/14/85	Columbia

Includes Harrison's track "I Don't Want to Do It" by Bob Dylan.

GREENPEACE	Various Artists	8/19/85 6/14/85	A&M

George contributes a remixed version of the song "Save the World" to this little-known charity compilation album.

WATER (original soundtrack)	Various Artists	6/28/85 No Brit. rel.	London (Filmtrax)

Harrison performs and lent a hand in composing here and there in this soundtrack to Hand Made Films' *Water* starring Michael Caine.

OHNOTHIMAGEN (bootleg)	George Harrison	1987	Loka Productions S.A.
CLOUD NINE	George Harrison	11/2/88	Dark Horse
THE TRAVELING WILBURYS (Volume One)	The Traveling Wilburys	10/25/88	Wilbury Records

Over the years there have been as many as fifty additional George Harrison bootlegs issued worldwide. However, since most were only rehashes of various live performances, they have not been included here.

SINGLES

A — SOUR MILK SEA B — THE EAGLE LAUGHS AT YOU	Jackie Lomax	8/26/68 9/6/68	Apple

George produced, and played guitar.

A — CAROLINA IN MY MIND B — TAKING IT IN	James Taylor	3/17/69 No Brit. rel.	Apple

George performs some harmony parts on the A side.

A — CAROLINA IN MY MIND B — SOMETHING'S WRONG	James Taylor	10/26/70 11/6/70	Apple

A — NEW DAY B — I FALL INSIDE YOUR EYES	Jackie Lomax	No Amer. rel. 5/9/69	Apple

Harrison produced.

A — NEW DAY B — THUMBING A RIDE	Jackie Lomax	6/2/69 No Brit. rel.	Apple

A — KING OF FUH B — NOBODY KNOWS	Brute Force	No Amer. rel. 5/16/69	Apple

George produced.

A — THAT'S THE WAY GOD PLANNED IT B — WHAT ABOUT YOU	Billy Preston	7/7/69 6/27/69	Apple

George produced.

A — HARE KRISHNA
    MANTRA
B — PRAYER TO THE
    SPIRITUAL MASTER
	The Radha
	Krishna Temple
		8/22/69
		8/29/69
			Apple

Harrison played several instruments and produced.

A — EVERYTHING'S ALL RIGHT B — I WANT TO THANK YOU	Billy Preston	10/24/69 10/17/69	Apple

George produced.

A — ALL THAT I'VE GOT B — AS I GET OLDER	Billy Preston	2/16/70 1/30/70	Apple

George produced.

A — INSTANT KARMA B — WHO HAS SEEN THE WIND	John Lennon Yoko Ono	2/20/70 2/6/70	Apple

Harrison plays guitar and piano on the A side.

A — HOW THE WEB WAS WOVEN	Jackie Lomax	3/9/70	Apple
B — I FALL INSIDE YOUR EYES		No Brit. rel.	

George produced.

A — AIN'T THAT CUTE	Doris Troy	3/16/70	Apple
B — VAYA CON DIOS		2/13/70	

George produced.

A — GOVINDA	The Radha Krishna	3/24/70	Apple
B — GOVINDA JAI JAI	Temple	3/6/70	

George produced as well as playing several instruments.

A — MY SWEET LORD	Billy Preston	12/3/70	Apple
B — LITTLE GIRL		No Brit. rel.	

A — MY SWEET LORD	Billy Preston	No Amer. rel.	Apple
B — LONG AS I GOT MY BABY		9/4/70	

A — JACOB'S LADDER	Doris Troy	9/21/70	Apple
B — GET BACK		8/28/70	

George produced.

A — MY SWEET LORD	George Harrison	No Amer. rel.	Apple
B — WHAT IS LIFE		1/15/71	

A — WHAT IS LIFE	George Harrison	2/15/71	Apple
B — APPLE SCRUFFS		No Brit. rel.	

A — TRY SOME BUY SOME	Ronnie Spector	4/19/71	Apple
B — TANDOORI CHICKEN		4/16/71	

George produced as well as composing both tunes.

A — BANGLA DESH	George Harrison	7/28/71	Apple
B — DEEP BLUE		7/30/71	

A — JOI BANGLA/OH BHAGAVAN	Ravi Shankar & Chorus	8/9/71	Apple
B — RAGA MISHRA-JINJHOTI		8/27/71	

George produced.

A — DAY AFTER DAY	Badfinger	11/10/71	Apple
B — MONEY		No Brit. rel.	

A — DAY AFTER DAY	Badfinger	No Amer. rel.	Apple
B — SWEET TUESDAY MORNING		1/14/72	

A — MY SWEET LORD	George Harrison	11/23/71	Apple
B — ISN'T IT A PITY		No Brit. rel.	

A — SWEET MUSIC B — SONG OF SONGS George produced.	Lon & Derrek Van Eaton	3/6/72 No Brit. rel.	Apple
A — BACK OFF BOOGALOO B — BLINDMAN Harrison produced the A side and plays guitar.	Ringo Starr	3/20/72 3/17/72	Apple
A — GIVE ME LOVE B — MISS O'DELL	George Harrison	5/7/73 5/25/73	Apple
A — PHOTOGRAPH B — DOWN AND OUT Harrison co-wrote the A side, produced and performed.	Ringo Starr	9/24/73 10/19/73	Apple
A — I AM MISSING YOU B — LUST Harrison produced and arranged.	Shankar Family & Friends	11/6/74 9/13/74	Dark Horse
A — DARK HORSE B — I DON'T CARE ANYMORE	George Harrison	11/18/74 11/22/74	Apple
A — DING DONG DING DONG B — I DON'T CARE ANYMORE	George Harrison	No Amer. rel. 12/6/74	Apple
A — DING DONG DING DONG B — HARI'S ON TOUR (EXPRESS)	George Harrison	12/23/74 No Brit. rel.	Apple
A — DARK HORSE B — HARI'S ON TOUR (EXPRESS)	George Harrison	No Amer. rel. 2/28/75	Apple
A — YOU B — WORLD OF STONE	George Harrison	9/15/75 9/12/75	Apple
A — THIS GUITAR CAN'T KEEP FROM CRYING B — MAYA LOVE	George Harrison	12/8/75 2/6/76	Apple
A — THIS SONG B — LEARNING HOW TO LOVE YOU	George Harrison	11/15/76 11/19/76	Dark Horse
A — CRACKERBOX PALACE B — LEARNING HOW TO LOVE YOU	George Harrison	1/24/77 No Brit. rel.	Dark Horse
A — TRUE LOVE B — PURE SMOKEY	George Harrison	No Amer. rel. 2/11/77	Dark Horse

A — IT'S WHAT YOU VALUE B — WOMAN DON'T YOU CRY FOR ME	George Harrison	No Amer. rel. 5/31/77	Dark Horse

A — BLOW AWAY B — SOFT HEARTED HANA	George Harrison	2/14/79 No Brit. rel.	Dark Horse

A — LOVE COMES TO EVERYONE B — SOFT HEARTED HANA	George Harrison	No Amer. rel. 4/20/79	Dark Horse

A — FASTER   George Harrison   No Amer. rel.   Dark Horse
B — YOUR LOVE IS FOREVER   7/30/79
(issued in special 45 picture disc)

A — LOVE COMES TO EVERYONE B — SOFT TOUCH	George Harrison	5/11/79 No Brit. rel.	Dark Horse

A — ALL THOSE YEARS AGO B — WRITING'S ON THE WALL	George Harrison	5/11/81 5/15/81	Dark Horse

A — TEARDROPS B — SAVE THE WORLD	George Harrison	7/24/81 7/31/81	Dark Horse

A — WAKE UP MY LOVE B — GREECE (INSTRUMENTAL)	George Harrison	10/27/82 11/8/82	Dark Horse

A — FREEDOM   Billy Connoly, etc.   No Amer. rel.   Dark Horse
B — CELEBRATION   5/31/85
George plays guitar on "Freedom" and co-wrote and plays guitar on "Celebration."

A — GOT MY MIND SET ON YOU B — LAY HIS HEAD	George Harrison	10/16/87	Dark Horse

A — WHEN WE WAS FAB B — ZIG ZAG	George Harrison	1/20/88	Dark Horse

A — THIS IS LOVE B — BREATH AWAY FROM HEAVEN	George Harrison	5/16/88	Dark Horse

A — HANDLE WITH CARE B — MARGARITA	The Traveling Wilburys	1988	Wilbury Records

A — END OF THE LINE B — CONGRATULATIONS	The Traveling Wilburys	1989	Wilbury Records

In addition, George Harrison has contributed his numerous producing, arranging, composing and performing talents to recordings from:

Joe Cocker	Cilla Black	Larry Hosford
Monty Python's Flying Circus	"Legs" Larry Smith	Delaney and Bonnie
Rick Grech	Bob Dylan	Rudy Romero
Duane Eddy	Jeff Lynne	
Roy Orbison	Tom Petty	

Dark Horse Records
(American Releases)

ALBUMS:

During 1975 and 1976 the following nine Dark Horse albums were distributed by A&M Records in the United States:

Dark Horse; GEORGE HARRISON — THE DARK HORSE RADIO SPECIAL (Promotion only, no commercial release)

The Place I love; SPLINTER

Shankar Family & Friends; RAVI SHANKAR

Jiva; JIVA

2nd Resurrection; STAIRSTEPS

Mind Your Own Business; HENRY McCULLOUGH

Harder to Live; SPLINTER

Ravi Shankar's Music Festival From India; RAVI SHANKAR

Attitudes; ATTITUDES

Since 1977 Warner Brothers Records has been the distributor of nine albums on the Dark Horse label in the United States:

A PERSONAL MUSIC DIALOGUE WITH GEORGE HARRISON AT 33 1/3; (Promotion only, no commercial release)

Thirty-Three & 1/3; GEORGE HARRISON

Good News; ATTITUDES

Keni Burke; KENI BURKE

Two Man Band; SPLINTER

George Harrison; GEORGE HARRISON

Somewhere in England; GEORGE HARRISON

Gone Troppo; GEORGE HARRISON

Cloud Nine; GEORGE HARRISON

DARK HORSE SINGLES:

There were eleven Dark Horse singles distributed by A&M Records in the United States:

I Am Missing You/Lust; RAVI SHANKAR

Costafine Town/Elly-May; SPLINTER

China Light/Haven't Got Time; SPLINTER

Ain't Live Enough/The Whole World's Crazy; ATTITUDES

From Us to You/Time; STAIRSTEPS

Something's Goin' On Inside L.A./Take My Love; JIVA

Which Way Will I Get Home/What Is It (If You Never Ever Tried It Yourself); SPLINTER

Honey Don't Leave L.A./Lend a Hand; ATTITUDES

Tell Me Why/Salaam; STAIRSTEPS

After Five Years/Halfway There; SPLINTER

Sweet Summer Music/If We Want To; ATTITUDES

To date Warner Brothers Records have distributed nineteen singles in the United States:

This Song/Learning How to Love You; GEORGE HARRISON

Crackerbox Palace/Learning How to Love You; GEORGE HARRISON

Sweet Summer Music/Being Here With You; ATTITUDES

Round & Round/I'll Bend for You; SPLINTER

In a Stranger's Arms/Good News; ATTITUDES

Shuffle/From Me to You; KENI BURKE

Keep on Singing/Day; KENI BURKE

Motions of Love/I Need Your Love; SPLINTER

Blow Away/Soft Hearted Hana; GEORGE HARRISON

Love Comes to Everyone/Soft Touch; GEORGE HARRISON (Promotion only, no commercial release)

All Those Years Ago/Writing's on the Wall; GEORGE HARRISON

All Those Years Ago; GEORGE HARRISON (12-inch DJ single, promotion only, no commercial release)

Teardrops/Save the World; GEORGE HARRISON

All Those Years Ago/Teardrops; GEORGE HARRISON (re-issue)

Wake Up My Love/Greece; GEORGE HARRISON

Wake Up My Love; GEORGE HARRISON (12-inch DJ single, promotion only, no commercial release)

I Really Love You; GEORGE HARRISON (DJ single, promotion only, no commercial release)

I Really Love You; GEORGE HARRISON

Got My Mind Set on You/Lay His Head; GEORGE HARRISON

When We Was Fab/Zig Zag; GEORGE HARRISON

Hand Made Films

1978   Hand Made Films founded by George Harrison and Denis O'Brien.

1979   THE LIFE OF BRIAN (comedy) starring Monty Python's Flying Circus. Written by the Pythons. Directed by Terry Jones.

1981   THE LONG GOOD FRIDAY (drama), starring Bob Hoskins and Eddie Constantine. Directed by John MacKenzie.

1981   TIME BANDITS (comedy), starring Sean Connery, Michael Palin, Shelley Duvall, John Cleese, Ralph Richardson, Katherine Helmond and David Warner. Directed by Terry Gilliam. Written by Michael Palin and Terry Gilliam.

1982   MONTY PYTHON LIVE AT THE HOLLYWOOD BOWL (comedy), starring Monty Python's Flying Circus with Neil Innes. Directed by Terry Hughes and the Pythons. Written by the Pythons, Carol Cleveland and Neil Innes.

1982   THE MISSIONARY (comedy), starring Michael Palin, Maggie Smith, Trevor Howard and Michael Hordern. Written by Richard Loncraine. Directed by Michael Palin.

1982   PRIVATES ON PARADE (comedy), featuring John Cleese and Denis Quilley. Directed by Michael Blackmore.

1982   SCRUBBERS (drama), directed by Mai Zetterling.

1982   BULLSHOT! (comedy), starring Alan Shearman, Diz White and Ron House.

1984   A PRIVATE FUNCTION (comedy), starring Michael Palin and Maggie Smith. Directed by Malcolm Mowbray. Written by Alan Bennett.

1984   WATER (comedy), starring Michael Caine, Valerie Perrine, Brenda Vaccaro and Fred Gwynne. Directed by Dick Clement.

1986   SHANGHAI SURPRISE (comedy/adventure), starring Madonna and Sean Penn. Written by John Kohn and Robert Bentley. Directed by Jim Goddard.

1986   MONA LISA (drama), starring Bob Hoskins and Cathy Tyson. Directed by Neil Jordan. Written by Neil Jordan and David Leland.

1987   WITHNAIL AND I (comedy), directed by Bruce Robinson.

1988   TRACK TWENTY NINE (drama), starring Theresa Russell and Christopher Lloyd. Directed by Nicolas Roeg. Written by Dennis Potter.

1988   THE LONELY PASSION OF JUDITH HEARNE (drama), starring Maggie Smith and Bob Hoskins. Directed by Jack Clayton.

1989   POW WOW HIGHWAY (drama), starring Gary Farmer. Directed by Jonathon Wacks.

1989   FIVE CORNERS (drama), starring Jodie Foster.

1989   CHECKING OUT (comedy), starring Jeff Daniels. Directed by David Leland.

1989   HOW TO GET AHEAD IN ADVERTISING (comedy), directed by Bruce Robinson.

1989   NUNS ON THE RUN (comedy), starring Eric Idle.

1989   THE RAGADY RAWNY (drama), directed by Bob Hoskins.

1989   COLD DOG SOUP (drama), no further information available.

Hand Made Distribution, a division of Hand Made Films was formed to aid the European marketing of foreign films.

1981   THE BURNING (horror), starring Brian Matthews and Lee Ayres. Directed by Tony Maylam.

1981   TATTOO (drama), starring Bruce Dern and Maud Adams.

1982   VENOM (drama), starring Oliver Reed, Klaus Kinski, Sarah Miles and Susan George.

A NOTE
ON SOURCES

Throughout more than a decade of research on the lives of the Beatles and the global effect of Beatlemania, I have had occasion to interview dozens of people who somehow landed right in the eye of the Beatles' hurricane. Given there has never before been a major biography on the life of George Harrison and that there may well never be another, I have endeavored to contact and interview as many people as possible who have played a part in Harrison's intriguing life. Some of these good people kindly consented to taped interviews, and some just spoke informally about their experiences with Harrison. In some cases the subjects asked not to be identified. Among the people who have spoken to me specifically for this project and also just generally on the lives of the Beatles over the years are:

IN HENLEY: Robbie Cain, Barrymore Barlow, Kirsten Grepne, Mary Hopkin, "Legs" Larry Smith and Jon Lord.

IN LIVERPOOL: Bob Wooler, Paddy Delaney, Julia Baird, Pete Best, Mike McCartney, Gerry Marsden, Allan Williams, Norman Birch, Leila Harvey, Millie Sutcliffe, "Father" Tom McKenzie and Clive Epstein.

IN LONDON: Paul McCartney (interview conducted through an associate), Neil Innes, Dezo Hoffman, Vivian Stanshall, Roy Kinnear, Roger Ruskinspear, Denny Laine and Dhananjaya Dasa.

IN NORTH AMERICA: Harry Harrison, Yoko Ono, Harry Nilsson, Ritchie Yorke, Ronnie Hawkins, Tony Mansfield, Jo Jo Laine, Pete Bennett, Horst Fascher, Julian Lennon, Alistair Taylor, Shambu Das, Sean Lennon, Steve Holly, Peter Brown, Scott Wheeler, Ritchie Havens and Mukunda Das Goswami.

I have also quoted from various Beatle and George Harrison press conferences held around the world over the past two decades. Most of the excerpts I have chosen have never before been published.

A Note on Sources

For brief quotations taken from the published work of other authors and journalists, I should like to acknowledge the following:

BOOKS

Baird, Julia with Geoffrey Giuliano. *John Lennon: My Brother*, Grafton Books, 1988. Copyright Julia Baird and Geoffrey Giuliano.

Bedford, Carol. *Waiting for the Beatles*, Blandford Paperbacks, 1984. Copyright Carol Bedford.

Bhaktivedanta, A.C. *The Bhagavad Gita, As It Is*, The Bhaktivedanta Book Trust, 1983. Copyright Bhaktivedanta Book Trust.

Blake, John. *All You Needed Was Love: The Beatles After the Beatles*, Perigee Books, 1981. Copyright John Blake.

Brown, Peter and Gaines, Steven. *Love You Make: An Insider's Story of the Beatles*, McGraw-Hill Publishers, 1983. Copyright Peter Brown and Steven Gaines.

Cepican, Bob and Ali Waleed. *Yesterday Came Suddenly: The Definitive History of the Beatles*, Timbre Books/Arbor House Publishing Company, 1985. Copyright Bob Cepican and Waleed Ali.

Crisp, Sir Frank. *The Friar Park Guide.* (No other information available.)

Davies, Hunter. *The Beatles: The Authorized Biography*, McGraw-Hill Inc. Copyright 1968.

Davis, Edward E. *The Beatle Book*, Cowles Publishers, 1967. Copyright information not available.

DiLello, Richard. *The Longest Cocktail Party*, Charisma Books, 1972. Copyright Richard DiLello.

Giuliano, Geoffrey. *The Beatles: A Celebration*, Methuen Carswell Publishers, 1986. Copyright Geoffrey Giuliano.

Harrison, George. *I Me Mine*, Genesis Publications, 1980. Copyright Ganga Publishing B. V.

Harry, Bill ed. *Mersey Beat: The Beginnings of the Beatles*, Omnibus Press, 1977. Introduction by Bill Harry.

Leary, Timothy, Ph.D., Metzner, Ralph, Ph.D. and Alpert, Richard, Ph.D. *The Psychedelic Experience: A Manual Based on the Tibetan Book of the Dead*, University Books, 1964. Copyright Timothy Leary, Ralph Metzner and Richard Alpert.

Lennon, Cynthia. *A Twist of Lennon*, Avon Books, 1978. Copyright Cynthia Lennon.

Michaels, Ross. *George Harrison: Yesterday and Today*, Flash Books, 1977. Copyright Flash Books.

Miles (compiled by). *Beatles in Their Own Words*, Quick Fox Books, 1978. Copyright Omnibus Press.

Miles (compiled by). *John Lennon in His Own Words*, Quick Fox Books, 1981. Copyright Quick Fox.

Shankar, Ravi. *My Music My Life*. No other information available.

Shotton, Pete and Schaffner, Nicholas. *John Lennon in My Life*, Stein and Day, 1983. Copyright Pete Shotton and Nicholas Schaffner.

Taylor, Alistair with Martin Roberts. *Yesterday: The Beatles Remembered*, Sidgwick & Jackson, 1988. Copyright Alistair Taylor and Martin Roberts.

MAGAZINE ARTICLES

"A Beatle's New Mania." Copyright IPC Business Press Ltd. *Motor*, July 25, 1979.

"A Conversation With George Harrison" by Mick Brown. Copyright Straight Arrow Publishers 1979. *Rolling Stone*, April 19, 1979.

"George Harrison: Alive and Kicking" by Timothy White. Copyright Musician. *Musician*, November 1987.

"George Harrison: Frets, Fame and Fortune" by Rip Rense. Copyright Harris Publications. *Guitar World*, April 1988.

"George Harrison: Helping Bangla Desh." Copyright Circus Enterprizes Corporation. *Circus*, Volume 6, Number 1, October 1971.

"George Harrison Speaks Out" by Lou Seal. Copyright Warner Brothers Records Inc. *Wax Paper*, February 9, 1979.

"Growing Up at 33 1/3: The George Harrison Interview" by Mitch Glazer. Copyright Crawdaddy Publishing Company Incorporated. *Crawdaddy*, February 1977.

"Lumbering in the Material World" by Ben Fong Torres. Copyright Straight Arrow Publishers, 1974. *Rolling Stone*, December 19, 1974.

Also consulted were these sources: *Cabbages and Kings, Beatles Monthly, The Harrison Alliance, Tiger Beat, Country Life Magazine, The Hollywood Reporter, People,* West Key Number Systems, *Look.*

It should be noted that at times I have taken the liberty of creating some lines of dialogue to more accurately depict George's life. I have done so, however, only after thoroughly checking the facts to ensure that what I wrote was a faithful approximation of the actual events in question.

Finally, there were my own observations gathered from living off and on for more than two years in Henley-on-Thames, with "Legs" Larry Smith at Jon Lord's country estate. During my time there I became privy to a good deal of sensitive material concerning the day-to-day lives of George Harrison and his friends. Throughout the long process of writing this book, it was this information that was personally the most difficult for me to share with the rest of the world. Were I to have left out some of the more sensational aspects of my life in Henley, however, I feel the book would have suffered in accurately portraying Harrison's life. As Yoko Ono used to say so often to John, "You can never unknow what you know."

It was in that spirit of attempting to write the definitive history of this great artist that I occasionally put aside my own apprehension in the interest of telling the tale in as honest and compelling a way as possible. In that, I hope I have not strayed too far from the mark.

ACKNOWLEDGMENTS

The author wishes to thank the following people for their kind assistance and encouragement in the production of this book:

Meher Baba, Barrymore Barlow, The Rt. Hon. Ezra Bean, Esq., Joe Bell, Pete Best, Deborah Lyn Black, Raymond and Sadie Black, Bloomsbury Publishing, Sam Brown, Robbie Cain & family, Stefano Castino, Arnold Comstock, Brant and Maria Cowie, Balabadra Dasa, Devi Deva Dasa & family, Jagannatha Dasa, Saraswati Devi Dasi, Paddy Delaney, Cynthia Webster Fogle, E.P. Dutton, Gregory Lyn Ford, David Germain, Brenda Giuliano, Robert and Robin Giuliano, Kirsten Grepne, Angel Guerra, William Hanna, Sandra Homer, Mary Hopkin, David Hooper, William Hushion, Jadurani Devi Dasi, Joseph and Mary Juliano, Alcides Antino King Esq., William King, Sri Bala Krishna, Pearl Littlefield Kuney, Denny, Helen and Lucy Laine, Jo Jo Laine and family, Jill Kathleen Lee, Donald Lehr, William Linehan, Allan Lysaght, Sri Chaitanya Mahaprabhu, B.H. Mangalniloy Maharaj, Bhaktimarga Maharaj, His Holiness Sridar Maharaj, George Martin, Jeanne Martinet, The Sri Chaitanya Gaudiya Math, Peter Michael McCartney, David Lloyd McIntyre, Alanna Nash, Nigel Newton, Niagara Computer, The Betsy Nolan Group, Tyre Reardon, MBE, David Reynolds, Steven Rosen, Charles F. Rosenay!!!, Dimo Safari, Marty Schiffert, Sesa, Devin, Avalon and India, Rajeswar Singh, Self Realization Fellowship (SRF), Skyboot Productions Ltd., Spiritual Realization Institute (SRI), Clint Starkey and family, Stoddart Publishing Co. Limited, A. C. Bhaktivedanta Swami, Alistair Taylor, Dennis Toll, Sandra Tooze, Vic's Auto Home & Trim, Anthony Violanti, Scott Wheeler, Bob Wooler, Ritchie Yorke, Myra Yahnkee, Ernie Williams, El Zombo, Ronald Zuker.

INDEX

Index

Index

Index

Starr, Ringo, 3, 13, 32, 40, 44-45, 50, 52, 56,
   61, 74, 76, 83, 84, 86, 91-92, 93, 95, 129,
   131-32, 139, 140, 143, 152, 164-65, 166,
   168, 172, 180, 186, 187, 188, 189, 192
Stewart, Jackie, 163, 180
Stewart, Les, 21
Stewart, Rod, 146, 170
Stigwood, Robert, 144
Strawberry Alarm Clock, 79
Sullivan, Ed, 43
SUMMER HOLIDAY (film), 43
Suresh (worker for Maharishi), 92
Surtees, John, 181
Sutcliffe, Millie, 40
Sutcliffe, Stuart, 28, 33, 34-35, 39
Sweden, 41
Swimmer, Saul, 135
Sylvester, Victor, 14

Taylor, Alistair, 39, 65, 66, 67-68, 70, 127
Taylor, Derek, 42-43, 50, 63, 67-68, 73, 79,
   166-67, 173, 181-82
Taylor, James, 70
Taylor, Joan, 79
"Tear Drops," 165-66
"Tears of the World," 165
Texas, 71-72
"That's the Way It Goes," 174
"That Which I Have Lost," 165
"There! I've Said It Again," 43
THIRTY-THREE & 1/3, 110, 111, 119, 154,
   157, 163
"This Guitar Can't Keep From Crying," 154
"This Is Love," 190
"This Song," 157
Thomson, Jane (grandmother), 4
"Those Were the Days," 74-75
"Three Cool Cats," 22
TIGER BEAT (magazine), 79
TIMES (London newspaper), 79
"Tired of Midnight Blue," 154
Tittenhurst Park, Berkshire, 98-99, 100, 104
Top Ten Club, Hamburg, 33-34, 38
Toronto, 109, 121, 170
Traveling Wilburys, 190-91
TRAVELING WILBURYS VOLUME ONE,
   THE, 191
Trident Studios, London, 71, 97
Troy, Doris, 74
"True Love," 155
Tucson, Arizona, 164
Tunisia, 162
Turner, Rodney, 162
"Twenty Flight Rock," 19
Twickenham Film Studios, 52
Two I's, London, 29
Tynan, Kenneth, 144

Uriah Heep, 2

Vancouver, 148, 150
Vaughan, Ivan, 18, 22
VEDAS (Hindu texts), 86
Vinton, Bobby, 43
Visconti, Tony, 170
Vivekananda (East Indian guru), 102-3
Vollmer, Jurgen, 32
Voormann, Klaus, 32-33, 53, 62, 74, 133, 140
Vrndavana, India, 107, 108

WAITING FOR THE BEATLES (book), 72
Waldheim, Kurt, 186
Waldorf Astoria Hotel, Manhattan, 187
Wales, 8, 18
"Walking on Thin Ice," 167
Wallace, Ian, 191
Warmflash, David, 82
Warner Brothers, 74, 154, 157, 165, 190-91
Washington, D.C., 46
Wavertree, England, 1, 5, 7
Weeks, Willie, 149, 165
Wenner, Jann, 83
West, Keith, 161
West, Michael, 64
West Key Number Systems, 156
"What Is Life," 130
Wheeler, Scott, 47
"While My Guitar Gently Weeps," 149, 187
White, Timothy, 128, 140
"Why Don't We Do It in the Road," 83
Wilbury Records, 191
Williams, Allan, 29-30
Windsor, England, 162
WITH THE BEATLES, 76
Wood, Ron, 144
Woodstock (festival), 88
Wooler, Bob, 37, 39
Woolton, England, 18, 19, 20, 21
"World of Stone," 154
Wright, Gary, 140, 145, 189
Wyman, Bill, 7

Yamuna (singer), 98
YELLOW SUBMARINE (film), 75
YELLOW SUBMARINE (soundtrack), 75
Yogananda, Paramahansa, 102-3, 109-10, 112,
   114, 153
Yorke, Ritchie, 30, 69
"Your True Love," 187
Yu, Dr. Zion, 153-54
Yukteswar, Sri, 110

Zappa, Frank, 105
Zapple Records, 173

242